MADNESS AND MORALS

By the same author

INTIMACY AND RITUAL:
a study of spiritualism, mediums and groups

MADNESS AND MORALS

Ideas on Insanity in the Nineteenth Century

Vieda Skultans

Department of Mental Health
University of Bristol

Routledge & Kegan Paul
London and Boston

First published in 1975
by Routledge & Kegan Paul Ltd
Broadway House, 68–74 Carter Lane,
London EC4V 5EL and
9 Park Street,
Boston, Mass. 02108, USA
Set in Intertype Lectura
and printed in Great Britain by
Clarke, Doble & Brendon Ltd
Plymouth

ISBN 0 7100 8022 0

Contents

PART TWO PSYCHIATRIC ROMANTICISM

Biographical Notes

John Abercrombie, 1780–1844
MD Oxon. and Edinburgh, FRCP Edinburgh. Physician to the Edinburgh Royal Public Dispensary and to the King in Scotland.

Rev. John Barlow, 1799–1869
MA Cantab., FRS. Secretary of the Royal Institution, rector of Little Bowden, Northamptonshire. Minister of Duke Street Chapel.

General William Booth, 1829–1912
Commander-in-Chief of Salvation Army. Director of its social institutions for destitute, vicious and criminal classes.

Sir John Charles Bucknill, 1817–97
MD London, FRCP, FRS. Medical Superintendent of Devon County Lunatic Asylum 1844–62; Lord Chancellor's Visitor in Lunacy 1862–76; President of the Medico-Psychological Association 1860; editor of the *Asylum Journal of Mental Science* 1853–62; co-founder and co-editor of *Brain: a Journal of Neurology* 1878.

George Man Burrows, 1771–1846
MRCS, LSA, MD St Andrews, FRCP. Owner of private asylum in Chelsea from 1814 and of the Retreat in Clapham (1823–43).

John Conolly, 1794–1866
MD Edinburgh, FRCP, Hon. DCL Oxon., Professor of the Practice of Medicine, London University 1827–31. Resident Physician,

Middlesex County Lunatic Asylum at Hanwell 1839–44; Consulting Physician 1845–8; Visiting Physician 1849–52; Chairman of the Association of Medical Officers of Asylums 1843 and 1851. President of the Medico-Psychological Association 1858.

Bryan Crowther, ?–1815
MRCS. Surgeon to Bridewell and Bethlem Hospitals. Also to the parish workhouse of St Clement Danes.

John Haslam, 1764–1844
MD Aberdeen, LRCP. Apothecary to Bethlem Hospital 1795–1816.

Robert Gardiner Hill, 1811–78
MRCS, LSA, LRCP Edinburgh. Resident Medical Officer at Lincoln Asylum 1835–40. Joint owner of Eastgate House Asylum, Lincoln 1840–63, and of Earls Court House Asylum, London, Wyke House and Inverness Lodge, Middlesex, from 1863 onwards.

Furneaux Jordan, 1830–1911
MB Roy. Univ. Irel. BCh 1889, FRCS. Demonstrator in Physiology, Queen's College, Birmingham.

Alfred Beaumont Maddock, 1816–63
MD Giessen University, Germany. Proprietor and Resident Physician of Malling Lunatic Asylum. Practice in Curzon Street, Mayfair.

Henry Maudsley, 1835–1918
MD University College, London. Medical Superintendent of Manchester Royal Lunatic Hospital 1859–62. Editor of *Journal of Mental Science* 1862–78. Physician of West London Hospital 1864–74. Professor of Medical Jurisprudence at University College, London 1869–79.

Charles Mercier, 1852–1919
MD London, LSA, FRCS, FRCP 1904. Physician for Mental Diseases at Charing Cross Hospital.

John Millar, 1818–88.
LRCP Edinburgh. Medical Superintendent, Bethnal House Asylum, London.

Sir Alexander Morison, 1779–1886
MD Edinburgh, FRCP. Fellow and President of Royal College of Physicians of Edinburgh. Inspecting Physician of private madhouses in Surrey. Consulting Physician to Bethlem Hospital 1835–53; to Middlesex County Asylum at Hanwell from 1832 and Surrey County Asylum, Springfield, from 1841.

Rev. William Willis Moseley, 1770–1863
AM, LLD, MRCS.

Daniel Noble, 1810–85
MD St Andrews 1853, LSA, MRCS, FRCP 1857, Hon. MA St Andrews. Consultant Physician at Wye House Lunatic Asylum, Buxton.

James Cowles Prichard, 1786–1848
MD Edinburgh, Hon. MD Oxon, FRS. Physician to St Peter's Hospital 1810, and Bristol Infirmary 1816. Commissioner in Lunacy 1844–8. Ethnologist.

James Sheppard, 1817–56
MD Aberdeen 1844. Stonehouse, Devon, LSA 1840.

Daniel Hack Tuke, 1827–95
MD Heidelberg, FRCP. Lecturer on Psychological Medicine at the York School of Medicine. Visiting Medical Officer to the Retreat at York.

Samuel Tuke, 1784–1857
Grandson of William Tuke, founder of the Retreat Asylum for the Quaker insane. Treasurer of the Retreat.

Andrew Wynter, 1819–76
MD St Andrews, MRCP 1861. Editor of *British Medical Journal* 1856.

Introduction

Dramatic changes took place in the theory and practice of psychiatry during the nineteenth century. Large county asylums were built and the insane, particularly the pauper insane, were gradually separated from the destitute and the criminal. They emerged as a distinct social category (see, for example, Kathleen Jones, 1972). Within asylums methods of treatment changed. In several institutions physical restraint was completely abolished, as at the Retreat in York and the Asylum at Hanwell. Elsewhere abolition, though not implemented, was seen as the ideal.

The eighty years covered by this book produced a wide and varied literature on insanity. It is not my intention to provide an all-embracing survey of this literature. There are, however, certain identifiable themes which emerge with some clarity and which have intrinsic merit. It is these themes which I have selected for development mainly because of their influence on the then contemporary attitudes to and treatment of the insane and also because of their relevance to today. Although to some extent this is a personal choice and, therefore, necessarily omits matters which in other contexts could be regarded as of equal interest, it is not a purely idiosyncratic selection. The extracts are all taken from English authors. In part this is the result of practical constraints and the need to limit the field of interest. However, it also relates to the conviction that ideas about the insane cannot be fully understood apart from the society which produces such ideas. For present purposes, therefore, it would have been confusing to introduce the writings of physicians from other countries.

At the theoretical level the nineteenth century provides much change and contrast. Despite these apparent contradictions a consistent importance is attached to moral concepts which gives unity to the whole period. During the earlier part of the century the idea of the individual as possessed of powers and the will to combat insanity was developed and widely popularized. For this reason I have described the period as one of 'Psychiatric Romanticism'. These ideas about insanity are, of course, consonant with the prevailing philosophy of individualism. During the latter part of the nineteenth century this view of insanity alters radically. Moral management (that is, the care of the insane without physical restraint and by appeal to the conscience and will of the patient) disappears. The reasons for its demise are in part practical and in part ideological. With the swelling of the asylum population, the earlier system of care devised for a few select patients becomes impracticable. There is also an intellectual reappraisal of the nature of insanity. Whereas earlier writers are interested in 'moral force' and 'will', later writers are interested in 'hereditary endowment' and 'character': an area of interest which Henry Maudsley aptly circumscribes with the phrase 'the tyranny of organization' (1873, p. 76).

Explanations of Insanity

Throughout the nineteenth century, and indeed throughout history, insanity has posed a challenge to man's explanatory powers as well as a threat to his self-image as a rational being. The investigation of the causes of insanity concerns all the nineteenth-century writers on insanity. The causes of insanity are typically classified under four headings: predisposing and exciting causes and physical and moral causes. The first pair of causes marks an obvious distinction; the second pair is by far the more important and calls for some comment. We can translate the term 'moral' as a rough nineteenth-century equivalent of the contemporary term 'psychological' which at the same time retains certain ethical implications. Throughout the century the literature is preoccupied with the relative weight to be attributed to physical and moral causes of insanity. During the early part of the century moral causes are thought to be of greater importance. During the latter part of the century physical causes assume ascendancy. Foremost among moral causes are lack of moderation and excesses of all kinds. Given this aetiology of insanity, moral factors are seen as forces against insanity. Habit, perseverance, the will and character may each constitute such a counteracting force. Daniel Hack Tuke offers practical advice on the prevention of insanity along the following lines: 'Remember that mental safety lies in pursuing the golden mean between unbridled indulgence and asceticism' (1878, p. 219). These ideas on moderation and excess are expanded and developed to account for systematic class differences in the aetiology of the neuroses. Roughly, these differences can be summarized as over-indulgence in the upper and working classes and over-application among the middle classes. Both conditions involve loss of moderation.

> Looking broadly at the facts . . . we may say . . . that the rich and poor, from different causes, though certainly in one respect the same cause, labour under a large amount of preventable lunacy; that beer and gin, malnutrition, a dreary monotony of toil, muscular exhaustion, domestic distress, misery and anxiety, account largely, not only for the number of poor who become insane in adult life, but who from hereditary predisposition are born weak-minded or actually idiotic; that among the middle classes, stress of business, excessive competition, failures and also, in many cases, reckless and intemperate living, occasion the attacks; while in the upper classes, intemperance still works woe—and under this head must be comprised lady and gentleman dipsomaniacs, who are not confined in asylums; and while multiplicity of subjects of study in youth, and excessive brain work in after life, exert a certain amount of injurious influence, underwork, luxurious habits, undisciplined wills, desultory life, produce a crop of nervous disorders, terminating not infrequently in insanity (ibid., p. 124).

Excess pertains to the imagination as well as to actual behaviour: '. . . the harpies (unwanted feelings and ideas) which may haunt our richest mental banquets, are often among the earliest symptom of a disordered brain' (ibid., p. 184). In short, the caution against excess provides a thread of continuity in the investigation of the causes of insanity.

Sexuality and Insanity

Another abiding interest of all nineteenth-century writers on insanity is sexuality. In 1782 Thomas Arnold wrote: 'Love between the sexes . . . too readily terminates in insanity' (p. 220). In claiming this, Arnold was merely giving elegant expression to the widespread conviction that sexuality is potentially dangerous. However, in men these dangers are associated with self-abuse and excess. In women such dangers are intrinsic in their very cycle of sexual development. Hence, the title 'Feminine Vulnerability' given to the section of this book about women and insanity. Puberty, menstruation, childbirth and the menopause are each fraught with peculiar moral dangers. Add to this the fact that women are thought to be more labile by their very constitution and the picture presented of womanhood is one of great fragility. The prevailing view is aptly summarized by Thomas Laycock: 'It is widely acknowledged that the affectability of the female sex has its counterpart in that of children, mental emotions and movements are excited in both with equal facility' (1840, p. 131). It is not, therefore, surprising to learn that insanity, like certain other dreaded diseases, is more often transmitted in the female lines.

As far as self-abuse and sexual excess are concerned, I have chosen not to deal with this as a separate category. The medical manipulation of information and hence the control of sexual behaviour have been described by Alex Comfort (1967). More specifically the relationship between masturbation and insanity has been explored by Spitz (1953) and Hare (1962). For this reason I have not singled out the subject for special consideration, but see it as part of the more general preoccupation with self-cultivation. In this context it is worth noting how attitudes towards masturbation changed. Comfort writes: 'The eighteenth and early nineteenth century, believing Masturbation to be harmful as well as a sinful practice, attempted to cure it, but from 1850 to 1879 surgical measures became increasingly popular' (1967, p. 103). These attitude changes are in line with the deeper changes which took place over the same period in ideas about insanity.

A final point relates to the act of procreation itself. It is widely held that the condition of body and mind at the time of conception influences the future development of the child. For example, Maddock writes of cases which are 'illustrative of the low condition of mental power in those children who have dated their origin from the drunken orgies of their parents; and the frequent and oft-remarked deficiency in mental calibre of the eldest child of a family to the rest, has been shrewdly attributed to the more sensual conditions under which its existence was commenced' (1854, p. 5).

Such ideas are interesting not only for the light which they throw on contemporary sexual mores, but also for what they reveal about held theories of inheritance. Maddock is clearly relying on a Lamarckian model, even though he does not make explicit reference to it. Later in the century when more importance is attached to heredity as an explanation of insanity the actual theories of inheritance used remain inexplicit and, hence, unexamined. Even though the influence of Darwin is apparent and sometimes explicitly acknowledged, traces of Lamarckism remain. At the level of biological theory the field is confused and models are used which best suit the explanation of a particular case of insanity.

Hobbes and Locke on Insanity

Nineteenth-century ideas on insanity form two streams of thought which are a development of Hobbes's and Locke's views on insanity. It is, therefore, worth describing the initial positions of the two philosophers. Hobbes presents a stereotyped view of the madman:

> that madness is nothing else, but too much appearing passion, may be gathered out of the effects of wine, which are the same with those of the evil disposition of the organs. For the variety of behaviour in men that have drunk too much, is the same with that of madmen: some of them raging, others laughing, all extravagantly, but according to their several domineering passions, for the effect of the wine, does but remove dissimulation, and take from them the sight of the deformity of their passions. For I believe that most sober men, when they walk alone without care and employment of the mind, would be unwilling the vanity and extravagance of their thoughts should be publicly seen; which is a confession, that passions unguided, are for the most part mere madness (1651; 1962 edn, p. 107).

The picture drawn is one of outrage and licentiousness in the absence of intellectual guidance. Contrast this with Locke's sober view of insanity: madness is a self-contained defect of reasoning. Locke writes: 'Madmen do not appear to have lost the faculty of reasoning: but having joined together some ideas very wrongly, they mistake them for truths, and they err as men do that argue right from wrong principles' (1690; 1959 edn, p. 209). These two seventeenth-century standpoints provide the point of departure for later schools of thought.

Moral Insanity and Monomania

The Hobbesian view is akin to that of the believers in moral insanity. The Lockeian view is shared by the moral managers. For example, their frequent reference to the condition of 'monomania' implies that a person can be mad in one respect only and remain unimpaired in other respects. Monomania consists of firmly held but false beliefs. In contemporary language they would be termed delusions. This approach is in contrast with the following: '. . . when a person is lunatic, he is, as Dr Bucknill has remarked, lunatic to his finger ends' (Maudsley, 1873, p. 41). The two positions, that of moral management and that of moral insanity, are totally opposed. Since these intellectual positions are strategic, both retrospectively in terms of the development which they represent of earlier philosophical ideas and prospectively in terms of their influence on subsequent psychiatric theory, it is worth taking time to explore the details of each position. First, a consideration of moral insanity is required. Although akin to the Hobbesian view of insanity, the actual term was first coined by James Cowles Prichard in 1833. Prichard defines moral insanity as follows: 'This form of mental disease has been said above to consist of a morbid perversion of the feelings, affectations, habits, without any hallucination or erroneous conviction impressed upon the understanding; it sometimes co-exists with an apparently unimpaired state of the intellectual faculties' (1833, p. 14). The focus of attention has moved from internal, private events to external ones. The emphasis is on disordered or antisocial behaviour, rather than on any 'lesion of the understanding' (ibid., p. 7). This account of moral insanity relates to a particular psychology. Namely, the view that each faculty of the mind is anchored to a particular locality in the brain. If the relevant portion of the brain is damaged or unsound then the corresponding faculty will be defective or absent. These are the theoretical underpinnings which support the notion of moral insanity. A number of interesting implications follow from this position. First, the distinction between eccentricity and insanity is blurred by the introduction of the term moral. Prichard himself recognizes the difficulties:

> It is often very difficult to pronounce, with certainty, as to the presence or absence of moral insanity, or to determine whether the appearances which are supposed to indicate its existence do not proceed from natural peculiarity or eccentricity of character. The existence of moral insanity is palpable and easily recognised only in those instances to which it comes on, as it often does, after some strongly marked disorder affecting the brain and the general state of health, such as a slight attack of paralysis, and when it displays a state of mind strikingly different from the previous, and habitual or natural character of the individual (1847, p. 31).

The inference which Prichard invites us to draw is that the trained eye of the physician is needed to discriminate between such niceties of conduct. Second, this account of moral insanity both determines a person's position in society and provides an explanation or sanction for it. It is a way of 'freezing' behaviour.

The notion of 'moral insanity' is clearly an early precursor of the contemporary notion of psychopathy. More immediately, however, it provides a starting point for the development of many of Maudsley's ideas. In particular, Maudsley's description of 'the tyranny of organization' and of 'moral degeneracy' have obvious affinities with Prichard's ideas. Both Prichard and Maudsley argue for an extension of the physician's area of professional competence. For example, Prichard claims: 'There is scarce any offence against public decorum that has not been frequently the result of mental disease.' Similarly, Maudsley argues for the existence of insanity even where it 'has so much the look of vice or crime that many persons regard it as an unfounded medical invention' (1874, pp. 170–1). More essential similarities relate to the account which both writers give of the nature of insanity. Like Prichard, Maudsley sees the central feature of most types of insanity to be the loss of what he calls moral sense. Maudsley refers to it in the following way:

> The last acquired faculty in the progress of human evolution, it is the first to suffer when disease invades the mental organization. One of the first symptoms of insanity—one which declares itself before there is any intellectual derangement, before the person's friends suspect even that he is becoming insane—is a deadening or complete perversion of the moral sense (1873, p. 136).

Elsewhere Maudsley describes the moral sense as 'the last acquisition in the progress of *humanization*, and of human degeneracy (1879, p. 102). Clearly moral sense is a fragile flower easily crushed. However, the recognition of moral insanity or degeneracy has wider social implications. For it points to the existence of a part visible, part submerged class of moral degenerates who by the very nature of their defeat, form an increasing sector of the population. Maudsley sees the origin of evil impulses to

> lie in the physical constitution of the individual, and, going still further back, perhaps in his organic antecedents. Because the fathers have eaten sour grapes, therefore it often is that the children's teeth are set on edge. . . . Assuredly of some criminals, as of some insane persons, it may be truly said that they are born, not made; they go criminal, as the insane go mad, because they cannot help it (1873, p. 127).

Thus with the help of the Book of Jeremiah Maudsley paints a dismal picture of the growing field of insanity. However, the early account of moral insanity, as, indeed, the later account of moral degeneracy suffer from certain logical weaknesses. Moral insanity implies loss, or deterioration of will, but does not indicate how this loss is to be established. Moral insanity is evidence for loss of will and conversely loss of will is evidence of insanity. The weaknesses of the position are ably demonstrated by a contemporary critic, John Charles Bucknill:

> To what extent, therefore, will sound reason justify him (the physician) in maintaining the deterioration or total loss of responsibility? To arrive at a perfectly just estimate it would be necessary for him, according to the phraseology of Lord Denman, 'to dive into the mind of the patient', to see what is going on below the surface, and in the mud at the bottom. This is not permitted man to do,—God only knows the heart; Omniscience alone can estimate accurately the degree of irresponsibility produced by cerebral disease, the degrees of moral freedom and responsibility left by the same (1854, p. 17).

According to Bucknill's account the physician must have quite extraordinary powers in order to be able to perceive loss of will. Similar logical difficulties attend the use of the contemporary term 'psychopathy'. These have been cogently pointed out by Barbara Wootton and are equally relevant to the historical antecedents of the term (1959, especially ch. 7).

Moral Management and Moral Force

The ideas of the moral managers provide a stark contrast with the development of both Prichard's and Maudsley's thought. The following quotation from *The Times* provides an apt illustration of the early and mid-nineteenth century attitudes towards insanity; in particular of the moral managers:

> In strictness, we are all mad when we give way to passion, to prejudice, to vice, to vanity; but if all the passionate, prejudiced, vicious and vain people in this world are to be locked up as lunatics, who is to keep the key of the asylum? As was very fairly observed, however, by a learned Baron of the Exchequer, when he was pressed by this argument, if we are all mad, being all madmen, we must do the best we can under such untoward circumstances (22 July, 1853).

Like the forces of social anarchy and disorder insanity was thought to be a universal presence ready to break loose. Samuel Johnson claimed: 'Of the uncertainties of our present state, the most dreadful and alarming is the uncertain continuance of reason.' This sentiment finds an echo in many hearts in the early nineteenth century.

Nineteenth-century psychiatrists[1] pride themselves on their enlightened attitudes towards the insane. They themselves contrast this newly acquired wisdom with the repressiveness of the eighteenth century. Moral management is seen as the achievement of an impartial and unselfish concern for the plight of the insane. I do not wish to dispute or undermine such self-awarded praise. However, moral management can also be seen as one among a number of attempts to combat the forces of disorder so threatening to the Victorians. In abandoning the methods of the eighteenth century,[2] nineteenth-century physicians were not abandoning their role as guardians of the moral order and agents of social control. Physical restraint, coercion and exile are replaced by a philosophy of the self which emphasizes the dual nature of man, the power of the will to prevent and control insanity and which elaborated the arts of self-government.

Interestingly, insanity was seen by the English as in some way their peculiar affliction. From the literature it appears that this is largely a self-appointed label. In 1734 George Cheyne had published a book called *The English Malady or a Treatise on Nervous Diseases of all Kinds*. Most nineteenth-century essays on insanity include a section on epidemiology wihch relates the incidence of insanity to particular social groups or categories and styles of life. Thomas Arnold (1806 edn) devotes a whole section of his book to the question of 'Whether Insanity Prevails more in England than in other countries' (ibid., pp. 14–25). The answer is, of course, that it does. Irrespective of whether such self-characterizations are deserved or not, it is significant that insanity was *thought* to be a peculiarly English problem. Why this is so needs explanation.

The ideas and practices involved in moral management must first be described. Their contribution to a more basic, underlying pattern of thought can then be identified. The word 'moral' in this context is ambiguous in that it is used in two ways. On the one hand it relates to the mental or emotional as opposed to the physical. This is the meaning still retained in the French and German uses of the word. On the other hand 'moral' can be used to evaluate human behaviour. In its first use moral causes of insanity are contrasted with physical causes. Moral treatment depends upon social interaction, mutual influence and malleability of feeling. According to the second usage moral causes of insanity include bad habits and consequently an undesirable and unprincipled character. Moral treatment consists of an appeal to the conscience, the cultivation of the will and the art of self-government. Kathleen Jones (1972) argues that these two meanings are quite distinct and that 'moral' management relies upon the first meaning, except in cases where treatment is obviously bound up with religious ideas, as in the case of the Retreat at York. She says: 'the term "moral" as used by some writers of the time had a specialized meaning. "Moral" causes were effective or emotional causes, and "moral" treatment was treatment through the emotions. This was probably not the sense in which the Tukes used the word, since their treatment was indispensably bound up with religious and ethical teaching' (1972, p. 100). This separation of meanings needs to be challenged. I argue that 'moral management' relies upon the concurrent use of both meanings and that there is a systematic ambiguity in the use of the term, whereby the second meaning is contained and sometimes hidden within the first.

First, a consideration of moral management as described by the moral managers. The first full length account of moral management as well as the best known is given by Samuel Tuke in his *Description of the Retreat an institution near York for Insane Persons of the Society of Friends* (1813). The Retreat was founded for the Quaker insane in 1792 by William Tuke, a Quaker and wholesale tea and coffee merchant. The Retreat became the major life interest of William Tuke and subsequently of his son Henry and grandson Samuel, although neither father, son nor grandson were medically qualified. Hunter and Macalpine (1964), the medical historians, describe the family, in particular Samuel Tuke, as having wide-ranging philanthropic interests.

> His philanthropy ranged from the York Dispensary and Hospital to the Faithful Female Servants' Society, from anti-slavery to Irish relief and Catholic emancipation, from popular education to prison reform, from providence societies to temperance movements. But living in the atmosphere of the Retreat, itself a family concern, he devoted himself above all to the care and conditions of the insane (ibid., p. 2).

The implications of this assimilation of an interest in the insane to wider philanthropic interests will be discussed later. For the present, the essence of the new ideas on moral management needs to be summarized. Samuel Tuke describes moral management as consisting of three distinct, yet interrelated methods. 'We shall therefore inquire,

1. By what means the power of the patient to control the disorder, is strengthened and assisted.
2. What modes of coercion are employed, when restraint is absolutely necessary.
3. By what means the general comfort of the insane is promoted' (ibid., p. 133).

The most important ingredient of treatment seems to be the cultivation of self-control. Comfort is provided in order to promote it and restraint is introduced in its absence. Treatment by domination and fear is rejected not so much on intrinsic grounds but because it is likely to have little chance of success. 'The natural tendency of such treatment is, to degrade the mind of the patient, and to make him indifferent to those moral feelings, which, under judicious direction and encouragement, are found capable, in no small degree, to strengthen the power of self-restraint; and which render the resort to coercion, in many cases, unnecessary' (ibid., p. 163). In short, internal control is proposed as a substitute for external control.

These ideas, first examined by the Quaker Tukes, are later developed by other writers and achieve their fullest expression in the mid-century works of such writers as John Conolly (1856) and John Barlow (1843). One of the most sympathetic and persuasive accounts of moral arrangement is given by Conolly. He describes the methods of moral management as being a revulsion against the past. Earlier methods proceeded by 'alarm and torture', thus subduing the patient into submission. 'In medical works of authority the first principle in the treatment of lunatics was laid down to be fear, and the best means of producing fear was said to be punishment, and the best mode of punishment was defined to be stripes' (1856, p. 13). Conolly rejects the therapeutic effects of fear and advocates kindness instead. In essence treatment consists of a gentle and attentive concern for the patient's physical and emotional well-being.

> Wherever they go they meet kind people, and hear kind words; they are never passed without some recognition, and the face of every officer is the face of a friend. In the evening, the domestic meal of tea refreshes them. Their supper and their bed are not negligently prepared. Day after day these influences operate, and day by day mental irritation subsides, and suspicions die, and gloomy thoughts gradually disperse, and confidence grows and strengthens, and natural affections re-awake, and reason returns (ibid., p. 58).

Despite its humanity the theoretical content of such therapy does, of course, seem limited.

The theoretical presuppositions of the moral managers need to be examined. A Cartesian view of the individual is involved. Within this broad framework there are two branches of thought. One line of thought maintains that insanity is a disease of the brain, but since man is also spiritual, spirit can be used to oppose matter. The second account of insanity sees it as a disease of the blood. The importance of bleeding as a therapeutic and prophylactic measure in insanity is well known from numerous eighteenth- and nineteenth-century accounts. Venesection, topical bleeding, dry cupping and refrigeration of the head were almost universally practised. What is less well known is the theory on which such therapeutic measures rest. One version of this theory is succinctly presented by James Sheppard in his *Observations on the Proximate Causes of Insanity* subtitled *Being an Attempt to Prove that Insanity is Dependent on a Morbid Condition of the Blood* (1844). The association of insanity with 'morbid conditions of the circulating fluid' (p. 34) is made in the context of rejecting an account of insanity as caused by disease of the brain, i.e. the structural account. Furthermore, the substitution of blood for brain or organization enables Sheppard to attribute to mind a more direct control over insanity. He claims there is a reciprocal influence between mind and blood, although he clearly indicates that the influence of mind over blood is greater (ibid., p. 51). Blood is the medium through which mind acts on organization. The chain of reasoning runs as follows: Thoughts and emotions are subject to individual control. These affect the content of the blood. Therefore, blood can be controlled by the individual. The condition of blood determines sanity and insanity. Therefore, insanity can be controlled. Unlike the brain which assumes greater importance later in the century, blood is fluid and malleable. It is introduced as an expression of confidence in the powers of the individual.

Both these accounts rely on Cartesian elements. The first relies on a straightforward account of man as being essentially dual. In the second version blood seems to play a role very similar to that of Descartes's 'animal spirits'. Both are mediators between spirit and matter.

This Cartesian outlook provides the theoretical background to the work of the Reverend John Barlow. *Man's Power over himself to Prevent or Control Insanity* ran to three editions, an indication of the popularity of the ideas expressed. The style of the book is well caught by the following expression:

> diseases of the brain and nervous system, however distressing, may and do, where the mind has been duly cultivated, leave the individual capable of knowing right from wrong, and of seeking exterior aid to combat the effects of mental derangement consequent on disease—a derangement of which he is either conscious at the time, or has an anticipatory

> knowledge of, which enables him rationally to provide against its violence (2nd edn, 1849, p. 47).

Thus the patient, no longer an enemy, becomes an ally in the struggle against disease. The preferred term is 'mental derangement' rather than 'insanity', emphasizing as it does disorder and lack of government. Immunity against mental derangement is secured by strength of character which, in turn, is nurtured by discipline and moderation. In fact, Barlow's book is offered as a practical manual outlining strategies of self-help in cases of derangement. However, not only was the will seen as force combating madness, its loss, however discovered, was constitutive of insanity. Thus the power of volition and self control were seen as the defining characteristics of sanity. Thus Daniel Noble, for example, writes: 'I will state insanity to consist in apyrexial disorder of the brain, penetrating thought or feeling, to the destruction and impairment of moral liberty' (1853, p. 11). John Charles Bucknill (1854) provides a definition of sanity along similar lines:

> what is the condition to which insanity, mental alienation, unsoundness, derangement, is opposed? It is that condition of the mind in which the emotions and the instincts are in such a state of subordination to the will, that the latter can direct and control their manifestations; in which moreover the intellectual faculties are capable of submitting to the will sound reasons for its actions. Such co-ordinate action of the faculties is termed sanity; a condition in which that is lost is termed insanity, or derangement, or alienation , or unsoundness, all terms having reference to the deprivation of the power of the will so directed (pp. 27–8).

Other examples illustrating the importance of the will could be taken from writers from the Tukes onwards and multiplied endlessly. Suffice it to say that the emphasis on the will reached a high point in the 1850s and thereafter gradually declined, although it did not disappear.

What are the insights which a survey of nineteenth-century ideas on insanity offers? First, it is worth noting that insanity is seen as a real problem both for the author and the reader. The problem is seen as being an explicitly moral one, intimately related to wider philosophical issues concerning the nature of man. Supporting this view is Kathleen Jones's statement (1972, p. 3) about eighteenth-century ideas on insanity: 'There was no clear definition of what mental disease was, and certainly no recognition of the mentally ill or handicapped as requiring a distinct form of treatment.' And, later she writes: 'The idea of insanity as a single social factor had not yet been evolved' (ibid., p. 25). The situation can be summarized by saying that insanity was seen as being a problem for mankind and not, as it was later to become, a problem for certain categories of men. This subjective approach to insanity is in the tradition of earlier classical works on the subject. Robert Burton, the melancholy divine, writes:

> I write of melancholy, by being busie to avoid melancholy . . . to ease my mind by writing, for I had *gravidum cor, foetum caput*, a kind of imposthume in my head, which I was very desirous to be unladen of, and could imagine no fitter evacuation than this . . . one must needs scratch where it itches (1621; 1806 edn, p. 7).

A similar commitment to the subject is found in George Cheyne's writing referred to previously. Cheyne describes himself as being afflicted with: 'Head-ache, Giddiness, Watchings, Bowness, Melancholy . . . perpetual Anxiety and Inquietude . . . so that I could scarce bear the sight of my patients.' He claims to have weighed over 32 stone and, understandably, singled out gluttony as one of the most important causes of insanity.

Throughout the first half of the nineteenth century the discussion of insanity follows the classical tradition and the problem is approached from a subjective viewpoint. Books on insanity like John Barlow (1843) and Thomas Bakewell, *The Domestic Guide in Cases of Insanity* (1809) were clearly intended as guides for laymen—even to the extent of being brought out in pocket-size editions. Presumably, they were meant to be carried around on one's person and consulted when need arose.

These ideas, interesting though they may be in themselves, form part of a whole cultural climate. The early and mid-nineteenth century was a period of unprecedented social change and seemingly unlimited economic expansion and promise. This social and economic setting provides the nurturing ground for a policy of *laissez-faire* and a philosophy of individualism. This relationship between the stages of economic development and philosophical outlook has, of course, been explored before. It is less widely recognized, however, that psychiatric ideas, too, contribute to the prevailing philosophy of individualism.

The importance attributed to moral training as a prophylactic against insanity and to moral force as controlling insanity is consonant with a philosophy of individualism. It depends, also, on an idealist philosophy which sees man's nature as being essentially dualistic. With each act of the will the individual is, as it were, made anew. His potentialities for development are, therefore, limitless. By contrast, the notion of 'character' which acquires popularity among physicians in the latter half of the century, implies a relatively unchanging set of qualities and imposes definite constraints on behaviour. Limits are set on what an individual may or may not achieve. However, the contrast between moral force and character is not altogether clear as the latter term was already widely used in early nineteenth-century society. But the term only acquired its meaning as an unalterable determinant of behaviour in late Victorian England. Prior to that character was a relatively malleable entity, open to influence by, for example, good habits. A similar etymological development belongs to the notion of 'psychological power'. First used in a medical context by Bucknill (1854, p. 59) and promising unimpeded success, it became later the overprotected offspring of 'organization'.

These ideas were not only the prerogative of physicians. They formed part of the outlook of poets, educationalists and men of letters. Ideas about the treatment of the insane and the education of the young have many similarities. The formation of character was central to educational theory of the newly founded public schools. There was the notion of a struggling and striving for the attainment of character. Second, the contribution of the public schools to the growth of the new middle classes is well known. Asa Briggs (1965, p. 153) says: 'the great social divide of the 1840's between landlords and businessmen was bridged. The public school, consequently provided for the gradual fusion of classes and their drawing upon a common store of values.' G. K. Chesterton's remark about public schools being for the fathers of gentlemen, rather than the sons of gentlemen is in point here. Thus both in educational and psychiatric theory, the cultivation of character provided a means of surmounting categorization, whether social or medical.

Coleridge shares the orthodox views on insanity. He talks specifically of 'mental anarchy': 'Why need we talk of a fiery hell? If the will, which is the law of our nature, were withdrawn from our memory, fancy, understanding, and reason, no other hell could equal, for a spiritual being, what we should then feel, from the anarchy of our powers. It would be conscious madness—a horrid thought!' (1835, p. 113). This view might equally well have been expressed by one of the moral managers. But Coleridge also gives a more detailed description of the dual nature of man and the interrelationship of the two parts in madness.

> Madness is not simply a bodily disease. It is the sleep of the spirit with certain conditions of wakefulness; that is to say lucid intervals. During this sleep, or recession of the spirit, the lower or bestial states of life rise up into action or prominence. It is an awful thing to be eternally tempted by the perverted senses. The reason may resist—it does resist, for a long time; but too often, at length, it yields for a moment and the man is mad forever. An act of the will is in many cases precedent to complete insanity. I think it was Bishop Butler who said that he was all his life struggling against the devilish suggestions of his senses, which would have maddened him, if he had relaxed the stern wakefulness of his reason for a single moment (ibid., p. 66).

Both the man of letters and the physician became interested during the same period of time with that private area of inner experience as the source of social and moral improvement.

However, the ideas most closely related to those of the moral managers were popularized by Samuel Smiles. His work summarizes in a pithy way the whole ethos of the mid-Victorianism. The titles of his books give an indication of his interests. *Self-Help* (1859), *Character* (1871), *Thrift* (1875), *Duty* (1880) all deal with the power to be derived from the inner resources of the individual. In *Self-Help*, for example, Smiles writes: 'It may be of comparatively little consequence how a man is governed from without when everything depends upon how he is governed from within' (1959, p. 36). Asa Briggs (1959, p. 23) describes Smiles as: 'content to accept the view which Shakespeare put into Iago's mouth—"our bodies are gardens to which our wills are gardeners . . . the power and corrigible authority lies in our wills".' Character according to Smiles is acquired by the development of inner force, not by the outward conformity of the eighteenth-century gentleman. Smiles recognized four qualities as being of special relevance to the development of character: energy, cheerfulness, prudence and industry. In the present context, energy is the most interesting ingredient of character in that it is a counterpart of the physician's term 'moral force'. 'It is will, force of purpose that enables a man to do whatever he sets his mind on being or doing' (ibid., p. 250). Such statements as these demonstrate the similarity between ideas on insanity and the spirit of the age. Like Mill and others of his time, Smiles thought that both the growth of the individual and of society depends on the development of character through a cultivation of the above qualities. 'Help from without is often enfeebling in its effects, but help from within invariably invigorates' (Briggs, 1959, p. 24). Interestingly, Smiles's popularity was at its peak in the 1860s and 1870s but declined by the end of the century. Smiles's ideas form part of the ethic glorifying individual effort and work. The ethic that provides the oppressive setting of Dickens's novels:

> 'But I like business', said Pancks, getting on a little faster. 'What's a man made for?' 'For nothing else?' said Clennam. Pancks put the counter question, 'What else?' It packed up in the smallest compass, a weight that had rested on Clennam's life; and he made no answer' (1855; 1967 edn, p. 201).

Thus, will, character and industry provide the ethical cornerstones of mid-Victorian society. Smiles himself, in a sociologically perceptive mood, describes characters as: 'human nature in its best form. It is the moral order embodied in the individual' (1859, p. 360). However, one needs to add that it is an expanding economy and a fluid social structure which permits a philosophy of individual power and effort. Similarly, a theory of insanity which attributes responsibility to the individual does not thereby bring about a decrease in the incidence of insanity, although it may have consequences for treatment. Rather it is the result of changes in the structure of society.

This analysis of the concepts of 'moral force' and 'character' and the way in which they relate to the social order is similar to Pitt-Rivers's consideration of 'honour' in Andalusia (1965). According to Pitt-Rivers (p. 31), 'honour' is important in situations involving equals: 'A man is answerable for his honour only to his social equals.' It can be a means of excelling where external criteria do not provide rules for precedence. The intention of a person (a private event) is important in establishing honour. Character, based on inner qualities, acquires importance in a different though not dissimiliar situation: one where social status is no longer dependent on certain external and fixed criteria. In a situation of social fluidity, inner worth replaces outward signs and accomplishments. There is, of course, a vast difference between the meaning of 'character' and 'personality'. The difference is nicely put by Anthony Quinton:

> It could be said that character, in view of its connection with the will, is an ethical notion, while that of personality is really aesthetic. Character is intrinsic and deep-seated, a rather central constituent of a person, something that is not easy for others to influence, or for the person himself to change. But personality can be put on and taken off with much less difficulty, there is something histrionic about it (1973, p. 372).

Unlike character-building, personality-building is a 'cosmetic art'. It is a situation in which 'nature's gentleman' comes into his own. One is reminded of the sad Victorian character who says of himself: 'I am not quite a gentleman but you would hardly notice it.' Like character, honour has both a descriptive and an evaluative component. 'The reconciliation between the social order as one finds it and the social order which we revere is accomplished thanks to the confusion which hinges upon the duality of honour and its associated concepts' (Pitt-Rivers, 1965, p. 38). It is quite clearly a situation where 'ought' is derived from 'is'. Similarly, our term character both refers to certain enduring aspects of an individual or of expressed approval of the individual's strength of will and moral force. The description of the context and uses of both terms indicates the direction which a sociology of morals should take. It conflicts with the approach of, for example, Ossowska (1971), as indeed of most philosophers. She says (p. 18): 'Descriptive ethics ought to be treated separately from normative ethics.' As a sociologist approaching a terrain hitherto occupied by philosophers, she promises a particularly barren start.

Parallels can also be drawn between ideas about insanity and the nineteenth-century philanthropic outlook. It is well known that the Victorians translated social problems into moral terms. Thus poverty, for example, was seen as the result of personal inadequacies. David Owen, in a comprehensive study of English philanthropy, writes (1964, p. 136): 'To them [i.e. the early

Victorians] the critical social evil was not mass poverty but pauperism, and this they ascribed largely to individual weakness. Unless the working classes could acquire the essential virtues of thrift, temperance, industry and family responsibility there was little hope for British society.' Given this analysis of social problems, philanthropy necessarily has a dual character. It is not simply a question of giving charity but also of moral elevation. Owen describes the principles of the Victorian philanthropic outlook:

> If charity was a response to human need, it was also the instrument of inculcating approved social attitudes. The new philanthropist frowned on alms-giving without careful investigation, and tended to judge charitable efforts by their success in encouraging recipients to stand on their own feet. Properly conceived charity should be limited to the 'deserving', that vaguely defined class of unfortunates which figures so heavily in nineteenth century writing on the subject (ibid., 98).

In other words, charity should be directed to those susceptible to moral improvement. But even with this class of the deserving poor caution should be exercised, for: 'To assist them unduly would be simply to pauperize, a word with terrifying implications for the Victorians' (ibid., p. 4). Terrifying, because charity is passively received and removes the need for individual moral force and acts of will so central to the early and mid Victorian moral order.

Heredity

Philanthropy leads inevitably to a consideration of class and thus directs attention to the changes which took place in psychiatry in the late nineteenth century. Philanthropists directed their attention towards what became known as the 'perishing and dangerous classes' (Carpenter, 1851). Included in this class are the pauper lunatics. By the end of the century General Booth is publicizing the existence of a 'submerged tenth'. This tenth is not a new arrival. John Bright had talked of a 'sunken sixth' much earlier. However, there is now an open and systematic acknowledgment of the most deprived sectors of the population. In part, this is the result of the work of such people as Charles Booth in the East End of London and Rowntree in York. (Whether or not the material conditions of the poor actually deteriorated is a point of debate among historians.) However, despite the philosophy of unhampered individualism and freedom, the poor and pauper lunatics did not disappear. As a consequence there was difficulty in reconciling the existing theories of insanity with the recognition of widespread destitution and with the swelling asylum population.

During the middle years of the century the middle classes had acquired the bulk of their members, aided by the appropriate philosophical and moral world-view. At the end of the century, however, the identity of the middle classes is threatened. The depression certainly involved a crisis of confidence and meant that further economic expansion was checked. Furthermore, the increasing cohesiveness of the working classes as measured, for example, by the formation of trade unions posed another threat to middle-class identity. Criteria for membership of the middle classes were, therefore, changed from acquired characteristics to inherited ones, thus firmly closing the door to newcomers. In part the differences between the mid-Victorian middle class and the late-Victorian middle class reduce to differences between families at different stages of their upward social climb. Those 'on the make' emphasize effort and acquired characteristics. Those who have arrived emphasize ascribed or inherited characteristics. Thus class boundaries and class consciousness are intensified during the latter part of the century.

To summarize: the 1870s are a time of economic depression. Prices fall; business no longer offers rewards to all with enterprise and industry. At the international level Britain no longer occupies its position of undisputed and unrivalled economic supremacy. The earlier sense of abounding optimism and progress is lost. The philosophy of the heyday of Victorianism is no longer adequate to changed circumstances.

How this contraction of social and economic opportunity affected ideas on insanity is particularly interesting. During the late Victorian period insanity is no longer seen as a problem either for the writer or the reader. Rather, it is a problem which afflicts certain categories of men. It is viewed from the outside as capable of measurement according to a number of objective yardsticks. The theme of moral power—so ardently pursued during the middle years of the century—is quietly forgotten. With this reinterpretation of the problem the philosopher is replaced by the physician: in the words of one ancient author: 'Ubi philosophia desinit, ibi medicina incipit.' The change in attitude can be brought out by the following reminder. For much of the nineteenth century a nervous breakdown was seen as a necessary stage in the development of any artist or, for that matter, of any man of sensibility. The madman is sometimes thought to be nearer to the fountainhead of truth. Dickens describes the oracular role which Mr Dick plays in the life of Miss Betsey Trotwood: in situations of uncertainty and crisis he is always consulted. Such ideas are radically different from later ones. For example, Bertrand Russell in the first volume of his autobiography describes his family's attitude towards his future wife. Apparently, his choice was not popular with them and among the arguments used to persuade the couple against marriage was the alleged existence of insanity in both families. Russell describes the 'thick atmosphere of sighs, tears, groans and morbid horror' (1967, p. 84) which the allegations generated. Although the warnings of relatives did not prevent the couple from marrying, they did decide not to have children 'on medical grounds'.

The implication is that there is a submerged category of the insane visible only to the clinical eye. Hence, the title of Andrew Wynter's book *The Borderlands of Insanity* (1875) is appropriate to the tone of late nineteenth-century thinking. The earlier note of apprehensive optimism is gone. Instead, caution and watchfulness are needed to guard against the hidden enemy. At bottom, however, men are helpless in the face of insanity: 'a passenger is every now and then missed from the ever-ebbing stream of life, and none but the physician notes that he has dropped through the pitfall on the bridge, and will never mix in the busy haunts of man again' (p. 31). There is a note of terrible finality about this disappearance. The most that can be done is to recognize the early warnings of insanity. These may be subtle indications apparent only to the physician. For example, the quiver of an eyebrow or the tremor of a lower lip can betray the incipient lunatic. (One is reminded of the *Malleus Maleficarum* and the apparently arbitrary signs which indicate witchcraft.)

In brief, a theme emerges which emphasizes the physical basis of insanity, or the importance of hereditary endowment. This outlook is epitomized in a much-favoured biblical warning: 'Because the fathers had stoned the prophets, therefore it was that the children rejected Him who was sent unto them' (Maudsley, 1873, p. 127). In fact, most psychiatric writing of the period has that solemn, carefully-measured tone of the Old Testament. Whilst earlier literature had instructed in the art of controlling insanity, now sub-headings appear on the 'Impossibility of Avoiding Insanity' (Blandford, 1878). Henry Maudsley, referring to John Barlow's book, writes: 'the author regards the subject entirely from a moral point of view and certainly in some respects overrates the power of control' (1874, p. 289). And writing about the will, Maudsley questions its power: 'No one can resolve successfully by a mere effort of will to think in a certain way, or to feel in a certain way, or even, which is easier, to act always in accordance with certain rules' (ibid., p. 289). These quotations clearly indicate a change of mind and mood on the subject of insanity.

The theme of heredity and organization is espoused by one physician after another. The writer whose influence was and remains greatest is, no doubt, Henry Maudsley. Throughout his writing the term 'heredity neurosis'[3] recurs. This interest expresses itself in many dire warnings such as: 'No one can escape the tyranny of his organization; no one can escape the destiny that is innate in him' (1873, p. 76). Or: 'Can the Ethiopian change his skin or the leopard his spots?' (ibid., p. 131). Even worse, Maudsley describes the man who has 'an enemy in his own camp, a traitor in his own nature, which is ever ready to conspire with external adversities' (1879, p. 103). Surely a situation of doom if ever there was one!

Even Daniel Hack Tuke, a descendant of the founder of the Retreat, introduced the notion of physical heredity as a causal factor in insanity. In an extraordinary passage, remembering his reputation as advocate for the gentle and humane treatment of the insane, Tuke (1878) concedes the power of native constitution. Having earlier characterized the delicate and fragile constitution he goes on to describe a further type:

> This constitution of the mind must be distinguished from an allied but different organization which is marked by native stupidity, and constitutes an infirm type of humanity largely met with in the lower classes and especially the population from which the great county asylums of England are fed. On admission 'No good' is plainly inscribed on their foreheads.

Diagnostic procedures were no doubt considerably helped with the aid of such simple guides! In sum, Tuke thought that 'the evils of bodily organization' cannot be 'set at nought by the will' (ibid., p. 152).

Other writers follow the lead set by Maudsley and Tuke. For example, Jordan writes about character or temperament and the way in which these relate to the body. He comes to the conclusion 'that each temperament has its cluster of special, distinctive, bodily signs. The more marked the temperament the more marked are the signs' (1896, p. 7). In fact, physical endowment determines character. 'Neither bodily nor mental characteristics are miscellaneous collections of fragments; they run together in more or less uniform clusters. With one particular kind of skeleton and skin there will be associated a particular kind of nervous organization, and, therefore, one particular kind of character' (ibid., p. 43). In fact, Jordan is so confident of a constant relationship between body and character that he is able to predict the physical attributes of the 'battered wife', even to the extent of drawing a diagram of her spinal curve. Character, as described by Jordan, is not shaped by the individual. It is inherited along with wealth, property and social standing. It is worth noting that the term inheritance refers primarily to the transmission of social assets and only by extension to the transmission of genetic characteristics.

What is the relationship between this view of the individual, particularly the pauper lunatic and criminal, and one's view of the nature of society? Jordan himself supplies the answer. 'On these terms the very existence of society is based—based on the dominancy of organization over the possibilities of circumstance' (ibid., p. 113).

This necessary residuum of bad heredity is recognized by General Booth under the label 'Objects of Infinite Compassion'. Of these objects Booth writes:

> There are men so incorrigibly lazy that no inducement that you can offer will tempt them to work; so eaten up by vice that virtue is abhorrent to them, and so inveterately dishonest that theft is to them a master passion. When a human being has reached that stage, there is only one course that can be rationally pursued. Sorrowfully, but remorselessly, it must be recognised that he has become lunatic, morally

> demented, incapable of self-government, and that upon him, therefore, must be passed the sentence of permanent seclusion from a world in which he is not fit to be at large. . . . Between them and the wide world there should be reared an impassable barrier, which once passed should be recrossed no more for ever (ibid., pp. 204–5).

To summarize, psychiatry in the nineteenth century is dominated by two contrasting themes. The literature is preoccupied with the relative weight to be attributed to physical and moral causes of insanity. The first theme which emerges gradually from the early nineteenth century onwards, stresses a number of moral factors which may act as counter-forces against insanity. Habit, perseverance, the will, character may each constitute such a counteracting force. The second theme emphasizes hereditary endowment or the 'tyranny of organization'. According to this theme insanity forms part of one's inheritance in the same way as does wealth and social standing. It emerges from the 1879s onwards and can be seen as a reversion to an earlier Hippocratic and platonic view. These two themes do not altogether exclude each other. To some extent they survive side by side. But the importance attached to each increases and decreases throughout the century so greatly, that it is necessary to look at the wider social context in which these theoretical changes take place.[4]

In part, this re-examination of psychiatric texts is prompted by the style of current writing in psychiatry. Recent writers, Szasz among them, have underlined the specific uses to which psychiatry has been put in the past, in order to make a more general claim about the nature of psychiatry as such. However, this review of the literature is related to a deeper conviction that nosology, particularly psychiatric nosology, is related to moral outlook and thus forms a part of the total social fabric of society. This connection can be seen more easily in other times and in other societies. We can afford to be more perceptive about the nineteenth century, since their categorizations exert less constraint over us than do our own.

Notes

1 Beginning with William Pargeter whose *Observations on Maniacal Disorders* published in 1792 first refers to the notion of 'management' as opposed to physical restraint of patients.

2 Order was maintained by the complete exclusion of deviants—this took such physical forms as for example the 'stultifera navis' or the ship of fools (Foucault, 1971).

3 It is worth noting that before Freud the terms 'neuroses' and 'psychoses' had, roughly speaking, meanings contrary to those which they possess today. The niceties of meaning are well explained by Hunter and Macalpine in their introduction of Schreber's *Memoirs of my Nervous Illness* (1955, p. 16):

> Neurosis, much the older term, derives from the Greek, meaning nerve, tendon or sinew, structures which were not differentiated. In our time, neurasthenia, nerve weakness, nerve strain, and, of course, treatment by nerve tonics show their origin in this old anatomical confusion. In 1661 a 'neurotic' was a substance having an action on the nervous system, particularly a bracing one; a book dealing with these more recently was entitled 'The Old Vegetable Neurotics'. (1869). In 1777 Cullen applied the term 'neurosis' to all diseases of the nervous system not accompanied by fever (all pyrexial diseases being grouped together irrespective of site or cause), the vasaniae, or mental diseases forming a sub-group.

In fact, the term 'psychosis' was introduced to replace the term 'neurosis' as well as to emphasize an alternative view of its aetiology. First used by Feuchtersleben in 1845, the term indicated the connection between insanity and the soul rather than the body or brain. The term was, of course, introduced at a time when this view of insanity was very popular. However, contemporary linguistic usage has, it seems, reversed these earlier meanings, since psychoses are more generally held to have an organic basis, whilst neuroses are thought to be 'functional'.

4 Gregory Bateson (1973) in a paper on the logic of alcoholism and the logic of Alcoholics Anonymous describes a world-view very similar to that popular in the first half of the nineteenth century and described here. Bateson describes the sober alcoholic as dogged by a particularly pernicious form of Cartesian Dualism, characterised by: 'the division between Mind and Matter, or, in this case, between conscious will, or "self", and the remainder of the personality' (ibid., p. 284). The return to the bottle indicates the inadequacy of the epistemology of sobriety and the 'rightness' of intoxication. AA challenges this epistemology and, according to Bateson: '. . . this change is from an incorrect to a more correct epistemology' (ibid., p. 287). The vicious dualism which makes sobriety insufferable for the alcoholic is demolished by the first principle of the AA: 'We admitted that we were powerless over alcohol—that our lives had become unmanageable.' According to Bateson this is a move to an epistemology which borrows the insights of cybernetics, namely that no part of a system can have unilateral control over that system.

Clearly, Bateson is in favour of the epistemology of the AA, and sees the epistemology of the sober alcoholic and, indeed, of common-sense thought, as wrong. My approach to theories of self should by now be clear, namely that, insightful though Bateson's paper is, it is not the task of social anthropologists to recommend epistomology, but rather to explore the social context and cultural climate in which they flourish.

Bibliography

ARNOLD, THOMAS (1782). *Observations on the Nature, Kinds, Causes and Prevention of Insanity*. London: Richard Phillips, second edn, 1806.

BAKEWELL, THOMAS (1809). *The Domestic Guide in Cases of Insanity.* Newcastle: C. Chester.

BARLOW, JOHN (1843). *Man's Power over Himself to Prevent or Control Insanity.* London: William Pickering.

BATESON, GREGORY (1973). *Steps towards an Ecology of Mind.* London: Paladin.

BLANDFORD, G. FIELDING (1878). *Insanity and its Treatment.* Edinburgh: Oliver & Boyd.

BOOTH, GENERAL (1890). *In Darkest England and the Way Out.* London: The Salvation Army.

BRIGGS, ASA (1965). *Victorian People.* Harmondsworth: Penguin.

BUCKNILL, JOHN CHARLES (1854). *Unsoundness of Mind in Relation to Criminal Insanity.* London: Longman, Brown, Green & Longmans.

BURTON, ROBERT (1621). *The Anatomy of Melancholy.* London: J. and E. Hodson, eleventh edn, 1806.

CARPENTER, M. (1851). *Reformatory Schools for the Children of the Perishing and Dangerous Classes and for Juvenile Offenders.* London: Gilpin.

CHEYNE, GEORGE (1734). *The English Malady or a Treatise on Nervous Diseases of all Kinds.* London: Strahan & Leake.

COLERIDGE, SAMUEL TAYLOR (1835; 1905). *Table Talk and Omniana.* London: George Bell & Sons.

COMFORT, ALEX (1967). *The Anxiety Makers.* London: Panther edn, 1968.

CONOLLY, JOHN (1856). *The Treatment of the Insane without Mechanical Restraints.* London: Smith, Elder & Co.

DICKENS, CHARLES (1855). *Little Dorrit.* Harmondsworth: Penguin edn, 1967.

FOUCAULT, MICHEL (1971). *Madness and Civilization.* London: Tavistock Publications.

HARE, E. H. (1962). 'Masturbational Insanity: the History of an Idea', *Journal of Mental Science.* 108, pp. 1–25.

HOBBES, THOMAS (1651). *Leviathan.* London: Fontana edn, 1962.

HUNTER, RICHARD and MACALPINE, IDA (1955, eds). Daniel Schreber, *Memoirs of my Nervous Illness.* London: Dawson & Sons Ltd.

HUNTER, RICHARD and MACALPINE, IDA (1964, eds). Samuel Tuke, *A Description of the Retreat* (1813). London: Dawsons of Pall Mall.

JONES, KATHLEEN (1972). *A History of the Mental Health Services.* London: Routledge & Kegan Paul.

JORDAN, FURNEAUX (1886). *Character as Seen in Body and Parentage.* London: Kegan Paul, Trench, Trubner & Co.

LAYCOCK, THOMAS (1840). *A Treatise on Nervous Diseases of Women.* London: Longman, Orme, Brown, Green & Longmans.

LOCKE, JOHN (1690). *An Essay Concerning Understanding.* New York: Dover edn, 1959.

MADDOCK, ALFRED BEAUMONT (1854). *Practical Observations on Mental and Nervous Disorders.* London: Simpkin, Marshall & Co.

MAUDSLEY, HENRY (1873). *Body and Mind.* London: Macmillan & Co.

MAUDSLEY, HENRY (1874). *Mental Diseases.* New York and London: D. Appleton & Co.

MAUDSLEY, HENRY (1879). *The Pathology of Mind.* London: Macmillan & Co.

NOBLE, DANIEL (1853). *Elements of Psychological Medicine*. London: John Churchill.
OSSOWSKA, MARIA (1971). *The Social Determinants of Moral Ideas*. London: Routledge & Kegan Paul.
OWEN, DAVID (1964). *English Philanthropy 1660–1960*. London: Oxford University Press.
PARGETER, WILLIAM (1792). *Observations on Maniacal Disorders*. Reading: for the author.
PITT-RIVERS, JULIAN (1965). 'Honour and Social Status' in *Honour and Shame: the Values of a Mediterranean Society*, ed. J. G. Peristiany. London: Weidenfeld & Nicolson.
PRICHARD, JAMES COWLES (1833). *A Treatise on Insanity*. London: Marchant.
PRICHARD, JAMES COWLES (1847). *On the Different Forms of Insanity in Relation to Jurisprudence*. London: Hippolyte Ballière.
QUINTON, ANTHONY (1973). 'The Continuity of Persons', *Times Literary Supplement*, 27 July, pp. 872–3.
RUSSELL, BERTRAND (1967). *Autobiography*. Vol. I. London: George Allen & Unwin.
SHEPPARD, JAMES (1844). *Observations on the Proximate Causes of Insanity*. London: Longman, Brown, Green & Longmans.
SMILES, SAMUEL (1859). *Self-Help*. London: John Murray.
SPITZ, R. A. (1953). 'Authority and Masturbation', *Yearbook of Psychoanalysis*, 9, pp. 113–45.
SZASZ, THOMAS (1971). *The Manufacture of Madness*. London: Routledge & Kegan Paul.
TUKE, DANIEL HACK (1878). *Insanity in Ancient and Modern Life with Chapters on its Prevention*. London: Macmillan & Co.
TUKE, SAMUEL (1813). *A Description of the Retreat: an Institution near York for Insane Persons of the Society of Friends*. London: Dawsons of Pall Mall, 1964 edn.
WOOTTON, BARBARA (1959). *Social Science and Social Pathology*. London: George Allen & Unwin.
WYNTER, ANDREW (1875). *The Borderlands of Insanity*. London: Robert Hardwicke.

PART ONE

OUTLINES OF INSANITY

Chapter I

Causes and Prevalence

1. John Haslam, *The Nature of Madness*

(Excerpt from *Observations on Madness and Melancholy*, London: Callow, 1810, pp. 15–16.)

Madness being the opposite to reason and good sense, as light is to darkness, straight to crooked, &c. it appears wonderful that two opposite opinions could be entertained on the subject: allowing each party to possess the ordinary faculties common to human beings in a sound and healthy state, yet such is really the fact: and if one party be right, the other must be wrong: because a person cannot correctly be said to be *in* his senses and *out* of his senses at the same time.

But there is considerable difficulty and some danger in applying logic to facts. Every person who takes the degree of Doctor becomes, in consequence of taking such degree, a learned man; and it is libellous to pronounce him ignorant. It is true, a Doctor may be blind, deaf and dumb, stupid or mad, but still his Diploma shields him from the imputation of ignorance.* It has also not unfrequently occurred, that a man who has been dubbed a Doctor of Medicine at Leyden, Aberdeen, or St. Andrews, and whose Diploma sets forth his profound learning, accomplishments, and competence to practise on the lives of His Majesty's good and faithful subjects, has been found incapable of satisfying the gentlemen in Warwick Lane that he possessed the common rudiments of his profession, and has been by them accordingly rejected: so that learning in many instances appears to be local.

* The feeblest intellect I ever commiserated was a Doctor of Laws from the University of Glasgow.

2. Alexander Morison, *Moral Causes of Insanity*

(Excerpt from *Outlines of Mental Diseases*, Edinburgh: MacLachlan & Stewart, 1824, pp. 66–71.)

With regard to the influence of Seasons, it appears that Spring and Summer are more conducive to Mania—Autumn to Partial Insanity with Depression—and Winter to Dementia.

The heat in summer produces exacerbation in many cases of insanity, and increases the tendency to suicide.

With respect to Age.

Infants are nearly exempted, although children under ten years of age occasionally exhibit symptoms of general and of partial insanity. It is sometimes coincident with rapid growth—and with the efforts of the constitution in establishing the menstrual discharge.

In old age, the first appearance of insanity (Dementia excepted) is rare, although instances have occasionally occurred in persons whose age has exceeded 80, and even 100. It is, however, most prevalent between the ages of 25 and 40.

Sex.—In some countries, as in Great Britain and France, there are more females insane than males; but this is not the case in all. Females are exposed to exciting causes from which males are exempted, as

The puerperal state, which seems to give a predisposition to insanity, and frequently calls it into action, when there is hereditary disposition; this cause acts more extensively in the higher than in the lower classes.

The critical period of female life also frequently leads to the development of insanity.

In the treatment of mental disease, it has been observed that there is a beneficial influence exerted by one sex over the other.

With regard to the influence of occupation and condition in life, in the production of insanity, it may be observed, that professions requiring great mental exertion, and those which lead to hazardous speculations, are more liable to insanity than others; persons who are most independent, in consequence of their rank and fortune, are comparatively speaking, more subject to it than the middle class. This may be accounted for in part by intermarriages and excesses.

Education conducted with too great severity may lead to insanity; but the opposite extreme is a more common cause of it—an education not conducted on the principle of bringing the inclinations and affections under the control of religious and moral principles, and of repressing ideas of hurtful tendency, but encouraging false and romantic notions, and ideas above the rank in life.

The minds of some have likewise been weakened by terrifying tales in early life.

Excess of ignorance, and excess of study, both tend to weaken the mind, particularly the latter, when directed to a few ideas. The consequences of this excess of study, or of application to business, are—an irritable state of body and of mind—restless nights—febrile symptoms—diminished power of attention—confusion of ideas—and, if persisted in, insanity.

The predominant ideas of the times, whether religious or political, have great influence in producing mental disorder.

With regard to the influence of religion, although excessive devotion, and contrition or remorse of conscience may occasionally lead to insanity, especially in melancholy dispositions, doubt of doctrines previously professed in general precedes madness from religion: the mind, in suspense as to what regards eternal salvation, is easily overset.

Religion has less influence in this respect in the warmer climates, and in the Catholic countries, than in the temperate climates, and in countries where latitude of religious opinion is permitted; free governments, and political commotions, being favourable to the production of insanity, while despotic governments are not.

The emotions of mind produced by ardent and ungratified desires—by domestic troubles—and by the affections and passions—are frequent causes of insanity.

Some of the latter, as terror, anger, and passions produced by reverse of fortune, act immediately; but more commonly the action is gradual and continued, as that of grief, love, jealousy, disappointed pride, shame, the struggle between religious and moral principles and passions, &c.

3. Alexander Morison, *Increase in Insanity*

(Excerpt from *Outlines of Mental Diseases*, Edinburgh: MacLachlan & Stewart, 1824, pp. 74–5.)

This leads to the question, whether insanity is on the increase or decrease? The former is said to be the case in this country, as both public and private establishments for the reception of the insane have increased. There can be little doubt that Insanity increases with civilization: in proof of which we find the number of insane stated to be very small in South America, and among the Indian tribes, &c. and to be very considerable in China.

It is therefore probable, that the increasing civilization and luxury of this country, co-operating with hereditary disposition, tends rather to increase the numbers in proportion to the population.

4. George Man Burrows, *Insanity: Disease of the Nerves or Blood?*

(Excerpt from *Commentaries on Insanity*, London: Underwood, 1828, p. 109.)

Most nosologists class insanity among the *neuroses*; and hence it has been popularly received as a disease exclusively of the nerves.

Let us examine if there be not ground to assume, that the disorders of the sanguiferous system have as great, or greater influence in originating insanity, than those of the nervous system.

Some authors advert to certain anomalies in the circulation in cases of insanity, especially in the earlier stages of the malady. But whether prepossessed with the opinion, that it be a disease only of the intelligent or thinking principle, or a disorder solely of the nerves themselves, as the instruments of this intelligent principle, I cannot decide; but it is clear such phenomena are rather incidentally than specially noticed.

The late Dr. Caleb Parry is an exception. He has exhibited, in a full and perspicuous manner, the disorders of the sanguiferous system, and their influence on health; and he especially applies his reasoning to prove the specific effects of such disorders on the operations of the mind.

5. George Man Burrows, *Brain, Heart and Will*

(Excerpt from *Commentaries on Insanity*, London: Underwood, 1828, pp. 112–13.)

Physiological experiments prove that an animal can live without a brain, but not without a heart; and in the instance of an acephalous child, we see the animal functions may be carried on without the former. Daily experience proves, that the brain, the seat of the sensorium, sustains great injuries and mutilations without injury to the intellectual functions. Life, therefore, it appears, as well as mind, is more dependent on the movements of the circulation than on the functions of the nerves.

Still, a disorder of the nerves may be, and frequently is, the immediate cause of insanity; for a violent moral impression being made on any of the senses, is first carried to the brain, which immediately acts synchroneously with the heart, and re-acts on the brain; and the last action may remain after the other has ceased. The same is seen in many morbid affections: the original induces a second affection, which is sympathetic; and the latter will continue long after the primary cause is removed.

Intense thought or abstraction exercises a powerful influence on the circulation. Great calculators have been known to pass days and nights without sleep, from having been deeply engaged in some intricate calculations. This want of sleep results from a preternaturally increased action of the vessels which supply the brain; and this action, if not relieved, soon runs on to delirium. Such pursuits being the effect of volition, may be suspended ere they proceed to this extremity.

All passions and emotions are said to be modifications of the will; and whenever the will stimulates the brain to violent exertion, the actions of the heart are always responsive, with a force proportionately augmented or diminished, according to the nature of the impression. Thus, joy, anger, desire, &c. increase the energy of the heart, and accelerate the circulation, and in excess super-induce apoplexy, palsy, mania, &c.; while, on the contrary, fear, horror, &c. diminish the action of that organ, and retard, or rather reflect, the current of blood on the large vessels, occasioning asphyxia, syncope, &c. But in this latter case, when the heart recovers its force, such a degree of re-action is produced, as sometimes either proves fatal to life, or otherwise deranges the intellectual faculties. Therefore, whether the impetus of the circulation be augmented or lessened; whether the blood, propelled by the heart, excite the brain, or the former be excited by the nervous influence of the latter,—still, if life be not extinguished in the conflict, the loss of reason is a frequent effect.

Whenever either of these important organs is preternaturally excited, the relation is so intimate, that a reciprocal and powerful action must be produced. The consequences are obvious; for, agreeably to a law of nature, extended as well to intellectual as to corporeal powers, when over-exerted, a state of relaxation or rest must follow, or a lesion of that power so over-exerted will ensue.

Even when the stimulus which has proved an exciting cause is withdrawn, or ceases to act before any lesion takes place, the extraordinary energy induced is necessarily succeeded by a state of diminished sensibility and weakness, or of collapse, subversive of the mind. It is in this way, probably, that moral or affective causes act on the nervous system.

6. George Man Burrows, *Moral Causes of Insanity as they Affect Different Social Classes*

(Excerpt from *Commentaries on Insanity*, London: Underwood, 1828, pp. 9–10, 18–20.)

The moderns divide the causes of insanity into moral and physical.

Every impression on the sensorium, through the external senses, and every passion in excess, may become a moral cause of insanity. Thus all, however opposite, act as exciting causes, and will produce this result: joy and grief, anger and pain, love and hatred, courage and fear, temperance and ebriety, repletion and inanition, application and indolence, may have the same effect. Vices, also, which occasion changes in the physical constitution, act as remote moral causes, and induce mental derangement.

All impressions that affect the feelings are conveyed to the sensorium, and operate according to the degree of constitutional susceptibility, and the nature and force of the impression. The action of the heart is correspondent with this impression, and re-acts on the brain and nervous system. Hence there are two impressions: the one primitive, affecting the sensorium; the other, consecutive, but simultaneously affecting the heart. Thus the nervous and vascular systems are both implicated; and in this manner moral impressions become causes of insanity. The moral cause, therefore, is always the remote cause; the physical, the proximate, or that state of the cerebral functions which immediately precedes the peculiar action denominated maniacal.

The influence of the passions on the operations of the mind is a subject which, to be examined as its merits, demands 'the eye of a natural historian, and the spirit and impartiality of a philosopher.' No author has discussed it with greater ability than Sir Alex Crichton.

The effect of intense emotions or passions, often repeated or long continued, not only disturbs the functions, but will occasion lesions of the brain. It is easy, says this author, to conceive, that an affection or change of structure of this organ does occur from an external impression being communicated to it by the nerves; but the effect on the mind produced by this impression on the brain, is what we cannot explain.

Many structural and functional diseases, which are ascribed to physical causes only, may be clearly traced to emotions of the mind.

Thus the heart, stomach, liver, intestines, kidneys, &c. are often violently acted upon by external impressions; but the effect is modified or altered, according to the force of the exciting cause, or the temperament of the person acted upon; and it commonly ceases with the cause that gave rise to it.

The upper classes, who are supposed to be most subject to maladies of the nervous system, have also been deemed almost exclusively liable to insanity. This, however, is a vulgar error, which an inspection of any of the pauper asylums for the insane instantly refutes. Habitual luxury, and the vices of refinement, are peculiar to the rich; and, consequently, a greater degree of susceptibility and irritability is superinduced. The lower orders, who ought more generally to be exempt from the concomitant of wealth and indolence, that is, disease, unhappily provoke it by their excesses; and thus voluntarily ingraft on themselves the evils which, from their condition, they might otherwise escape.

If, therefore, the nervous system be immediately acted upon, through greater susceptibility in the upper classes, from luxury, an equal susceptibility to morbid affections of the viscera is induced in the lower classes, though more slowly and remotely, from intemperance.

The moral causes of insanity will naturally affect the rich and educated differently to the poor and uneducated. Indeed it will be found, that the former, with the exception of hereditary insanity, are most frequently deranged from affective or moral causes, while the latter are principally so from physical causes.

Extensive as I conceive the influence is of moral causes in the production of insanity, I cannot assign it so wide a scope as many foreign writers.

I entertain very strong doubts of the fidelity of the catalogue of moral causes which they enumerate with so much affectation of minute accuracy. For, although very inquisitive on this point in every case on which I am consulted, yet it very frequently happens, that I can trace no moral cause at all. The majority originate in direct physical causes, which the privations and consequent misery, the poor suffer in all countries, as well as their vices, greatly multiply.

A recent English author, going to the other extreme, asserts, that he never could trace, in several hundred cases, more than one originating in a moral cause. The necessary inference is, that he could have made no inquiry.

Different professions, occupations, and trades, have been supposed to exercise a greater moral influence in inducing insanity than others. Hence the French Registers embrace a most extensive list of them, and the number of insane of each calling. But this evidence, I repeat, is too vague to afford any conclusion.

Insanity bears always a striking relation to public events. Great political or civil revolutions in states are always productive of great enthusiasm in the people, and correspondent vicissitudes in their moral condition; and as all extremes in society are exciting causes, it will occur, that in proportion as the feelings are acted upon, so will insanity be more or less frequent.

7. George Man Burrows, *Civilization and Insanity*

(Excerpt from *Commentaries on Insanity*, London: Underwood, 1828, pp. 21–3.)

As the multiplication of moral causes is co-relative with the degree and progress of civilisation, it might be inferred, that savage nations are exempt from insanity—the curse of polished life. Rush asserts, that it is unknown among the North American Indians, and the infrequency of it has been noticed among those of South America. But the more remote and savage, the less likely are the natural habits to be ascertained; and hence I suspect some fallacy in this conclusion.

The passions of barbarians are always strong, and sometimes furious; and most evince that their affections are violent. Their organisation is the same as the more civilised; and when such people become contaminated by association, they contract the same diseases. Why, therefore, should it be imagined savages never go mad?

The natives of the Indian peninsula, who are far more temperate in diet, and have their passions much more under control, are yet very prone to insanity; and several asylums are now established in the different presidencies for their reception. It is true, they are more civilised than the American aborigines; but if civilisation bring not with it the wants, and vices, and consequent diseases, of Europeans, the exciting causes of mental derangement among the Peninsular Indians appear to be inadequate to produce this physical effect. As they are, indubitably, a very ancient race, hereditary predisposition probably exercises a considerable influence upon them.

Moral philosophers love to theorise on the passive virtues of unsophisticated aborigines, and fancy them as void of vice as the fabulous race who adorned the golden age,

——'When man, yet new,
No rule but uncorrupted reason knew.'

Viewing man, however, as he really is, wherever he inhabits, I judge him to be always so much the slave of his passions, as to be liable, among other ills, to insanity.

All emotions of the mind, it is evident, are capable of disturbing the corporeal functions; and though in themselves moral causes, they become physical in their operation. Hence physical causes grow out of moral causes, and these frequently lead to insanity; not, however, by direct impressions on the organ of the mind, but through the means of those morbid changes in the system which they gradually effect.

Habitual drunkenness is a moral lesion, productive among the common people of the larger number of the insane. Excessive venery is another fruitful source. So, in fact, in peculiar constitutions, is indulgence to excess in any sensual pleasure. A certain solitary vice, which youth are so apt to contract through bad example, is a moral vice, and wide-spreading cause of insanity, in its worst form—fatuity, and even idiotcy. Tissot has fearfully depicted the progress of the consequences of this odious practice; and those who are unhappily addicted to it, will do well to consult this author's work. They will there read a picture that must, if any sense be retained, check this unnatural propensity, ere it has actually brought on mental alienation.

Could we imagine a human being void of all feeling, moral or religious, mental derangement is not there to be expected through a moral cause. But even where reason is wanting, instinct prevails; and brutes have their passions, which, when excited to excess, or thwarted, produce madness.

8. George Man Burrows, *Enthusiasm and Insanity*

(Excerpt from *Commentaries on Insanity*, London: Underwood, 1828, pp. 29–30, 33.)

In England, where the mass of the people are piously and morally inclined, and where the liberty of theological discussion and religious worship is tolerated, every variety of schism and sectarism abounds. Consequently, numbers exchange one form of faith for another; and hence the work of proselytism is exceedingly prolific. This, in truth, is the great predisposing cause to what is designated religious madness.

One author avows the obligations of a particular establishment to *Methodism*; another, in his experience, has had no such evidence. The discrepancy may be accounted for without oppugning the correctness of either. They were placed in situations very dissimilar; the patients coming under their cognizance were as opposite in their natural character and habits, as in religious opinions; and hence their conclusions are at variance. It is possible, however, that there may be more lunatics of the methodistic persuasion than of any other; and for this reason: converts have multiplied relatively with the number and the mental capacity of that class of society to which such doctrines are principally directed. Therefore, in a lunatic asylum appropriated for the relief of the lower orders, there will of course be more of this description of dissenters. But this is no proof that the peculiar doctrine of that sect is the cause of mental disorder.

Enthusiasm and insanity bear such close affinity, that the shades are often too indistinct to define which is one and which the other. Exuberance of zeal on any subject, in some constitutions, soon ripens into madness: but excess of religious enthusiasm, unless tempered by an habitual command over the affective passions, usually and readily degenerates into fanaticism; thence to superstition the transition is in sequence; and permanent delirium too often closes the scene. Enthusiasm and superstition, however, are not necessarily in sequence; for they are as opposite in character as, generally, in effect. The one is almost always the concomitant of genius or a vigorous mind, and may inspire the purest piety or benevolence, or emulate deeds of the highest glory: while the other seldom invades genius, except when extenuated by some corporeal disorder; but is commonly confined to the weak, the timid, and the uninformed; and in them produces either the blindest fury or the most gloomy despondency, and sometimes the wildest schemes for propitiating the offended DEITY.*

9. William Willis Moseley, *Predisposing and Exciting Causes of Insanity*

(Excerpt from *Eleven Chapters on Nervous and Mental Complaints*, London: Simpkin, Marshall & Co., 1838, pp. 123–40.)

That disease in the organ of the brain, and not in the mind, is the cause of nervous complaints and insanity, is therefore now admitted.

There are several agencies, one of which is sufficiently powerful, to cause the brain that is healthy to sink into a morbid state.

These causes are of two kinds—predisposing and exciting.

If there exists in us any physical preponderance in favour of any *inclination, passion*, or practice, we are said to be under

* Works on insanity abound in instances of this horrible superstition. Few, perhaps, more clearly expose the source and effect of extravagant fanatic excitation in a weak mind, than the following abridged report of a trial, at Launceston Assizes, April 1824:—
Amy *alias* Emma George, a young woman 19 years of age, was indicted for the murder of her brother, Benjamin George, a child under seven years of age, by strangling him with a silk handkerchief.

the influence of a predisposing cause. The following are some of those which operate as predisposing causes to mental disease or insanity.

1st. Family connections. In all ages, in civilized countries an opinion has prevailed that certain tendencies exist in some families to certain principles, practices, and diseases. This opinion has grown up on the evidence of plain and numerous successive facts. The working of hereditary tendencies is too obvious to be disputed in consumption and scrofula; nor is it less generally admitted in diseases of the mind. Times of great national excitement are very fertile in the production of proof of this kind. Without going back to the days of the Charles, in England, and of Wallace, in Scotland, let us hear what has been said by an eminent physician on the influence of the late revolution in France.

'Many of the women,' says *Esquirol*, 'who conceived during the violent agitations of these unhappy days, were delivered of children whose infantine years were associated with spasmodic affections, convulsions, &c., and in youth to idiocy, imbecility, and madness.' And there are few, who have visited the poor in large towns, who have not heard of the brutal conduct of husbands towards their wives while pregnant; and have not also heard that such children become timid, melancholy, and mad. 'I have been nervous from my childhood, I inherit this from my mother,' is the chief subject of conversation of many who apply for our advice.

2ndly. Ill-conducted nurseries, hot cradles, cribs, and beds; heated rooms without air, constant indulgence or continual severity, infantine and youthful days passed in constant excitement, cause a large race of both sexes to be constitutionally feeble and tremulously weak. These sink soon into nervousness and timidity, become incompetent to bear the trials of time or discharge its duties, fall beneath the load of life, deprecate their birth, and sigh for the grave.

3rdly. Strong passions are dangerous adjuncts to all, but especially to youth. The violence of passion exhibited under circumstances of great provocation, by a spoiled boy or a petted girl, compared with the self-control displayed by the son or a daughter of a Quaker under similar circumstances, demonstrate the position that children are, in their habits and manners, what their education makes them.

Unable to bear the mortification of being denied at the family dinner-table a single article, the petted son of Mr. J—— rose from his chair, fled for a pistol, rushed to the door and in a minute blew out his brains!

How many volumes would the details of the evils of violent passions fill! And who can tell the melancholy, the weariness of life, the suicides, the murders, the insanity, which violent passions have predisposed multitudes to suffer or to commit.

4thly. The absence of appropriate exercise and occupation is another predisposing cause.

'Every organ of the brain should be employed to secure its improvement, and to prevent mental deterioration and daily wretchedness.'

The well-being of man and his happiness depend on his activity; and the brain is constituted in conformity to this great law; and, if not exercised, it becomes relaxed, and sinks into a condition of incompetency.

The physiological explanation of this fact is simple and interesting. Arterial or oxyginated blood is the essential element of nutriment to every organ. It is the means of repairing their lost power, and of stimulating their vital energies. The chief local effect of exercise is, to increase the action of the blood-vessels, and the nerves, &c.; to cause a more rapid and plentiful supply of blood and of nervous energy, and thereby to increase the vigour of every part.

Keeping these principles in view, it will excite no surprise, to find that *non-exercise* of the brain and the nervous system, or inactivity of intellect and feeling, is a very frequent predisposing cause of every form of nervous disease and insanity itself. For demonstrative evidence of this position, we have only to look at the numerous victims to be found among females of the middle and higher ranks who have no strong motives to exertion, or any cause to exert themselves for honour or gain; no interests that call forth their mental energies, or to prevent, by their employment, these energies sinking into feebleness by disuse.

If we look round us we shall see from this cause innumerable examples of nervous or mental debility. Yes! their minds having become apathetic, and possessing no grounds of sympathy in common with others, they have sunken into extreme sensitiveness; shrink within themselves; live in a circle of their own construction, and try in vain to protect themselves against annoyances by living out of society.

To go into society now requires an effort they can no longer make without painful associations. In this state, home, with its little interests, is the centre of attraction; and the mind, which is constituted for a wide range of employment and pleasure, is confined within boundaries too limited for the range of a worm.

Among young ladies, of the most respectable circles, from twenty to thirty years of age, as well as among females of the middle ranks of society, many suffer from these and similar causes. We have such now under our care in town and country.

Young men, whose days are entirely without the occupations of the state, church, army, navy, or business, and who find it difficult to kill their time, are sometimes among the sufferers of this class. Nor are military men, when occupying retired positions, and are obliged for weeks to be much alone, strangers to these feelings; feelings which, without much caution, will terminate in very distressing symptoms. But excess of mental activity must be as much guarded against as the want of exercise.

5thly. The brain requires more blood than any other organ, and it requires that it should be of the best kind. The nature of the case suggested this. Facts, in many instances, have made it probable. Experiments made by oxygen have demonstrated it. The *langour* and *nervous debility* that attend long continuance in crowded places of worship, or amusement, or of business, as factories, &c., are produced by the *bad air* of these places deteriorating the blood. This vital fluid, under such circumstances, cannot receive a sufficient supply of oxygen to keep it in vigorous health; and, deprived of this *quickening power*—this essential ingredient of vigour in all nature—langour, nervous debility, &c., follow as naturally and as certainly, as ice will melt on the disc of the sun.

This theory is established by this fact:—Bring those who suffer in these circumstances from the places deprived of a due proportion of oxygen into the open air, and they will soon recover, without any other aids, their lost energy, &c.

The excesses of the excitements of joy, sorrow, watchfulness, weariness, unexpected losses, the unexpected accession of wealth, the excitements of love, mortified ambition, pride or vanity, sudden and unexpected honour, and every other cause of great excitement or heavy depression, will, by degrees, operate as most powerful predisposing causes, when they do not appear at the time to put forth all their vigorous powers, and produce an immediate effect.

The more acute feelings, the greater sensibilities, the more retired and solitary habits, the absence of the bustling occupations, and of the great absorbing *external* interests of Lloyd's, and of the stock exchange, and of the Royal Exchange, &c., is each sufficient to predispose females to nervous diseases; and, in proportion as these several agencies combine their *great non-exercise* influence, and act on the nerves of one of this higher class of created beings, she unhappily becomes a victim to strong predisposing agencies. Oh! that she may never fall a victim to the martyrdom of the disease itself.

To these it is unnecessary I should add, that the ardent application of the mind to any study, classics, mathematics, metaphysics, or even the lower branches of intellectual delights, as the composition of poetry, &c.: indeed, close reading on any subject, and sedentary occupations of every kind, will predispose all of both sexes to nervous sufferings, if long and severely pursued.

Let moderation, therefore, govern thee, O, Reader!

Having hastened through a few observations on the predisposing causes of nervous or mental disease and insanity, I must more hastily run through a few observations on the *exciting* causes of these sad complaints.

1st. That the liquids which have an immediate influence on the organ of the brain, should produce disease in it, can create no surprise. Man is so constituted, that all liquids which contain *alcohol* act immediately on the brain, through nerves which it meets with in the *mouth* and in the *throat*, and in its passage to as well as when it arrives in the stomach.

And this action of *alcohol* is as certain to produce a deteriorating effect on the brain, as the spur which stimulates the horse, inflicts a wound in his flesh, and the cruel goad makes a deeper wound in the sensitive legs of the poor ox. But wounds of this kind will also inflame and suppurate; and so will the wounds of alcohol produce disease in the brain.

The repeated use of liquids containing alcohol cannot, therefore, leave the brain of any undisturbed.

In fact, these liquids are the destructive agents which have caused mutinies in our navy, disobedience to orders in our army, have filled our prisons with all kinds of victims; our hospitals and mad-houses with every description of mental and bodily disease; our domestic circles with strife; our cellars and garrets with want and misery; and our streets with blasphemy and obscenity.

Inebriation is temporary madness. If often repeated it may become permanent madness. But wines, spirits, malt liquors, cider, perry, &c., are not the only liquids which contain alcohol, and are in daily use. No! Eau de Cologne, and other *waters*, scents, &c., are common odoriferous accompaniments of the toilet. These, yes! these have alcohol, and these are no less causes of mental disturbance, and will produce low spirits, nervous debility, *delusion, irresolution, sleepless nights*, wretchedness, &c. They may brighten the eye for the moment, but they will inflict deadly wounds in the head and the heart by and by.

2ndly. Determination of blood to the head is another common exciting cause. It is not my intention to detail the various assigned causes of the determination of blood to the head, or to examine these various assigned causes, with a view to ascertain the correctness of any particular theory of such causes.

No; this would carry my reader from the point in view; which is the simple fact, that when this disease state of the circulation exists, it is an absolutely certain cause of nervous or mental disease, and not unfrequently of insanity itself.

3rdly. Solar heat. Exposure of the head to the heat of the sun can never do good. The harm it does varies in kind, depending on the constitutional tendencies of the patient, and on the intensity of the heat, regulated by the climate, season of the year, time of the day, &c.

Head-ache, fever, sickness, nervous debility, delirium, idiocy, insanity, are some of the various effects produced by this powerfully exciting agent.

4thly. Tumours in the head sometimes (not often) become the exciting causes. It is not correct to suppose that tumours exist, unless the constitution is deteriorated by the scrophulous virus. A gentleman,* well read on this disease, can at once from the lips, eye-lids, or complexion, determine if this virus is making its ravages on the health.

Miss W—— was suffering much from pains in the head, nervous symptoms, &c., and knowing that Mrs. G——, of the same town, had been cured by us, was induced to come to town with her mamma last November, to be cured. At the first interview, the

* The writer published an octavo volume on this disease twenty years ago.

existence of the scrophulous virus was suspected. Two subsequent interviews confirmed the opinion; and the removal of the pain of the head was accordingly attempted by a more appropriate method of cure.

This has been accomplished; every symptom of disease has disappeared. The pain has not been felt for a long while, and every nervous suffering has given way to pleasurable feelings.

This young lady was the previous patient of the best medical men in Northampton for near two years before she came to town. She was an only daughter. Her mamma's life appeared to depend on hers; and all hopes of this had been nearly abandoned.

5thly. Extreme cold and heat produce nervous diseases, and insanity in some constitutions. The retreat of the French army from Moscow, and the voyages of Captain Parry, supply proof of this; and the log-books of many vessels, sailing eastward, as well as the domestic history of the three Asiatic capitals, Calcutta, Madras, and Bombay, supply too many sad details in confirmation of the effects of heat on the nerves.

Many visitors say, 'I have been in India, and I trace my nervous sufferings to the influence of the heat of that climate.'

6thly. Long-continued watchfulness. This ought to be guarded against, as it often produces nervous disease. Mrs. T——, through watchfulness during [her husband's] illness, became very nervous. Numerous subsequent cases of a similar kind are before us among our correspondents.

7thly. Suppressed discharges. If eruptions, discharges, or evacuations of any kind, whether cutaneous, uterine, or intestinal, are suppressed, the first effect must be the increased fulness of the vessels. As the number of these suppressed discharges increases, and the period of their suppression is extended, the vessels must become gorged.

The vessels of the head suffer in common with the rest.

In some cases the force of suppression will fall on the lungs and produce consumption; but in many it will fall on the brain and produce nervous diseases, perhaps madness.

Some medical men have charged too much to the account of suppressed evacuations, others too little. But reasoning on the facts of the great evils which are often produced by the suppression of *common perspiration*, what reader is incapable of comprehending the greater evils that may be produced by the suppression of the *much greater ordinary periodical discharges?*

Many such cases have been subjects of correspondence and interviews with us, and *much nervous disease has been produced by these agencies.*

8thly. Wealth and poverty, affliction, speculations, &c., all create a deep interest in most minds. The acquisition and losses of wealth often rouse strong emotions and excite intense and incessant feelings. These create violent cerebral action, indicated by pain in the head, fever, sleeplessness, diseased elevation, vertigo, fear, aberration, &c. Out of one hundred and sixty-four patients in the private mad-house of Esquirol, fifty were merchants. Two respectable brothers, out of three, were torn away as conscripts for the army, during the French revolution, whom *Pinel* knew, and one being shot by the side of the other, the survivor instantly went mad; and when he was conducted home to the third brother, the excitement occasioned in his brain by this sight, and the tale of shooting, caused him to go mad also.

We have before named the cause of Miss L—— becoming awfully nervous through her mamma being forced into the mad-house of Dr. Mon——.

9thly. Nymphomania. This is another name for certain strong feelings which keep the brain in a state of feverish excitement: it is sometimes called cerebellar disease, and at other times amativeness. The cause is, no doubt, the size and peculiar sensitiveness of the nympha. The enlargement of the cerebellum is the consequence or sign of this, and not the cause. This disease is unjustly attributed to a worse nature and a more corrupt heart: to a class of human passions of a demoralizing tendency; to the want of a good education; and to the absence of good moral and religious feelings. But the reverse of all this is true, and has been so fully and frequently demonstrated to us, by facts in our practice, as to teach us to *pity, sympathise,* and *not to blame.* Yes! it is an *organic disease,* against the tide of which neither the firm resolutions, nor good principles, nor *frequent fervent prayers* of Miss A——, nor of Miss S——, the daughter of a clergyman, nor of Mrs.——, a married lady, with children, could make sufficient head to stifle these feelings, or keep their distressed minds in a state of self-approval.

10thly. Strong attachments; separation, &c. Strong attachments arise from many causes. Their influence is often increased by the concentration of our best and strongest passions, and all the tender sympathies and kindly feelings of our nature. Tranquillity, happiness, peace, and life itself, are felt at the moment to depend on their continuity; and if any cause rend this bond of union asunder, the separation is often attended with great mental disturbance. This evil, so powerful, and so frequent, has obtained an appropriate position in the list of diseases, under the name *Nostalgia*. Many extraordinary instances of its power have been displayed in this country during war, when *pressgangs*, as in former years, were allowed to tear husbands from the arms of their wives, and children from the embraces of their parents! The revolution in France supplied numberless strong illustrations of the evils of breaking the bonds of attachment, by producing all kinds of mental disease. Dr. Perfect has given us, in his 'Annals of Nervous Disease and Insanity,' several interesting proofs of lacerated attachments. Among others, he names a lady, aged thirty, who sunk into the depth of despair by the death of a friend. She passed days and nights without uttering a word. Sometimes she shed floods of tears, and, at other times, uttered the most piercing shrieks! Her face became pale and swelled, her spirits melancholy, and her mind deranged! Mrs. T——, of B——, Northamptonshire, became melancholy when separated from her husband. Arrangements were made for Miss —— to go out to her brother, holding a high civil appointment in India; her passage was paid, her dress prepared; all her family, that was in England, were with her, to accompany her to the ship. In a state of the greatest excitement, from reluctance to leave England and be separated from her friends, she fled here. *The scene was painfully interesting!*

Incapable of enduring separation from her mother, another young lady became herself mad, when her mamma was sent to a mad-house, by the advice of the medical man who kept it!

11thly. Domestic disturbances and quarrels have made more husbands, wives, and daughters nervous, than the sword has slain; and ought, on this ground, to be most religiously guarded against.

12thly. Disappointed love has ruined the constitutions, broken down the mental powers, and inflicted more intense misery on a greater number of females, than LOVE ever made happy. The number which become nervous from this cause, is greater than from most others.

13thly. Onanism. To this baneful practice, the deterioration of early beauty, the loss of brilliancy in the eye, and a smooth surface of the forehead; the appearance of premature age; fidgetiness, eccentricity, *unevenness of temper*, unnatural quickness, or great dullness and stupidity; incompetency, impotency, idiocy, wretchedness, and aberration of mind, are to be frequently ascribed. It is true, that it is not always, but very often, to *this cause*, in both sexes, these symptoms can be traced.

14thly. The excessive desire of children.

15thly. Extreme hunger, continued some days.

16thly. Love of admiration.

17thly. Self-esteem.

18thly. Great fear.

19thly. Mistaken perceptions of real religion and of Christian doctrines, and the grounds of acceptance both of our prayers, duties, and persons with God.

20thly. Hard, intense, and *long-continued studies*.

21stly. Blows on the head.

22ndly. Mal-formation of the *cranium*.

23rdly. Lightning.

24thly. Gambling.

25thly. Jealousy.

26thly. The sudden death of persons in our presence.

27thly. The horrors of a storm at sea.

28thly. The fearful associations of being awoke from sound sleep while the house is on fire.

29thly. The sight of a public execution.

30thly. Sudden and unexpected changes of fortune.

31stly. And INFLUENZA—are but a few of the exciting causes of nervous disease that have come under our notice. But we have not leisure to select more, nor time to offer any remarks on these, or give any more cases of illustration.

10. James Sheppard, *Insanity and Morbid Conditions of the Blood*

(Excerpt from *Observations on the Proximate Causes of Insanity*, London: Longman, Brown, Green & Longmans, 1844, pp. 33–7, 44–6, 72–4.)

1st—That insanity does not *depend* on disease of the brain.

2nd—That insanity cannot consist either in a disease, or an impairment of the entire mind, or of what is termed its powers and faculties.

3rd—That insanity cannot result from unappreciable lesions of structure.

4th—That no conclusive evidence can be advanced in support of the position, that insanity can result from morbid conditions of the nervous system.

We must now extend the enquiry to *what relation exists between insanity and morbid conditions of the circulating fluid*; and shall endeavour to prove that insanity, when developed, results *manifestly*, at times, from a morbid condition of the blood, and that there is, at least, *presumptive evidence*, that insanity may *always depend* on a morbid condition of the circulating fluid.

While reflecting on the phenomena exhibited by man in a state of intoxication, my mind was first impressed with the idea, that insanity is, at times, connected with morbid conditions of the blood. Further reflection and observation strengthened that impression, and raised in my mind *presumptive evidence*, not only that insanity is intimately connected with some morbid conditions of the blood, and is often dependent thereon,—but that insanity is *universally* and *essentially* dependent on morbid conditions of the blood.

Let it be observed, that the insanity which is especially the subject of my consideration, is not that which results—or, rather, which is supposed to result—from congenital malformation of the brain, or of the cranium; but such as occurs in one whose previous sanity demonstrates the pre-existence of a perfectly organized structure.

Even if insanity does result from congenital malformation *alone*, I do not consider that it affects my conjecture, that this disease is dependent on certain morbid conditions of the blood, in cases where the brain is, or has been, perfectly organized.

It is, in my apprehension, an anomaly to suppose that an organ, imperfect, either in relation to itself, or to its immediate vital relations, can produce perfect functions; though I do not pretend to decide on the degree of malformation, &c. which is requisite to produce such a lesion of the intellectual faculties as may be fairly termed insanity, or as to whether any degree of malformation *at all* is equal to its production.*

* What is the cause of the malformation? There must have been some absolute physical cause, otherwise there could, of course, be no malformation. May not the malformation be dependent on some morbid conditions of the blood?

Let me remind those who, without hesitation, refer the insanity of malformed idiots *solely* to their malformation, that, in many persons who have died without any symptoms of insanity, there has been found such extensive disease of the brain, as must be allowed to constitute a much greater departure from the perfect condition of that organ than is ever found in congenital malformation, with this distinction, that, in the latter case, the malformation generally exists on both sides of the head, while the disorganization, &c. is for the most part, but not always, confined to one side.

If insanity be dependent on morbid conditions of the blood, how easy is its transmission by hereditary descent to be understood. When we consider the results I have before alluded to, which prove that in cases of insanity other diseases frequently coexist with organic lesions of the brain, proving a *general* cause; and take in conjunction with this the fact of the very frequent hereditary transmission of many of those diseases—diseases which are universally believed to descend through the medium of the blood —I do think, that every reflecting mind must allow, that it is more easy to comprehend how insanity, if it be dependent on morbid conditions of the blood, can be transmitted hereditarily, than if it be the result of diseased organization, whether that disease be appreciable or unappreciable.

May not the luxurious habits, &c. of civilized nations, be the cause of their being more frequently the subjects of insanity than savages?

May not those habits give rise, as it were, to a national predisposition in the blood to assume the condition that is equal to the production of insanity?

When tumours, disorganization, &c. of the brain, are accompanied with insanity, may not that disease be produced by these tumours, &c. inducing a certain morbid condition of the blood?

To set the subject in as clear a light as I am able, I shall now endeavour to support the following propositions.

1st—That a morbid *quantity* of blood is frequently the exciting cause of insanity.

2nd—That *deficiency* of blood is frequently the exciting cause of insanity.

3rd—That a morbid *quality* of the blood is, undeniably, *at times*, the cause of insanity; and that there is, at least, *presumptive evidence*, that insanity may *always be dependent thereon.*

PROP. 1st.—That a morbid quantity of blood is frequently the exciting cause of insanity.

That it is quite possible for an abnormal quantity of blood to exist in the cavity of the cranium, is proved by the experiments of Dr. Burrows; besides which, I think that the phenomena of hypertrophy of the brain, without increased cranial development, stand diametrically opposed to the idea, that the contents of the cranium are *invariably* the same.

Dr. Marshall Hall, in his *Principles of Medicine*, relates the following case—'A. B. æt 40, became ruined in character and in fortune; and, when in the midst of his difficulties, experienced a sense of heaviness and pressure in his head, and passed restless nights. After several days, he attempted suicide, by dividing the blood-vessels and muscles of the arm. He lost a large quantity of blood, and became faint. On recovering from this state, he said to his medical friend, "Had you bled me a few days ago, I should not have done this act; my feelings are altered, and I regard suicide with abhorrence." '

If insanity be not dependent on a morbid condition of the blood, I confess that I am at a loss to know how bleeding, or revulsive treatment, can relieve it.

May not such treatment act by enabling the vital power to restore the vital equilibrium of the blood?

How congestion of the brain can exist, in some cases, to such an extent as to cause its pathognomonic signs, without producing mental derangement, while in another case a much smaller quantity of blood appears sufficient to call insanity into existence, I do not know, unless it be, that when quantity of blood is the exciting cause of insanity, it acts by inducing a *morbid quality* of that fluid.

11. Daniel Noble, *Blood and Brain in the Etiology of Insanity*

(Excerpt from *Elements of Psychological Medicine*, London: John Churchill, 1853, pp. 223–4.)

The etiology of insanity, like that of other diseases, comprises the circumstances of predisposition and exciting cause. By predisposition is understood some inherent vice or imperfection of structure, which renders the function unusually liable to disorder, and the structure itself inordinately susceptible of physical deterioration. A constitution of brain exists in particular persons, which, although quite compatible with the due exercise of mind, involves great liability to mental perversion. This condition is very often inherited, but frequently it is induced. An individual whose brain is predisposed to insanity, may pass through life, and die of some other disease, without at any time suffering from disordered mind, the same thing happening with reference to all constitutional diseases. Many persons predisposed to phthisis take great care of themselves, and thus prevent the development of pulmonary tuberculosis.

The physical characters of strucuure do not always reveal the presence or absence of predisposition to disease, and the physical conditions upon which it depends are somewhat obscure; but, in whatever it essentially consists, it would appeai to be strengthened by certain vices in the circulating fluid, congenital or otherwise, which indeed, in some circumstances, may operate as exciting cause; the blood, in its relations to the function of structure, being in some respects analogous to steam in the working of a steam-engine.

But inherent fault in the constitution of brain, with vicious blood superadded as an accessory circumstance, may be incompetent to produce insanity; the concurrence of other circumstances may be demanded. Physical violence done to the head may supply the vacant link in the chain of effective causation, or some intellectual effort over-taxing the strength, or serious perturbation of the emotional sensibility; in such instances, the exciting causes have an immediate action upon the mind itself.

An introduction within the blood of certain quasi-poisonous substances, deranging the cerebral functions through the circulation, may constitute the last circumstance required for the production of mental disorder; or, finally, injurious impressions made upon structures and organs remote from the brain, may operate as exciting cause, such impressions being communicated, in correspondence with well-known pathological laws, to the brain as the seat of consciousness, the centre of all affectibility, and the converging point of organic unity.

12. Daniel Noble, *A Vitiated State of Blood*

(Excerpt from *Elements of Psychological Medicine*, London: John Churchill, 1853, p. 238.)

Amongst the circumstances that more immediately determine those forms of cerebral disorder which manifest themselves in insanity, is a vitiated state of the blood. But of the particular conditions of the circulating fluid which operate in this way, we have no very exact knowledge. It is well known, however, that when the blood has adventitious ingredients of several kinds mingled with it, the functions of various organs become perverted, and especially those of the brain and nervous system. Particular substances exert a prejudicial influence upon certain structures and functions, rather than upon others; and this elective affinity, so to speak, obtains with regard to divisions of the encephalon and to the other ganglionic centres. Alcohol, opium, cannabis indica, and chloroform, amongst other ingredients, act upon the brain and nervous system generally, though not upon all the parts uniformly.

13. Daniel Noble, *A Loaded Colon*

(Excerpt from *Elements of Psychological Medicine*, London: John Churchill, 1853, pp. 250–1.)

The prejudicial effects of a loaded colon upon the temper and moral disposition, are the subject of universal experience. Indeed, premonitory symptoms of insanity are sometimes dissipated by procuring a free and vigorous action of the large intestines. 'Could we penetrate,' says that eminent medical psychologist, Feuchterleben, 'into the secret foundations of human events, we should frequently find the misfortunes of one man caused by the intestines of another, whom the former endeavoured to inspire with sympathy in his fate at a moment when the frame of mind of the latter was affected by impeded secretion. An hour later, and his fortune would have been made.'

Derangement of the colon, indeed, is eminently prejudicial to the functional integrity of the encephalon. Esquirol first observed that a displacement of this structure, which caused it to have the vertical, instead of its usual transverse position, was an occasional feature in the pathological anatomy of the insane. 'In combination with this state of the colon, Bergman found the following morbid phenomena: plethora of the abdomen and the encephalon; hæmorrhoidal disease; tumefaction of the spleen, liver, and uterus; distension of vessels in the brain. The symptoms during life were in these instances peculiar; viz., hardness, and tumefaction, and tenderness of the abdomen; slow and difficult progress in a bent forward position; anxiety in the præcordia; obstinate constipation, with vomiting; coldness, and a blue colour of the skin; trembling and agitation, convulsion, rigor, diarrhœa ushering in the final catastrophe.'

14. Alfred Beaumont Maddock, *The Spread of Insanity*

(Excerpt from *Practical Observations on Mental and Nervous Disorders*, London: Simpkin, Marshall & Co., 1854, pp. 12–13.)

As the disorders which are dependent on, or are essentially connected with, the nervous temperament, are, as has been just shown, undoubtedly of an hereditary nature, and therefore peculiarly liable to transmission, they must, according to the common course of events, necessarily multiply or suffer aggravation to a very considerable extent, subject of course to those chances of occasional decay and obliteration mentioned in the former chapter. These ailments, by the continual additions which a lapse of years has the inevitable tendency to produce, must, to the unhappy victims of their attack, eventually acquire a huge preponderance over the rest of the vital phenomena. To check the steady and insidious march of this silent enemy, it is probable, no mode would be so effectual, as a gradual revolution in the dietetic, sanatory, and moral habits of the people. Neither physical strength of body, nor mental vigour can long maintain themselves, under enervating or debasing modes of life. As that elegant Roman poet Horace has observed—

Fortes creantur fortibus et bonis,

and appositely adds—

Doctrina sed vim promovet insitam,
Rectique cultus pectora roborant.

The illustrious Sydenham, father of the modern school of physic, writing at the close of the seventeenth century, computed febrile diseases to constitute two-thirds of the maladies of mankind; but had his erudite and sagacious pen been employed in these our days, he would doubtless have affirmed, what we now perceive to be the fact, that nervous diseases had usurped the place of fevers and disorders of a more active type, and constituted by far the larger proportion of the cases which fall under the treatment of the physician. Dr. Cheyne, who wrote his celebrated work on the 'English Malady' in the year 1733, appears seldom to have met with nervous disorders among the bulk of the population, but to have observed them more particularly, among the higher classes of society. Unhappily, however correct his views may have been at the period in which he lived, the present times offer a marked contradiction to them, for disorders of the nervous system are no longer limited to the superior ranks of life, or to the idle and luxurious, but extensively co-exist, and have taken deep root, among the poorer, as well as the middle orders of society. If any difference exists in the prevalence of these widely-spread afflictions, perhaps the rural and agricultural districts may claim some degree of exemption, over the more densely-crowded population of the manufacturing cities.

In no other country, compared with England, do we find such numerous and formidable examples of this extensive scourge. In some measure, this may arise from the habitual pride and hauteur of the English character; partly from the commercial greatness which it has long been her boast to enjoy; and partly from the unnatural style of living too generally adopted.

15. John Millar, *The Dangers of Masturbation*

(Excerpt from *Hints on Insanity*, London: Henry Renshaw, 1861, pp. 37–40.)

When insanity is suspected in young men under twenty-five years of age, particularly those who have been carefully brought up under the anxious supervision of their friends, and have lived apparently in a most exemplary and becoming manner, and who, from not being allowed to mix freely with the world, have escaped the trials and temptations of life; and if the symptoms are chiefly of a negative character, shown more in the absence of any positive indication of derangement than otherwise, such as secluding themselves from society, avoiding conversation; if they are at the same time pale and out of health, generally morose and apathetic, occasionally impulsive, violent, and irritable; if they speak to you in a pert manner, with averted face, have a peculiar leaden appearance of the cornea, dull expression, damp, clammy hand, and languid circulation; there is every reason to fear that these symptoms are due to habits of a most pernicious character.

From the frequency with which this class of persons have been brought under my observation, after the mind has become affected, and from the symptoms being as distinctly recognisable as those of any other special disease with which I am acquainted, I do not hesitate to ascribe this form of the malady to self-abuse; and an unblushing admission of the fact will often at once confirm the diagnosis. On inquiry, it will be found that the practice has been followed for years; and that there is a persistence in it will be painfully evident on careful examination. To hope for any amendment until the exhaustion produced by the drain of the vital fluid and from nervous excitement is stopped, is out of the question; and I believe that it is only in the early stage of the complaint that any real or permanent good can be effected; for once the mind becomes palpably disordered, I have seen, in a very extensive experience, but few recoveries, and for that reason I refer to it here.

An appeal to the moral feelings, and reference to the inevitable consequences of the habit, generally meet with due attention and promises of immediate amendment; but as a present gratification cannot be sacrificed to a prospective evil, the practice continues unabated. Involuntary emissions are sometimes excited from the irritation which the constant excitement of the parts has set up about the orifices of the ejaculatory ducts (for there is often a tenderness at this point), or upon a loaded state of the rectum. As they cannot be trusted, I would urge the propriety of placing the patients under the constant supervision of some elderly person to watch them night and day; let them sleep on a hard mattress, lightly clad; keep the parts cool, and remove any irritation about the prepuce or rectum by frequent washing, and the occasional administration of large enemata of warm water. The passage of a full-sized bougie will sometimes relieve the irritation, and, in obstinate cases, the application of caustic to the orifices of the ejaculatory ducts may be necessary. If the urine be avid, carbonate of soda will be found useful; but if the practice be checked, the irritability will gradually diminish. At the same time, I would recommend the free use of sedatives at bed-time, and astringent tonics, such as tinct. ferri sesquichlor., with infusion of calumba, &c.

In severe cases, acute maniacal symptoms often come on, which must be treated in the usual way; whilst in this condition, the patients should be carefully watched, as they often attempt to mutilate themselves.

Though nymphomanic symptoms are constantly present when young females are insane, I have met with only one instance in which I could say that the mental disturbance was due to this vice; and this patient continues in a hopeless state of dementia.

16. John Millar, *The Importance of Sleep*

(Excerpt from *Hints on Insanity*, London: Henry Renshaw, 1861, pp. 6–7, 2–3.)

It is most desirable, therefore, that even the public in general should be fully alive to the vast importance of sleep for those who are engaged in the struggle for position and existence; and also to the dangerous influence which the want of it exerts in producing constitutional disturbance and mental derangement. Medical men would then be consulted oftener than they now are upon this apparently trifling point; and, instead of being sent for after the disease has become fully developed, merely to sign a certificate of lunacy, they would be enabled, in a great majority of cases, to avert so terrible a calamity, and save most of those valuable lives which are now sacrificed during incipient insanity by suicide. There is abundant statistical evidence to prove that the recoveries of patients whose disorders arise from functional derangement, and who are admitted to asylums within the first year of their attack, amount to 60 or 70 per cent.; and it is perfectly well known that this result is due entirely to early treatment. If, then, success bear a direct ratio to the shortness of the duration of the attack before being subjected to treatment, it follows, as a necessary consequence, that the disorder itself would be cut short, or possibly averted, by the early treatment of its cause. Let it be remembered, that insanity is not—like scarlet fever, measles, or small-pox—incapable of being arrested when once it has set in; but, as I have shown, it becomes developed by slow degrees, gives ample warning of its approach, and is the inevitable result of an infringement of well-known laws.

If, then, the manifestation of mind be dependent upon the evolution of some power by the brain, it follows that the normal development of this power in any sane person must also be dependent upon the maintenance of those conditions which are requisite for the healthy action of the brain; and any disturbance of those conditions must operate through the organ upon the power, and so affect the healthy manifestation of mind. Now the brain, like other organs of the body, is subject to waste and disintegration of tissue, in proportion to its functional activity, and requires a period of rest or cessation from action to enable it to repair the waste, and continue to perform its customary functions. Like other organs of the body also, its healthy condition is best maintained by exercise alternating with rest. Hence, as we almost invariably find that the attack of insanity is preceded by an interference with these conditions, indicated by continuous and uninterrupted action of the mind, without sleep, I am of opinion that mental aberration in such cases is merely a symptom of an exhausted condition of the power; in fact, a functional derangement. In no other way can I satisfactorily account for the beneficial results attendant upon the employment of those remedies which procure sleep or rest to the brain, or for the effect which follows the administration of a full and liberal supply of nutritious food to the insane; nor can I in any other way explain the reason of the utter absence of any constant recognisable pathological change in the substance of the brain of those who die whilst suffering from mental alienation.

17. Henry Maudsley, *Physical and Mental Derangement*

(Excerpt from *Body and Mind*, London: Macmillan & Co., 1873, p. 41.)

Mental disorders are neither more nor less than nervous diseases in which mental symptoms predominate, and their entire separation from other nervous diseases has been a sad hindrance to progress. When a blow on the head has paralysed sensibility and movement, in consequence of the disease in the brain which it has initiated, the patient is sent to the hospital; but when a blow on the head has caused mental derangement, in consequence of the disease of brain which it has initiated, the patient is sent to an asylum. In like manner, one man who has unluckily swallowed the eggs of a tænia, and has got a cysticercus in the brain, may go to the hospital; another who has been similarly unlucky goes to an asylum. Syphilitic disease of the brain or its arteries lands one person in an asylum with mental symptoms predominant, another in an hospital with sensory and motor disorder predominant. The same cause produces different symptoms, according to the part of the brain which it particularly affects. No doubt it is right that mental derangements should have, as they often require, the special appliances of an asylum, but it is certainly not right that the separation which is necessary for treatment should reach to their pathology and to the method of its study.

18. Henry Maudsley, *Self-Abuse*

(Excerpt from *Body and Mind*, London: Macmillan & Co., 1873, pp. 86–7.)

The development of puberty may indirectly lead to insanity by becoming the occasion of a vicious habit of self-abuse in men; and it is not always easy to say in such cases how much of the evil is due to pubescence and how much to the vice. But the form of mental derangement directly traceable to it has certainly characteristic features. There are no acute symptoms, the onset of the disease being most gradual. The patient becomes offensively egotistic and impracticable; he is full of self-feeling and self-conceit; insensible to the claims of others upon him and of his duties to them: interested only in hypochondriacally watching his morbid sensations and attending to his morbid feelings. His mental energy is sapped; and though he has extravagant pretensions, and often speaks of great projects engendered by his conceit, he never works systematically for any aim, but exhibits an incredible vacillation of conduct, and spends his days in indolent and suspicious self-brooding. His relatives he thinks hostile to him because they do not take the interest in his sufferings which he craves, nor yield sufficiently to his pretensions, but perhaps urge him to some kind of work; he is utterly incapable of conceiving that he has duties to them. As matters get worse, the general suspicion of the hostility of people takes more definite form, and delusions spring up that persons speak offensively of him, or watch him in the street, or comment on what passes in his mind, or play tricks upon him by electricity or mesmerism, or in some other mysterious way. His delusions are the objective explanation, by wrong imagination, of the perverted feelings. Messages may be received from heaven by peculiar telegraphic signals; and there are occasionally quasi-cataleptic trances. It is strange what exalted feelings and high moral and religious aims these patients will often declare they have, who, incapable of reforming themselves, are ready to reform the world. A later and worse stage is one of moody or vacant self-absorption, and of extreme loss of mental power. They are silent, or, if they converse, they discover delusions of a suspicious or obscene character, the perverted sexual passion still giving the colour to their thoughts. They die miserable wrecks at the last. This is a form of insanity which certainly has its special exciting cause and its characteristic features; nevertheless, I think that the vicious habit seldom, if ever, produces it without the cooperation of the insane neurosis.

19. Henry Maudsley, *Tuberculosis and Insanity*

(Excerpt from *Body and Mind*, London: Macmillan & Co., 1873, pp. 97–100.)

There has long been an opinion, which seems to be well founded, that tubercle of the lungs is more common among the insane than among the sane. For although the proportion of deaths in asylums attributed to phthisis is one-fourth, which is the same proportion as that for the same population above fourteen years of age, Dr. Clouston has shown, by careful scrutiny of the records of 282 post-mortem examinations made in the Edinburgh Asylum, that phthisis was the assigned cause of death in only a little more than half of the cases in which there was tubercle in the body. The symptoms of phthisis are so much masked in the insane, there being usually no cough and no expectoration, that its diagnosis is difficult, and it is not always detected during life. The relation between it and insanity has been noticed by several writers: Schröder van der Kolk was distinctly of opinion that a hereditary predisposition to phthisis might predispose to, or develop into, insanity, and, on the other hand, that insanity predisposed to phthisis; and Dr. Clouston found that hereditary predisposition to insanity existed in 7 per cent. more of the insane who were tubercular than of the insane generally. When family degeneration is far gone, the two diseases appear to occur frequently, and the last member is likely to die insane or phthisical, or both; whether, therefore, they mutually predispose to one another or not, they are often concomitant effects in the course of degeneration. However, in weighing the specific value of these observations, we must not forget that, independently of any special relation, the enfeebled nutrition of tuberculosis will tend to stimulate into activity the latent predisposition to insanity; and that, in like manner, insanity, especially in its melancholic forms, will favour the actual development of a predisposition to phthisis.

In the cases in which the development of phthisis and insanity has been nearly contemporaneous, which are about one-fourth of the cases in which they coexist, the mental symptoms are of so peculiar and uniform a character as to have led to the inclusion of the cases in a natural group under the designation of *phthisical-mania*. They have no positively distinctive symptom, it is true; they cannot be separated from other cases by a well-defined line of demarcation; yet they do exhibit, Dr. Clouston believes, certain common and uniform characters which justify their description as a separate variety. They often begin in an insidious way by irritability, waywardness, and capriciousness of conduct, and apparent weakening of intellect; yet the patient converses rationally when he chooses to talk, and shows that he still has his intellect, albeit there is a great disinclination to exert it. To sign a certificate of his insanity would be no easy matter. Or they begin with an acutely maniacal or melancholic stage, which is, however, of very short duration, soon passing into a half-maniacal, half-demented state. If there be a single characteristic feature, it is a momomania of suspicion. As the disease advances, the symptoms of dementia predominate; but there are occasional brief attacks of irritable excitement and fitful flashes of intelligence. And in these cases, more often than in other cases, there occurs a momentary revival of intelligence before death. We shall the more readily admit the special features of phthisical mania when we call to mind that there is in most phthisical patients a peculiar mental state; and that brief attacks of temporary mania or delirium sometimes occur in the course of phthisis. The phthisical patient is irritable, fanciful, unstable of purpose, brilliant, and imaginative, but wanting in calmness and repose; quick of insight, but without depth and comprehension; everything is fitful—fitful energy, fitful projects, fitful flashes of imagination. The hectic is in his thoughts and in his actions. The whims and imaginings of his mind become almost wanderings at times, his fancies almost delusions.

20. Henry Maudsley, *The Growth of Civilization and Insanity*

(Excerpt from *The Pathology of Mind*, London: Macmillan & Co., 1879, pp. 127–9, 131–3, 168–70.)

A question has been much discussed, and is not yet settled satisfactorily, whether insanity has increased with the progress of civilisation and is still increasing in the community out of proportion to the increase of the population. Travellers are agreed that it is a disease which they seldom meet with amongst barbarous peoples. But that is no proof that it does not occur. Among savages those who are weak in body or in mind, the sick and the helpless, who would be a burden to the community, are often eliminated, being either killed or driven into the bush and left to perish there; certainly the weak units are not carefully tended, as they are among civilised nations. In this way not only is the amount of existing insanity rendered small, but its propagation to the next generation is prevented. Admitting the comparative immunity of uncivilised peoples from insanity, it is not difficult to conceive reasons for it. On looking at any table which sets forth the usual causes of the disease, we find that hereditary predisposition, intemperance, and mental anxieties of some kind or other cover nearly the whole field of causation. From these three great classes of causes savages are nearly exempt. They do not intermarry, the prohibition of marriage extending among them to distant blood-relations, and, as I have just pointed out, they do not much propagate the disease from one generation to another, because it is got rid of to a great extent among them by natural or artificial means of elimination. Secondly, they do not poison their brains with alcohol, at any rate not until the white man brings it to them; when they do obtain it, they no doubt abandon themselves to great debauches, but they cannot obtain the regular supply which would enable them to keep their brains day after day in a state of artificial excitement; and it may fairly be questioned whether alcohol, however and in whatever quantities it may be taken, is so likely to produce mental derangement in the undeveloped brain of a savage, which has so little mental function to perform, as in the more complex and specialized structure of a civilised brain.* Lastly, the savage has few and simple wants springing from his appetites, and them he gratifies: he is free from the manifold artificial passions and desires which go along with the multiplied industries, the eager competitions, the social ambitions of an active civilisation; he is free too from the conventional restraints upon his natural passions which civilisation imposes, and suffers not from a conflict between urgent desire of gratification and the duty to suppress all manifestations thereof, a conflict which sometimes proves too great a strain upon the mind of a civilised person.

On the other hand, it may be thought that the savage must suffer ill consequences from the unrestrained indulgence of his fierce sensual passions. But it might not be amiss to consider curiously whether savage nudity provokes sensuality so much as civilised dress, especially dress that is artfully designed to suggest what it conceals. There is no scope for the imagination where nothing is concealed and suggested, and it may be that clothing is sometimes a stimulus to immodest thoughts, and that, like the conventional covering of the passions, it inflames desire. Be that as it may, the savage is not disquieted by fretting social passions: with him there is no eager straining beyond his strength after aims that are not intrinsically worth the labour and vexations which they cost, no disappointed ambition from failure to compass such aims, no gloomy dejection from the reaction which follows the successful attainment of an overrated ambition, no

* Cameron, in his *Journey across Africa*, says that he met with one man only who was suffering from delirium tremens: it was the only instance of this disorder which he saw in Africa, though drunkenness was common. The supply of pombé, the intoxicating liquor, often falls short, because the corn from which they make it is not abundant.

pining regrets, no feverish envy of competition, no anxious sense of responsibility, no heaven of aspiration nor hell of fulfilled desire; he has no life-long hypocrisies to keep up, no gnawing remorse of conscience to endure, no tormenting reflections of an exaggerated self-consciousness; he has none, in fact, of the complex passions which make the chief wear and tear of civilised life. His conscience is a very primitive affair, being no more than a sense of right attaching to the beliefs and customs of his tribe, but such as it is he seldom goes against it; he may cheat, lie, steal, violate all the dictates of a true moral sense, especially in his relations with the members of other tribes; but he obeys his tribal conscience, as the animal obeys its instinct, without feeling a temptation to violate it. He is extraordinarily conservative, the custom of his fathers being for him the fullest justification of any belief or practice, however monstrous or irksome; he is free therefore from the perils which to unstable natures lie in the excitement produced by revolutionary change and in the adjustment to new relations exacted thereby. So it comes to pass that he is not subject to the powerful moral causes of mental derangement which act upon the civilised person, and that he cannot suffer from some of the forms of derangement which afflict the latter.

These considerations favour the accepted notion that insanity is less common among uncivilised than among civilised peoples, and that there is an increased liability to mental disorder going along with an increase in the complexity of the mental organization. Certainly it is in accordance with common sense to suppose that a complex machine, like the civilised brain, which is constructed of many special and delicate parts working together in the most nicely adjusted relations, will be exposed to more risk of derangement of action and be more likely to go wrong than a simpler and coarser machine, the less various parts of which have less fine and complicated relations.

Alarming statements are often made concerning the rapid increase of insanity which is supposed to be going on year by year in civilised countries; and the figures which are quoted certainly look formidable. In 1844 there were in England and Wales 20,611 registered insane persons; in 1859 the number had risen to 36,762; in 1869 it was 53,177; and on the 1st January, 1878, it was 68,538. Or, calculating the proportion of idiots and lunatics to the increasing population, it was, in 1859, 18·67 to

10,000; in 1869, 23·93; on the 1st January, 1878, 27·57.† The broad truth is that there is about one registered insane person to 365 of the population now, while the proportion in 1859 was one in 540. The very greatness of this increase, however, might well raise a suspicion that it has not been due mainly to an increased production of insanity in the population; for whether the course of human events during the last quarter of a century has been good or bad, it certainly has not differed so much from that of former times, or differed so much and so capriciously during the quarter of a century, as such a difference in the quantity of insanity, were it due to it, would mean. Without doubt the main part of this increase is owing to the more stringent regulations which from time to time have been made and enforced for the registration and protection of insane persons, whereby many that were never heard of officially at one time are now duly registered and counted. When the admissions of each year into asylums are examined, which represent pretty fairly the numbers of occurring cases, it is observed that a marked rise in the numbers has followed the enactment of some new Act of Parliament, the direct effect of which has been to force insane paupers into asylums: the increase has not been steadily progressive, but has taken place rather by leaps and bounds which have answered the stimulus of each fresh parliamentary enactment. It will be noted furthermore that the increase is mainly among paupers, since the ratio of private lunatics to the population (per 10,000) has been as follows:

Year—	1859	1865	1873	1874	1875	1876	1877	1878
Males	2·81	3·16	3·43	3·49	3·47	3·44	3·42	3·45
Females	2·26	2·34	2·61	2·69	2·72	2·77	2·78	2·76
Total	2·5	2·74	3·01	3·08	3·09	3·10	3·09	3·09

Thus there has been little change during the last five years—an increase of only half a lunatic in 10,000 persons since 1859.

On examining the admissions of private patients each year and calculating their ratio to the increasing population of the country, it will be found that the figures do not point to a steadily increased production of insanity in the non-pauper class; and they are the more significant when it is borne in mind that the more numerous and powerful causes which are supposed to be

† *Thirty-Second Report of the Lunancy Commissioners*, 1878.

at work to augment the liability of the community to mental disease will affect the classes from which private patients come at least to an equal degree with, and probably to a greater degree than, the classes which supply the pauper patients. It cannot be said that they yield real support to the opinion of the alarmists that so many more persons go mad now than in the days of our grandfathers.

Agricultural counties furnish a larger proportion of lunatics than manufacturing districts, and those counties in which the wages are low, like Wilts, a larger proportion than those in which the wages are high. Low wages of course mean poverty and bad nourishment, and lunacy shows a distinct tendency to go hand in hand with pauperism. Moreover the stagnant, unintellectual life of an agricultural labourer is less conducive to mental health than the more active and varied intellectual life evoked by the pursuits and interests of a manufacturing town. Mental exercise is the true foundation of mental health; and when a person who by virtue of being born of civilised parents has inherited the mental organs and aptitudes fitting him for a certain height and variety of moral and intellectual development, makes no use of them, but allows them to waste and degenerate, so initiating decay of his higher nature, he is in favourable conditions for the occurrence of some form or other of more positive mental derangement. He is not like the savage who, having no such inheritance, suffers not any ill consequences from mental stagnation; being the heir to ages of culture, he has the responsibilities of his inheritance; he cannot divest his nature of the privileges of its higher birth, nor himself of the duty to exercise them fitly, nor exempt himself or his posterity from the sure penalties of neglect of them.

Whether one profession, trade, or pursuit more than another favours the occurrence of insanity is not really so much a question of the effect of the particular pursuit as of the habits of those who follow it and of the spirit in which they follow it. Among the lower classes of society it is for the most part a question of sobriety and temperance against intemperance and riotous living. In the classes that are above the lower, when a man sets before himself as his aim in life riches or social position, not for any good use of what he gets by his toil and cares and heart-burnings, but as an end in itself, let his business be what it will, he is pursuing a not very worthy end, and will be likely to do so in an intemperate way, if not by actually unworthy means. If the social system be one in which riches are held in great esteem, and his passionate ambition is to get rich, he will not boggle much at the knavery which helps him to his end, and which will be overlooked by such a society in the admiration which it bestows upon success. Even when a man has made success or reputation in business the exclusive aim of his life, not out of a mere desire to become rich, but out of an eager energy and honest love of doing his work well; when he has by long concentration of desire and work upon it grown so completely to it as to make it the entire current of his life, that to which all his thoughts, feelings, and actions turn habitually, and in which they are engrossed—other interests being as it were little and accidental eddies that escape for a short time only the attraction of the main stream—he is ill fortified by mental culture against the shock when hope is shattered, his pride of opinion brought low, and the fabric which he has raised with all the eagerness and energy of an intense egoism levelled to the ground by a crushing blow of misfortune. Nay, the belief only that such a catastrophe is threatened may be enough to overthrow him; for if nine out of ten parts of his being and energies are absorbed in the successful prosecution of his work, and that has had a severe check, where is an adequate recuperative and distracting force to come from? He is not unlikely to sink into an agitated apprehension, and from that state to lapse into despairing melancholy.

It was a common notion at one time that governesses were victims of insanity out of all proportion to their numbers, and much sympathy was spent upon them in consequence. But the opinion was not well founded. It originated in the observation that a great number of governesses were received into Bethlehem Hospital—as many as 110 in ten years; the reason of which was not that so many more of them than of other classes went mad, but that they were just the persons who fulfilled best the conditions of charitable admission into that hospital, being poor enough to be unable to pay for care and treatment in private asylums, but yet not poor enough to be paupers and suitable for admission into county asylums.

If it be true, as is said, that persons who work with the head are more liable, on the whole, to mental disease than those who work with the hand, and that they are less likely to recover when they have had an attack, we may easily understand the reason to be that a more complex and delicate mental organization, with its greater variety and activity of function, will furnish more frequent occasions of disorder, and that the disorder will do greater hurt to the finer and more delicate instrument. But it would probably be a fuller statement of the truth to supplement it by adding that those who work with the heart are more likely to fall insane than either headworkers or handworkers; for the causes of the derangement are to be found not so much in the strain of the intellectual work as in the passion and feeling which are put into it, and which are the real wearing force. It is not in fact the nature of the occupation, but the temperament of the individual, which determines mainly what emotional wear and tear there shall be; one person may fret and consume his heart with anxiety in the small cares of a petty business, while another shall conduct the complex affairs of a mighty nation with unconcern of feeling.

Chapter II

Signs and Symptoms

21. Alexander Morison, *The Physiognomy of Insanity*

(Excerpt from *Outlines of Mental Diseases*, Edinburgh: MacLachlan & Stewart, 1824, pp. 131–2, 142–3, 146–9, 156–9.)

The appearance of the face, it is well known, is intimately connected with, and dependent upon, the state of the mind. The repetition of the same ideas and emotions, and the consequent repetition of the same movements of the muscles of the eyes, and of the face, give a peculiar expression, which, in the insane state, is a combination of wildness, abstraction, or vacancy, and of those predominating ideas and emotions which characterize, the different species of mental disorder, as pride, anger, suspicion, love, fear, grief, &c.

Besides this moveable physiognomy, as it has been termed, other external signs, by which the different modifications of mental disorder might be ascertained, have been suggested. Some of those who adopt the phrenological ideas of Dr Gall, conceiving mental disorder to proceed from disease in the departments of the brain exercising the functions disordered, allege that this disorder is marked, in recent cases, by increased heat in particular parts of the head, and in cases of long standing by external enlargement or diminution, and internal diseased structure in those parts.

Masks of the insane have likewise been taken, to ascertain whether or not there exists any connexion between what is termed the fixed physiognomy, or form and position of the bones of the face, and the different species of insanity.

The following series of Plates is intended to convey an idea of the *moveable* physiognomy in certain species of mental disease.

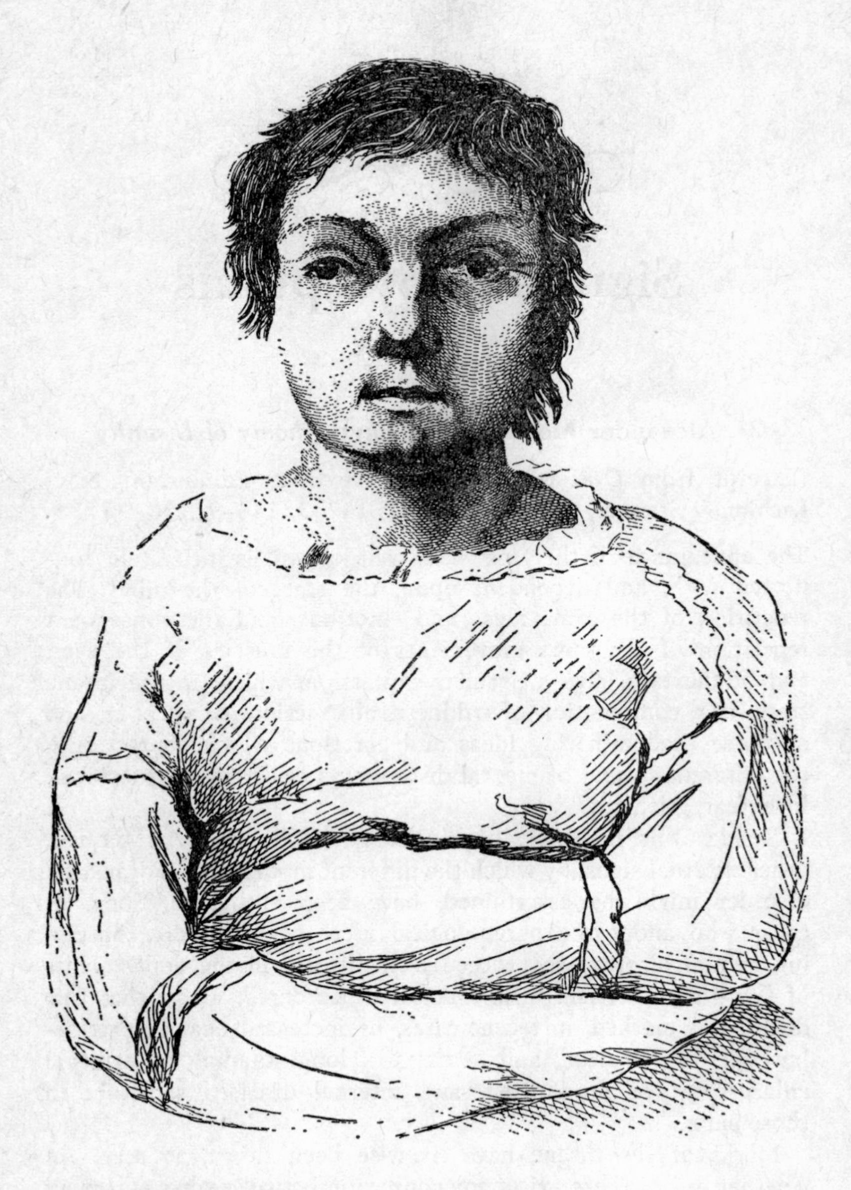

Monomania with Pride

This Plate represents a Female, in whom, although a Pauper, ideas of wealth and grandeur are predominant. She is liable to violent fits of fury, when her delusions are called in question, but talks rationally enough on subjects unconnected with them.

Religious Monomania

This Plate represents a Female labouring under the variety of partial insanity to which the name of *Theomania* has been given. She conceives herself to be more than mortal, and is full of self-complacency and benevolence to those about her; she is, however, thrown into a state of fury and agitation if her divinity be questioned.

Monomania with Love

This elderly Female, in whom lascivious ideas predominated, constituting the variety termed *Nymphomania*.

Monomania with Depression

This Plate represents a Female labouring under partial insanity with depression, or, as it has been termed by Dr ESQUIROL, *Lypemania*. The cause of her malady was grief, occasioned by the loss of a brother.

She continued in a state of insanity two years and a half. Her death was preceded by marasmus, with slow fever.

She frequently refused her food; and used to sit in a state of complete abstraction, without speech or motion.

Imbecility

This Plate represents a Man in a state of Imbecility. He had received a good education, but indulgence in solitary vice brought on a state of general imbecility.

Idiotism

This Plate represents a Female Idiot, with a *large* head and good-humoured expression.

She attended to the calls of hunger and thirst, but was never able to dress herself, and her evacuations were passed involuntarily. She had been taught some words, and appeared grateful to those who attended her.

22. George Man Burrows, *The Odour of the Insane*

(Excerpt from *Commentaries on Insanity*, London: Underwood, 1828, pp. 296–8.)

The odour of perspirable matter is often very strong and peculiar; and in some adults it is very offensive. There is also an effluvium peculiar to infants.

Dogs are known to recognise their master among a crowd, or trace him a great distance, by his particular odour; and thence we may suppose that every healthy person emits a different one, though not perceptible to our obtuser senses. Humboldt remarks, that the difference of odour is so striking in some climates, that the Indians of Peru can distinguish by it, even in the night, a European, an American Indian, or a negro, from each other.*

Many diseases are distinguished by a particular fetor, as hydrocephalus, rheumatism, and gout; the pelagra is distinguished by a smell like mouldy bread; but mania especially is characterised by a peculiar odour. It is not the *hircum olet* of Horace, but is a smell quite unique; and when once recognised, it never can be mistaken for any other. It has been compared to the scent of henbane in a state of fermentation; but I know nothing which it resembles.

This odour does not always attend on mania; and it differs in intensity. Personal cleanliness of the skin, and frequent changes of body-linen, much modifies, and perhaps may remove it. Where it is generated, it is easiest detected by going in the morning into the chamber of the lunatic before he has risen, and before fresh air has been admitted.

The maniacal odour is not noticed by every writer on the signs of insanity. Nor, as I have said, is it always present; but I consider it a pathognomonic symptom so unerring, that if I detected it in any person, I should not hesitate to pronounce him insane, even though I had no other proof of it.

I remember the case of a very delicate young lady, of good family, and highly educated, who became insane; but whose family would not admit the correctness of their physician's judgment, till her mother, having somewhere heard of this character-

* Polit. Essay, vol. i, p. 246.

istic symptom, upon entering her daughter's chamber before she had risen, detected this peculiar fetor; and then she yielded to conviction of the nature of the malady.

The knowledge of this physiological fact may be found very useful, as a test of mental derangement, when there is difficulty in deciding.

The breath of maniacal persons has been remarked by Esquirol and other practical authors to exhale a very fetid smell, which some compare to that of stinking fish; but I have never observed it as peculiar to the insane. As the stomach is often very much disordered, and the teeth from that cause are frequently carious and become loaded with sordes, the breath may thence be very offensive, especially where the patients consist of the lower orders, who are unaccustomed to personal cleanliness. Esquirol may well complain of it in La Salpetrière; for the inmates, according to his own report, are much affected by scurvy,—a disease in which the gums of course are spongy and putrescent.

The dejections of maniacs have commonly a very offensive, but not peculiar smell. Neither is it always the effect of vitiated biliary secretions, or unconcocted ingesta; for strong mental impressions often occasion singular changes in all the excretions.

23. George Man Burrows, *The Character of Insanity*

(Excerpt from *Commentaries on Insanity*, London: Underwood, 1828, pp. 260–2.)

The ancient Stoics conceived that a wise man might become furious, but could not be insane; and that every foolish or vicious person was morally mad, and not to be distinguished from those actually or physically so, except by the degree of the disorder.

We certainly sometimes meet with those who are not only considered sane, but who possess superior minds, nevertheless entertaining projects so preposterous, and committing themselves so unreasonably, that none can coincide with them.

Some yield to first impressions and their immediate gratification. Others cherish prejudices uncorrected by reason, and thus voluntarily shut out the light of truth. Many good and otherwise sensible people are in these senses morally mad. Others, again, indulge in reveries, talking to themselves, regardless of all around, till they become insane. The danger of insanity, it has been truly said, is perhaps in a ratio with the habit of abstraction. The one is not a necessary consequence of the other, else Newton could not have escaped; yet this malady certainly more frequently attends on those who devote an exclusive and intense application to a solitary object.

These moral madmen constitute, doubtless, a very large class of mankind; but they have not arrived exactly at that point to be considered physically or legally mad. Yet whenever these conditions of the moral faculties concur, as they sometimes do, very little more is required to convert them into a state of real insanity.

In the common acceptation, that person is insane or mad, or in a delirium, when any single or several faculties, which synthetically constitute the mind, exhibit signs of disordered function.

Whether one or more of the intellectual faculties be deranged, the pathognomonic of every species of insanity is delirium, continued or intermittent, general or partial.

To describe insanity in all its varieties, would not only be difficult, but it would also be a work of supererogation. In every language of the civilised world, and in every system of medicine, descriptions, sufficiently accurate, of all the forms of mental derangement, are to be found. I shall confine myself, therefore, to a very general description of the characters of insanity.

Madness, says Sauvages, is the dream of him who is awake; and really I know nothing that can be compared to the ideas of an insane person but the delusive images of sleeping visions.

This waking dream may consist in an unnatural rapidity of thoughts, or in a morbid association of them with some known or recollected object, or in the substitution of illusions for realities. Sometimes perception is correct, but memory and judgment are defective, or the reverse may obtain.

Sometimes sensation and volition are equally affected: one, or several, of the external senses shall be perfect, and the others changed; and sometimes all are implicated, or the mind and the will may be at variance. Every sensation, thought, or idea, may have place; but have neither order, object, connexion, nor stability. Neither, though they perceive and think, can the insane always connect, compare, or abstract. These must be received as general propositions, but with exceptions. For instance, the faculty of associating their ideas with words and things, and of applying them to their own situations, so as to combine and execute plans, is sometimes exhibited in a manner most correct and wonderful. Often, the most trivial thing will induce certain ideas, which at their birth are correct; but the judgment being lesed or perverted, the catenation is broken, their application mistaken, and the most wild and incoherent thought, expressions, and actions follow.

Hence, impressions may be either strong or weak; the mind in the one case pertinaciously adhering to one illusion, to the exclusion of every other idea; in the other, the delusive impression is so evanescent as to induce us to presume that the memory is impaired; and yet, hereafter the last idea may revive, and recur with vivid force.

Sometimes the attention to internal feelings supersedes that to all external objects, or the reverse; or one faculty may acquire such an excessive acuteness, while the others retain their natural condition, that such a preponderance of the trains of thought and actions connected with the objects of that sense ensues, as constitutes insanity.

24. George Man Burrows, *Disordered Functions*

(Excerpt from *Commentaries on Insanity*, London: Underwood, 1828, pp. 262–3.)

The will, unconnected with sensation, is often solely occupied in voluntary exertion, and is under no control: hence there is no sense of shame or apprehension of consequences, and the muscular powers are intensely exalted, and every action is an irresistible impulse. Such are equally regardless of natural appetites, or of surrounding objects, except those which administer to their designs. To extremes of temperature, hunger, and other privations, they are insensible; and they display immense strength, and exercise it with great perseverance, with little apparent injury to their general health. On the contrary, some are imbued with a morbid sensibility, are extremely susceptible of the variations in temperature or of any privation, and capable of little muscular exertion; and yet their speech and actions seem independent of volition.

One or several of the exterior senses are usually obtunded, perverted, depraved, or alienated. The sense of hearing usually suffers the first and most. Their fancies 'impart to things inanimate a voice,' and whisperings, or loud and strange noises, as of talking, movements of animals, machines, and sometimes ventriloquous sounds, are imagined. The taste and smell are occasionally singularly perverted. The most disgusting matters, even their own ordure, is eaten; while they will reject with horror the purest and most nutritive food. The sense of touch is often so much impaired, that it does not rectify the errors respecting size, form, or weight of substances.

In mania especially, they are impetuous, irascible, and often malicious: the impressions are many, but generally less strong and more fugacious. In melancholia they are sad and gloomy, and limited to few, or perhaps to one idea or object exclusively—as in monomania, which is most pertinaciously adhered to. The melancholic is less easily roused to anger, except when interruption or opposition be given to his cherished and fixed delusion, and then he is often furious. Sometimes, however, he is subject to rage as well as to great dejection, and equally without occasion.

Some melancholics are so wholly abstracted, that it is quite impossible to discover from them the nature of their hallucination, or anything in which they ever took an interest.

25. John Charles Bucknill, *The Delusions of the Insane*

(Excerpt from *Unsoundness of Mind in Relation to Criminal Insanity*, London: Longman, Brown, Green & Longmans, 1854, pp. 74–7.)

Not unfrequently, but by no means constantly, the delusions of the insane possess characteristic features, by which they may be distinguished from the absurd opinions of the foolish and ignorant. The following are some of the most prominent.

1st. The delusions of the insane are generally independent of the opinions of others; they isolate the person who entertains them from his kind: whereas the sane portion of mankind are gregarious in their absurdities; fools who are to be considered sane, follow each other through a gap like a flock of sheep; oftentimes indeed following some bell wether who is more rogue than fool; they have neither the confidence nor the courage to walk alone. Mr. Dadd was probably the only person in England who believed in

Osiris; had there been a few hundreds or even a few scores of persons entertaining the same belief, his ideas on this subject would have been of infinitely less value as a symptom of insanity.

2nd. The faith of the insane in the truth of their delusive opinions is stedfast and unflinching. It almost surpasses the religious faith of the Mahomedan or Hindoo, and renders pale by contrast the attenuated belief which sane men accord to the absurdities of the hour. The dilettanti philosopher or religionist concedes to clairvoyance, to rapping spirits, or to Mr. Prince, a certain amount of belief, which may give way under the assault of ridicule, or logic, or misfortune; but the lunatic believes in his delusion with all his soul; he may outlive it or be cured of it, but can never be driven from it by any influences, however potent; 'no one who has not been insane,' says a convalescent patient, 'can imagine how terribly real the delusions of lunatics are.'

3rd. The delusions of the insane come on after some physical or moral shock, and often present strange contrasts to the previous habits of thought, or have no relation thereto. The absurdities of the foolish or the ignorant have no such starting point, and are generally consistent with their customary attempts at thinking.

4th. The delusions of the insane in many instances have relation to the patients alone, and are often of a kind which renders their nature apparent; no one could for an instant doubt that a man was insane who conceived himself turned into the screw of a cider-press, and for months revolved on his own axis, making a creaking noise with his mouth. The idea of loss of personal identity in an infinite variety of ways is a frequent source of delusion, and indicates so complete an overthrow of the normal action of the mind, that it must generally be considered the result of disease. Even where such delusion is to a certain extent endemic, and therefore loses its isolated character, as in the '*loup garous*' of France it is found to be caused by disease.

These characteristics of insane delusions are not constant. In a great number of instances they afford a clue to the formation of a right judgment, but not unfrequently they are altogether wanting. In such doubtful and difficult cases the psycopathist can only form his opinion by a careful estimate of all concomitant circumstances.

26. John Charles Bucknill, *Bad Habits*

(Excerpt from *Unsoundness of Mind in Relation to Criminal Insanity*, London: Longman, Brown, Green & Longmans, 1854, pp. 30–1.)

For many years much of our own time has been occupied in subduing the vicious habits of persons of weak intellect: these efforts have been attended with a sufficient amount of success to convince us that no amount of emotional or instinctive self-indulgence, however established and confirmed by inveterate habit, can maintain its ground against a corrective discipline, watchful, patient, untiring, and systematic. The corrective discipline of society, systematized into the form of law, 'supplies those motives which strike the senses, and which are necessary to prevent the despotism of each individual from plunging society into its former chaos. Such motives are the punishments established against the infraction of the laws.' Such agencies may well be employed to correct or to cure insanity dependent upon vicious mental habit alone.

Whether insanity can exist founded upon habit alone, without disease, may be left to be determined by future research, and such a condition, like that of drunkenness, must be held to confer but a partial immunity from punishment.

27. John Charles Bucknill, *Deterioration of Behaviour*

(Excerpt from *Unsoundness of Mind in Relation to Criminal Insanity*, London: Longman, Brown, Green & Longmans, 1854, pp. 31–3.)

As the element of disease, therefore, is essential to a strict medico-legal definition of insanity, it becomes necessary to enquire in what manner its existence is to be ascertained. Care must be taken at this point to avoid the *argumentum in circulam*, educing disease from insanity, and insanity from disease. The real test of cerebro-mental, as of physical disease, appears to be a change for the worse from the normal condition of the individual, an appreciable deterioration from the normal state of the functions: a change distinct from developement and from natural decay. The term disease, as generally understood, implies a change from a previous state. We should scarcely call a congenital malformation of any of the organs of an infant a disease, though one born with the small-pox would correctly be said to be diseased from a previous though fœtal state of health. To prove cerebro-mental disease, therefore, the existence of a changed condition must be established; and this can only be done by comparing the individual with his former self. But it may with truth be said, that the character of all men is subject to constant change, without the suspicion of disease; that no man lives through a year of his life without undergoing modifications of opinion and sentiment. The deteriorating change produced by cerebro-mental disease is, however, sufficiently different in its degree and nature from this; and it might as well be said that, because a man's outward appearance is ever undergoing a gradual development from infancy to manhood, and a gradual decadence from manhood to age, that therefore a physician can never pronounce, from a change in the aspect of any man, that he is the subject of bodily disease. A change therefore, with impairment or perturbation of function, is the chief test of cerebro-mental disease.

It may take the same direction as the original character, and persons naturally timid or daring, cautious or reckless, generous or selfish, may have their natural bias of mind quickly developed in excess. Or the change may reverse the character, and the patient may exhibit a striking contrast to his former self; or it may take some strange direction which no one could guess at beforehand. Nothing can appear more wayward and uncertain than the direction which insanity takes in its development. Doubtless there are facts and laws, could they be seized upon and subjected to computation, by which, the original character and the disturbing cause being given, the extent and direction of the diseased movement might be predicted; but as yet, if cerebro-mental science is in its infancy, the science of Ethology may be said to be in a fœtal condition; and where such knowledge exists it appears to be the intuitive and incommunicable privilege of genius.

28. John Charles Bucknill, *Inappropriate Behaviour*

(Excerpt from *Unsoundness of Mind in Relation to Criminal Insanity*, London: Longman, Brown, Green & Longmans, 1854, p. 34).

Another test of cerebro-mental disease is the relation between cause and effect, and the operation of remedies. Continuing the parallel illustration of bodily disorder, if a stimulating substance taken into the stomach instead of a feeling of comfortable warmth produced intense pain and vomiting; if to allay these symptoms large doses of opium were given, and large quantities of blood extracted without producing the usual effects of opium and loss of blood in healthy persons; no doubt could be left in the mind of any one capable of reasoning, that a state of bodily disease (gastritis or something else) had been induced. In like manner, if a mental shock of grief or disappointment instead of producing the usual consequences of sorrow or chagrin, has been followed by extravagant and unbounded spirits, and if such excitement, bidding defiance to advice and reason, gives way under the judicious administration of pharmaceutical remedies, and to the influence of that atmosphere of control designated moral treatment; such circumstances will not admit the insinuation of a doubt concerning the existence of disease.

29. Henry Maudsley, *Illustrations of a Variety of Insanity*

(Excerpt from the *Journal of Mental Science*, July 1868, pp. 153–61.)

The miserable sinner whose mind suffers by reason of self-abuse becomes offensively egotistic; he gets more and more closely wrapped up in his own narrow and morbid feelings, and less and less sensible of the claims of others upon him and of his duties towards them; he is full of self-feeling and self-conceit; insensible to the feelings of others; his moral nature is blunted or lost. His mental energy is sapped, and though he has extravagant pretensions, and often speaks of great projects engendered of his conceit, he never enters seriously into any occupation nor works systematically at the accomplishment of any object, but spends all his time in indolent and solitary self-brooding, and is not wearied of going on day after day in the same purposeless and idle life. Hypochondriacally occupied with his health, his sensations, his feelings, he imagines that his relatives are hostile to him because they do not take the interest in him which he does in himself, or make the estimate of him which he makes of himself. His own family are especially hostile to him, because they are distressed by his indolence and pretensions, and try to instigate him to do something. If they speak of the impossibility of always maintaining him in complete idleness, they are unfeeling and do not understand him. His manner is shy, nervous, and suspicious, his dress often untidy or slovenly; there is a want of manliness of appearance as of manliness of feeling. The pupils are often dilated, the breath bad, the face sallow, and the body somewhat emaciated. When we are consulted about a case presenting these general features, we may hardly feel justified in signing a certificate of insanity, but we have little doubt of the nature of the mental degeneration which is beginning.

The first class of patients of this kind to which I may direct attention is that comprising youths of about 18 years of age. They are brought for medical advice by their parents or other relatives, because they are not doing any good at the business to which they have been put, and their masters complain that they can make nothing of them. They show no interest, and put no energy, in what they are set to do; they are forgetful, moody, careless, abstracted, perhaps muttering to themselves, and waste a long time in doing badly very simple things, or fail to do them. It is a thought at first that their conduct is the result of laziness, viciousness, and a desire to shirk work; but after a while it becomes apparent that there is something wrong in them, and those who have the superintendence of them are convinced that there is some failure of mind. Meanwhile, at home they are selfish, irritable, exacting, very deceitful, and passionate; they are entirely wanting in reverence for their parents, or in proper feeling for others; and their pretensions are outrageous. They themselves by no means admit that they give any just ground of complaint; but make some excuse for their conduct by putting the blame of it on persons or circumstances, or deny it altogether. One youth, who spent most of the day in leaning against a door-post, or in wandering about in a vacant and abstracted way, maintained that he had always done his work well; but that his master was jealous of him, and therefore had determined to get rid of him. Another asserted that his relatives were hostile to him, that he was superior in talents to them, and that, therefore, they had done all they could to injure his character and reputation. Another considered the business in which he was employed beneath his dignity; and when another business was tried, he found it equally unsuitable to his merits. It is always so; always some excuse for failure and faults, which are entirely in themselves—for a course of conduct really due to a sort of moral insanity.

If you question these youths about their vicious habit, or charge them with it, you are not likely to get an acknowledgment of it; the most they will admit probably is that they have erred once or twice; but they will deny solemnly that they are continuing the habit. There is no faith to be put in their most solemn assertions, their moral nature being thoroughly vitiated. One youth, whom I was questioning upon the point, after first pretending not to hear me, and then not to understand me, confessed that he had practised self-abuse once or twice, but certainly not oftener. When further pressed upon the subject, he acknowledged that he had been suspected and accused of the continuance of the vice by his father; but this he attributed to his father's nasty ideas, and to a jealousy of him because of his mental superiority. And I may add, as an illustration of how completely all proper feelings had been destroyed by the evil habit, that he actually maintained that his father, being jealous of his superior strength, and believing that this superiority might be due to such practice, had himself been guilty of it, in order to try to equal him; but that, having failed, he had thenceforth cherished the bitterest ill-feeling against him. A striking illustration of the utter moral perversion of these patients! Good moral feeling has been acquired gradually by cultivation through generations, as the highest mental endowment of the human kind; the loss of it is one of the first symptoms of that degeneration of mankind which insanity marks, and the loss of it in its most effective form one of the most striking symptoms of insanity caused by self-abuse.

Though you will not usually get a candid confession from these youths, observation of their habits will soon decide whether the practice is continued. They are much given to being alone; spend a long time in their bedrooms or in the watercloset; and they are often found to have bought some of the books published by the spermatorrheal quacks. They are very hopeless beings to deal with, and it is very difficult to know what to recommend should be done with them. It is no easy matter to write a certificate of their insanity, for they betray no delusion, unless their estimate of themselves and whole manner of thought be a delusion. Moreover, if they are sent to an asylum, they invariably get worse. Their life there is idle, uninteresting, and monotonous; there is nothing to stimulate their better feelings, or to call forth their energies; they continue their evil practice without any effectual check, and they sink lower and lower in degradation. The only plan which offers a chance of success is to place them with some kind, but firm and judicious, person, who will be at the pains to exercise a close supervision, without appearing to watch too much; who will not try to bully them out of their vice—for no one yet was ever bullied out of such a vice—but who will endeavour by their influence of manly feeling and kindly advice to awaken an interest in some work, and to wean them from their ruinous vice. When they get worse, as they are very apt to do, their general suspicion of the hostility of people to them takes some special form; they come to think that persons speak of them in the streets, or that their relatives or others attempt to poison them.

Such cases are examples of the sapping of the mental health before the sexual life has really taken its place in the intellectual life—before the individual's character has had time to exhibit its influence. The natural evolution of it in consciousness is prevented by reason of the vice having been begun so early. Consequently, we have degenerate beings produced, who, as regards moral character, are very much what eunuchs are represented to be—cunning, deceitful, liars, selfish, in fact, morally insane; while their physical and intellectual vigour is further damaged by the exhausting vice.

But when the mental failure caused by self-abuse occurs at a later period of life—when the vicious habit, though it may have been commenced early, has not produced its disastrous consequences until the sexual life has entered into the circle of the ideas and feelings, then the features of the mental derangement witness to the perversion of the sexual instinct. The victim of the vice, though shy of women's society, and silent and constrained in general company, will fall in love, or think he does, with some female whom circumstances may have made him intimate with. He is then apt to be unpleasantly close and pressing in his attentions, which have a lascivious look about them. If he has the opportunities which an engagement offers, there is no small danger of his demoralising her mind; for his thoughts run much on nasty subjects. In one case of this nature I had occasion to see the letter which a young lady, accomplished, and apparently most virtuous in thought and deed—of whom one would have dreamt nothing but purity—had written. Many of these were proper and becoming letters, but in two of them, after writing as a young lady should, she adds—'Now I will say something which will please you,' and then enters upon the most disgusting beastliness. In any case, the manner of a masturbator under these circumstances indicates to an experienced eye a lustful feeling without the power of natural restraint or of natural gratification. In fact, his behaviour betrays the actual state of things—a morbid sexual feeling, in the excitement of which he finds pleasure, and a want of restraint of manliness, which is an indication of a real sexual impotence.

He often talks in high poetical or idealistic style, speaks of absurdly exalted plans, but is entirely unpractical; he does not find sufficiently exalted feelings and high aims in the world, and cannot sympathise with, but is distressed by, its low aims and rude ways. He has great projects, but no resolves; abundant self-conceit, but no self-knowledge; a spasmodic sort of self-will, but no true will. When he is alone and has the opportunity and inclination, he practices self-abuse, and afterwards is depressed, gloomy, troubled with all kinds of anomalous sensations, and full of fancies and complaints about his health. However, his system recovers energy after a time, and then the same thing is repeated. If he has become engaged, it is when the day of marriage is fixed that his troubles begin; he is doubtful, anxious, fearful, dreading what is to come; and after rendering his betrothed miserable by his vacillations, uncertainties, doubts of compatibility, or by some overstrained religious scruples, he is almost sure to break off the engagement under some hypothetical pretext or other; if he marries, it is the lady who marries him. I have met with more than one instance in which, almost at the last moment, the gentleman, driven by the pressure of the closely impending event, has written a long accusatory letter, full of apprehensions of the serious responsibility, apprehensions having the semblance of hyperconscientious qualms or scruples. Now if any medical man were consulted in such a state of things I have a strong opinion that he ought to oppose the marriage. Little save sorrow and mischief can come of it afterwards. Certainly marriage need not be recommended to the confirmed masturbator in the hope or expectation of curing him of his vice. He will most likely continue it afterwards, and the circumstances in which he is placed will aggravate the misery and the mischief of it. For natural intercourse he has little power or no desire, and finds no pleasure in it;

the indulgence of a depraved appetite has destroyed the natural appetite. Besides, if he be not entirely impotent, what an outlook for any child begotten of such a degenerate stock! Has a being so degraded any right to curse a child with the inheritance of such a wretched descent? Far better that the vice and its consequences should die with him. In one case which came under my notice, a confession was obtained from the gentleman of the practice to which he was addicted; and the lady, after everything had been explained to her, resolved to go on with the matter, taking him for better or worse. For worse, certainly; for a few days after the event she was compelled to send to her friends for help and protection, on account of his capricious conduct and violence.

In another case the engagement was broken off, but after a time the gentleman became attached to another lady, who was inferior to him in social position; and she, being a woman of remarkable intelligence and great force of character, kept him in the course until the goal was reached. In the first week after marriage he proposed a separation, talking of incompatibility and want of sympathy. That was the excuse he found for himself for his inability satisfactorily to consummate the marriage. Before the honeymoon was over, he had dragged her out of bed by her hair in a paroxysm of capricious and irritable violence, and beaten her as severely as such a spasmodic being could. Such persons always behave brutally, and often cruelly, to their wives.

In another case a gentleman, long addicted to self-abuse, married a beautiful and amiable woman; his father, who was aware of the vice, having urged on the marriage in the hope of curing his son. For a time nothing extraordinary happened, though he was cold and indifferent to his wife, full of fancies, anxieties, and precautions about his own health, and indolent in the extreme. At the end of a year a dead child was born, after an extremely difficult labour. When his wife had recovered from the effects of her confinement, he manifested no inclination or desire to return to her society; and one morning he entered his father's library, and calmly explained to him his firm resolve never to do so. He had no complaint to make of his wife; but he was so deeply impressed with the tremendous responsibility of bringing a child into the world, that he would not again have intercourse with her. The father reasoned and expostulated with him; and the end of the matter was that he consented as a matter of obedience to return to his wife. But they did not remain together long; he was cold and indifferent, and entirely absorbed in elaborate cares about his own health; and there could be no doubt regularly continued his vicious practices. What a position for a virtuous woman to be placed in, for the purpose of saving a degraded being, in whose life nothing could be so reasonably desired as the end of it! Note again in this case the high-pitched and hypocritical excuse for a coldness and indifference springing from an emasculation of character by a debilitating vice.

These cases are examples of evil effects which fall short of actual insanity, although they are sure to reach it ultimately. When the mischief has gone further, the symptoms of mental derangement become unmistakable; positive delusions, usually in reference to their own importance, are engendered. But their conduct is often more insane than their intellect. We observe in them an intense conceit of self in a quiet or an offensive way; large discourse concerning their peculiar feelings which other people fail to appreciate; a complete paralysis of moral feeling, so that they are dead to all their obligations and responsibilities; at the same time excited enunciation of exalted sentiments of a benevolent or religious character, which are commonly the expression of their assumed superiority in noble feelings and exalted aspirations; a disorder of intelligence not manifested in any actual incoherence, but in outrageously exaggerated notions of their own importance, and ultimately in positive delusions of grandeur with regard to themselves, or of persecutions which they undergo by reason of the envy and jealousy of others. Some of them reveal in their gait—in a turkey-like strut—the pride with which they are possessed; while others shuffle along in a slouching and slovenly manner, with eyes bent upon the ground. In the former we see, if I may so speak, the convulsion of conceit; in the latter, the paralysis of self-respect—both equally indications of the extreme degradation. When their selfish ways or personal projects are interfered with, and especially when they are challenged with their vicious practices, they break out in most violent outbursts of anger and abuse, intermingling often with their abusive raving a great deal of religious rant. Incapable of reforming themselves, they are quite prepared to reform a wicked world. Thus, one of my patients who, apart from his insufferable conceit, was tolerably sensible in his calmer moods, would exclaim, in the midst of his passionate invective, that he was not a person to be controlled; that God had given him superior gifts of intellect, and would some day make manifest his superiority; that he would be the means of regenerating a world dead in trespasses and sins; that his family, who had confined him in an asylum because of their jealousy of him, would have to bow down to him, as Joseph's brethren did of old. Another, similarly exalted in his profession of religious sentiments and in his self-esteem, used always to address his mother as 'madam' on the rare occasions when he deigned to write to her.

As an example of the high-pitched and absurd sentiments professed sometimes by these degraded beings, I may mention the case of a gentleman who had a plan for curing the social evil. He set forth with great feeling and energy the miserable and wicked thing which it was that so many of the most beautiful women should be degraded to gratify the worst lusts of men; and professed himself to be grievously distressed by the sin and evil which were caused thereby. How were so much vice and misery to be done away with? His plan, which he practised himself and proposed that others should follow, was to masturbate every morning into a tumbler of water and then to drink it. He argued that the lust was thus gratified without injury to any other person, while the man himself was strengthened by the nourishment afforded to his brain. Here, then, as in other cases, was a mind enervated by vicious practices, dwelling continually on sexual subjects, and concocting, not designedly, but with unconscious hypocrisy, an excuse for the vice which wrecked his life. It is a curious thing that to such a state of moral degradation have patients of this class come, that they will actually defend their vice on some pretence or other.

As matters get worse, hallucinations occur: the patient fancies that persons are aware of everything that passes in his mind, and reply to it, or comment upon it; or he has strange feelings, which he attributes to mesmeric, electric, or other mysterious agencies; and sometimes he is subject to a kind of trance or ecstacy, in which lies for hours in a sort of cataleptic state. Days of deep gloom, depression and wretchedness occur, in which he is a very pitiable object.

A later and still worse stage at which these degenerate beings arrive is one of moody and morose self-absorption, and of extreme loss of mental power. They are sullen, silent, and indisposed to converse at all; but if they do enter into conversation, they reveal delusions of a suspicious or obscene nature. They believe themselves subjected to strange influences, especially in the night, and sometimes that unnatural offences are practised upon them. Their minds seem to dwell much on such disgusting subjects; the perverted sexual passion still giving the colour to their thoughts. They are extremely suspicious, intensely and offensively conceited, and their outbreaks of abandoned passion and of furious, blasphemous, and obscene raving, are most painful to witness. They make suicidal or homicidal threats, but they are usually too fearful of pain and deficient in resolution to hurt themselves, and too cowardly to attack others deliberately. In a frenzy of passion they might do some sudden violence; but their loud threats, though full of sound and fury, do not signify much. It is needless to say that they have lost all healthy human feeling and every natural desire. The body is usually much emaciated, notwithstanding they eat well; and although they often last for a longer period than might be thought possible, they finally totter on to death through a complete prostration of the entire system, if they are not carried off by some inter-current disease.

Such, then, is the natural history of the physical and mental degeneracy produced in men by self-abuse. It is a miserable picture of human degradation, but it is not overcharged. When we meet in practice with its painful features we know what has been the cause of the disease, and what must be its inevitable termination. I have nothing to add concerning treatment; once the habit is formed, and the mind has positively suffered from it, the victim is less able to control what is more difficult of control, and there would be almost as much hope of the Ethiopian changing his skin, or the leopard its spots, as of his abandoning the vice. I have no faith in the employment of physical means to check what has become a serious mental disease; the sooner he sinks to his degraded rest the better for himself, and the better for the world which is well rid of him.

30. Henry Maudsley, *The Insane Temperament*

(Excerpt from *Body and Mind*, London: Macmillan & Co., 1873, pp. 62–4.)

What are the bodily and mental marks of the insane temperament? That there are such is most certain; for although the varieties of this temperament cannot yet be described with any precision, no one who accustoms himself to observe closely will fail to be able to say positively in many instances whether an insane person, and even a sane person in some instances, comes of an insane family or not. An irregular and unsymmetrical conformation of the head, a want of regularity and harmony of the features, and, as Morel holds, malformations of the external ear, are sometimes observed. Convulsions are apt to occur in early life; and there are tics, grimaces, or other spasmodic movements of muscles of face, eyelids, or lips afterwards. Stammering and defects of pronunciation are also sometimes signs of the neurosis. In other cases there are peculiarities of the eyes, which, though they may be full and prominent, have a vacillating movement, and a vacantly-abstracted, or half-fearful, half-suspicious, and distrustful look. There may, indeed, be something in the eye wonderfully suggestive of the look of an animal. The walk and manner are uncertain, and, though not easily described in words, may be distinctly peculiar. With these bodily traits are associated peculiarities of thought, feeling, and conduct. Without being insane, a person who has the insane neurosis strongly marked is thought to be strange, queer, and not like other persons. He is apt to see things under novel aspects, or to think about them under novel relations, which would not have occurred to an ordinary mortal. Punning on words is, I am inclined to think, sometimes an indication of the temperament, and so also that higher kind of wit which startles us with the use of an idea in a double sense; of both which aptitudes no better example can be given than that of Charles Lamb. His case, too, may show that the insane temperament is compatible with, and indeed it not seldom coexists with, considerable genius. Even those who have it in a more marked form often exhibit remarkable special talents and aptitudes, such as an extraordinary talent for music, or for calculation, or a prodigious memory for details, when they may be little better than imbecile in other things.

31. Andrew Wynter, *Early Warnings*

(Excerpt from *The Borderlands of Insanity*, London: Robert Hardwicke, 1875, pp. 15–17, 34–5.)

The more the fact of the physical nature of insanity is acknowledged, the more it is recognized as an ailment, which can be reached by physical agents, the greater will be the chance of its successful treatment. If a man shivers, and feels depressed, he seeks the advice of his physician that he may meet the coming fever with the best resources of his art. If a man feels his brain disturbed—if he feels the 'early warnings' of which his friends as yet know nothing—would it not be equally wise of him to summon the aid of medicine before it is too late? Insanity when not clearly hereditary, if taken in its earliest stages, is more easily cured than many diseases which a man passes through without any great fear; for instance, we question if pneumonia is not less curable than a first attack of insanity. If such a mystery were not made of mental disease, it would be deprived of half its terrors, and of half its evil consequences at the same time.

Whilst we should be keenly alive to the first symptoms of a departure from an ordinary state of mind or habit, it must not be supposed that we see a madman in every individual who thinks for himself, or acts in a manner different from his neighbours. We wish to drag no garden-roller, as it were, over character, and to declare that any person who goes out of the general dead level is to be suspected of being what is called 'touched.' There are naturally crooked sticks as well as straight ones. If, however, a man habitually of an eccentric turn of mind, were to become all at once like other people, and remained so, we should feel certain that some mischief was brewing. *It is the sustained departure from the normal condition of mind and mode of life which should suggest a grave suspicion of impending insanity.*

There are certain significant, although but slightly-marked signs of softening, which tell clearly to the eye of the practised physician the approach of the disintegration of the cerebral matter. The trained eye will observe a loss of muscular power; the patient will slip on one side; the leg is put forward with great premeditation; volition ceases to act unconsciously; certain acts are performed as though the sufferer were pulling the wires of a doll; the hand cannot grasp with a firm, healthy grip. A minute degree of facial paralysis will sometimes disturb the wonted expression of the countenance, without even friends knowing the cause. A very slight elevation of one eyebrow, a drawing aside of the mouth a hair's breadth, will materially alter the look of a person; and paralysis of this kind often exists without any one suspecting that softening of the brain is impending. This partial paralysis, which is indicative of approaching apoplexy, very often shows itself in a person's speech. When we remember the number of muscles which must co-ordinate to enable a man to articulate, it will be readily understood that any loss of power in these delicate muscles must show itself in the speech. It often happens that the first signs will be a clipping of the queen's English: the person will speak as though he were drunk; indeed, drunkenness does produce the very temporary paralysis we allude to.

Chapter III

Treatment

32. Bryan Crowther, *Bleeding*

(Excerpt from *Practical Remarks on Insanity*, London: Underwood, 1811, pp. 102–6.)

Venesection is performed by the surgeon of the Hospital; and attentive as I have been to the state of the patients directed by the physician to be bled, my remarks are but few.

Patients are not brought to the charity for admission at the commencement of their insanity, and therefore we can form no opinion of the condition of their blood at that time.

At one of the bleedings* I noticed in several of the patients, an extraordinary heat of skin, foulness of tongue, offensive breath, and sallowness of complexion. I was induced to select for examination a porringer of blood from those who appeared to me most affected by these symptoms, but it exhibited no sizy appearance.

The lancet has been found a very communicative sort of instrument, not by a disclosure of much information, with respect to insanity, but in as much as it has tended to invalidate the claim of phrenitis to the consideration of being the general cause of mania: I have no hesitation in insisting, that if inflammation of the brain and its membranes is the general exciting cause of madness, its existence would be indicated by the appearance of the blood drawn from the patient. We find it also recorded in a work on insanity, that 'in more than two hundred patients, male and female, who were let blood by venesection, there were only *six*, whose blood could be termed sizy.'

The utility of venesection, at a suitable period, is acknow-

* The curable patients in Bethlem Hospital are regularly bled about the commencement of June, and the latter end of July.

ledged; and the propriety of adopting it is farther sanctioned, by the following extract, from Burdin's Medical Studies. 'Warm seasons have a striking influence upon the return of the paroxysm in mania.'

As noisy and riotous mad persons are more subject to apoplectic and epileptic attacks, the medical attendant will duly appreciate the advantages of phlebotomy, especially to such who are of apoplectic make.

Professor Pinel, p. 253 mentions, that, 'out of fourteen patients who died at Charenton, ten were carried off by apoplexy.'

This writer also enquires: Is it not probable that a fatal termination of this kind might be frequently prevented by a copious bleeding from the vessels of the feet?' To this observation I shall subjoin the very appropriate answer given to the question, in Dr. Davis's own words, as contained in a foot note of his translation of Pinel's Treatise on Insanity; I conceive his sentiments to be valuable: I embody them in the present work.

'Had the author prescribed blood to be taken from the temporal artery, from the jugular, occipital, frontal, angular, or nasal internal vein, or by cupping from the vessels of the scalp, his suggestion would have been valuable. Founded as it is, solely upon the exploded theory of revulsion, and calculated to excite false confidence in a very inactive method of depletion; it is equally injudicious and dangerous.'

Dr. Cox seems to have entertained an unnecessary fear, with respect to insane patients after bleeding, for they do not require any other precaution than that which is requisite in persons not of that description.

I have bled 150 patients at one time and have never found it requisite to adopt any other means of security against hemorrhage, than that of sending back the patient to his accustomed confinement: not a single instance can be adduced of deleterious consequences from the occurrence of a fresh bleeding.

The hazard of bleeding is very great; but let the operator direct the blade of the lancet by his fore-finger and thumb, and open the vein horizontally, and he will avoid all danger of doing mischief. The most violent I have been obliged to place on the floor, and then secure them by assistants, and place myself in the like situation, in order to perform the operation without danger.

33. Bryan Crowther, *Purging*

(Excerpt from *Practical Remarks on Insanity*, London: Underwood, 1811, pp. 106–8.)

The generally received opinion that insane persons are subject to costiveness, I believe to be very correct. Those who superintend the management of mad patients cannot be too attentive to the state of their bowels. In my practice I have witnessed very criminal neglect as to this point: I have seen evacuations which, from their volume and bulk, one would suppose had passed from an over-fed quadruped, instead of a human subject.

In one case, the intestines were so distended, that the transverse arch of the colon gave way, and I shall leave the medical reader to conclude what followed.

It is the duty of persons who have the management of the insane, every morning to enquire into the state of the bowels; and they should know that it is not barely sufficient that they be kept soluble, but that the evacuations should be coloured completely by bile. Calomel, with purgatives, will be found very beneficial in such cases of constipation. Mad persons will occasionally retain their urine for a long time; this circumstance is therefore deserving of attention.

Having adverted to the use of Mercury, I will just observe, that I have employed it, on account of insane persons having syphilitic complaints; but, as these were slight, I did not feel justified in pushing the remedy so as to produce ptyalism, especially as the state of their minds had improved. But I confess I should like to see what effect a mercurial course would have on a driveling case of insanity, such a one as I have depicted in the next article.

34. Bryan Crowther, *Vomits*

(Excerpt from *Practical Remarks on Insanity*, London: Underwood, 1811, pp. 108–13.)

I embrace the consideration of this subject, to settle the discordant opinions of writers, as to the propriety of giving emetics in cases of madness.

In this investigation I feel a peculiar delicacy, having pledged myself to avoid personality, and hitherto, it is hoped, I have adhered to that determination.

But, let me ask, is it any reason that, because the physician of one insane hospital declines the employment of any particular method of treatment, that another belonging to a similar establishment should deny himself the adoption of a plan, which his progenitors have exercised with advantage? Every intelligent reader will give his own answer to this question.

From my own personal knowledge, I state, that vomits have their use; for the servants of Bethlem have repeatedly told me of the quantity of phlegm, with other offensive matters, which have been evacuated by them; in a degree that really excited their astonishment.

I will now portray a character of a maniac to my reader's mind. Let him view one reduced in health, of emaciated form, the eyes shedding tears, although the organs of sight be unimpaired, and the palpebræ in a healthy state.

To these symptoms, I add the snivelling condition of the nostrils, and the saliva flowing from the mouth, I ask my reader what remedies he would propose under such circumstances.

It is presumption in me to give even an opinion; but would the medical man employ the lancet in these cases? I think not: if he agrees with me, then what more suitable plan could he adopt than that of emetics?

Dr. Cox, of Bristol, and Dr. Halloran, of Ireland, speak in high commendation of emetics, but to settle this point the more decidedly, I subjoin the observations of the late Dr. Monro on the efficacy of vomits.

'The evacuation by *vomiting* is infiinitely preferable to any other, if repeated experience is to be depended on; and I should be very sorry to find any one frightened from the use of such an efficacious remedy, by its being called a* *shocking operation, the consequence of a morbid convulsion.* I never saw or heard of the bad effect of *vomits*, in my practice; nor can I suppose any mischief to happen, but from their being injudiciously administered; or when they are given too strong, or the person who orders them is too much *afraid of the lancet*.'

'The prodigious quantity of phlegm, with which those abound who are troubled with this complaint, is not to be got the better of but by repeated *vomits*; and we very often find, that *purges*

* Remarks on Dr. Battie's Treatise on Madness.

have not their right effect, or do not operate to so good purpose, until the phlegm is broken and attenuated by frequent *emetics*.'

'Why should we endeavour to give the world a shocking opinion of a remedy, that is not only safe, but greatly useful both in this and many other distempers? however, to obviate the apprehensions, that may be conceived from such an account, it would be worth while to peruse some cases related by* Dr. *Bryan Robinson*, who does not seem to have been at all alarmed at this *shocking operation*, which, he tells us, he has prescribed for a whole year together, sometimes once a day, sometimes twice, and that with the greatest success.'

'I lately received from a worthy friend of mine the case of a gentleman, who had laboured under a melancholy for three years; he himself calls it an hypochondriacal, convulsive disorder, *from which he was relieved entirely by the use of vomits*, and a proper regimen. So very sensible was he of their good effects, that he did not scruple to take sixty-one from the third of *October* to the second of *April* following; and for eighteen nights successively one each night; by which means he got rid of a prodigious quantity of phlegm, and obtained a perfect recovery. The first seventeen were composed of one ounce of the vin. ipecacuan. with one grain of emetic tartar, and afterwards he made use of no more than half an ounce of the wine. And those, who are much used to hypochondriacal people, will find them in general less weakened with *vomits* than *purges*.'

It may be inferred that those who employ this remedy very sparingly are but imperfectly qualified to judge of the propriety of the practice of those who adopt this plan on a much more extensive scale.

I refer my reader to three cases in Dr. Cox's book on Insanity, p. 105, 6, 7, in which he states, that a single emetic, in a very wonderful manner removed every maniacal symptom: these cases are the more valuable in as much as no other remedy was employed.

35. Bryan Crowther, *A Successful Case of Treatment by Bleeding*

(Excerpt from *Practical Remarks on Insanity*, London: Underwood, 1811, pp. 72–5.)

* Observations on the virtues and operations of medicines, p. 145, & seq.

I was called on to see a gentleman who had sustained an injury of the head: being intoxicated he had a fall from his horse, and in consequence received several severe contusions on the scalp. I was glad that he had been the preceding evening bled pretty largely at the arm, in the country, where the injury occurred. He was removed to his chambers, in one of the Inns of Court, in my neighbourhood, on the following morning. I found him insensible and comatose; but never relying on the state of pulse, in injuries of the head, proceeding from accidental violence, I opened a vein in the arm, and took from him a pint and a half of blood. Not finding him relieved on the third day after the accident, although he had frequent evacuations (by medicine) from the bowels, I requested that the late Mr. Pitts, Surgeon to St. Bartholomew's Hospital, should visit him. This gentleman examined the head, and gave it as his opinion, that nothing beyond the occasional use of the lancet, cathartics, and keeping open a blister which I had previously directed between the shoulders, could be done. This advice was strictly attended to, and in a few days the patient was relieved from the comatose symptom; but in two days afterwards he became furiously deranged. In this state he continued a fortnight, during which period he was bled three times, taking his purging medicine when the state of his bowels required it. The demeanour of this gentleman, during his mental derangement, was shrewd and cunning. He one day prevailed upon his wife to release him from the confinement of a strait waistcoat, promising her to be very submissive and orderly in his behaviour. But instantly on regaining his liberty he fought with his wife and a female servant, the former of whom he treated with a pair of black eyes. I was sent for, and on my entering the room my patient seated himself quietly in an elbow chair, as if nothing had happened. On remonstrating with his wife, upon the impropriety of her conduct, he burst out into a fit of laughter, saying, '*She had what she deserved.*' From the state of his pulse, and the strength of his constitution, I bled him once more; at the same time firmly impressing upon his mind, that so often as he behaved in this riotous manner, I would cool his disposition to mischief. On the following morning I directed opening medicine for him. In short, my mode of treatment, coupled with efforts of his own violent disposition, unattended by sleep, induced such a state of exhaustion, both of mind and body, that he at length fell asleep, and continued in that state upwards of sixteen hours; at length, on awaking, full of surprize at the condition in which he found himself, he was altogether perfectly calm and rational. When he was informed of the state from which he had been relieved, he perfectly acquiesced in the propriety of the coercion which had been employed.

36. John Haslam, *The Therapeutic Value of Confinement*

(Excerpt from *Considerations on the Moral Management of Insane Persons*, London: R. Hunter, 1817, pp. 13–16, 22–3.)

From long established practice, there has been an usual association between BEING MAD, and confinement in a MADHOUSE. That insanity is a disease, which fare its cure, and also for the prevention of mischief, ordinarily requires seclusion, must be admitted; and in many instances, that persons so confined, enjoy a larger portion of comfort than they could attain by being at large is equally certain. Still it is my opinion that confinement is too indiscriminately recommended and persisted in. It may be expected that some rules should be laid down, or directions given on this important subject, as a guide to practitioners, but this is nearly impossible.

That many persons of deranged intellect are at liberty, and for some years have been permitted to be so, who have conducted themselves in a quiet and harmless manner, is well known. Perhaps when insanity exists without a desire to harm others or themselves, there can be no necessity or even justification for seclusion. But the difficulty is in predicting what will be the conduct of a person whose intellect is deranged: he may be harmless one month and disposed to violence the next, and such conversion of character oftentimes takes place. I recollect a female lunatic, who for many months was of a remarkably placid and amiable disposition, but who without any evident cause became transformed into a most furious and vindictive patient, and in which state she continued for several years.

In many instances an intercourse with the world has dispelled those hallucinations which a protracted confinement, in all probability, would have added to, and confirmed. In its passive state insanity has been often known, if the expression be allowable, to wear off, by permitting the patient to enjoy his liberty, and return to his usual occupation and industrious habits: indeed it might be naturally expected that bodily labour in the open air, with moderate employment of mind, directed to some useful object, would more contribute to health and rationality than immuring a person, so circumstanced, within the walls of a madhouse, provided his derangement be of a mild and inoffensive character. In this view of the subject a pauper has considerably the advantage of a man of rank and fortune. The former being an incombrance to the parish during the time he is secluded, the parochial officers are disposed to afford him a trial by way of probation, rather than continue him in confinement at a considerable expense.

Before the pure spirit of benevolence and christian piety devised the foundation of charitable institutions for lunatics, these miserable objects were allowed to wander, and considered as interdicted persons—when they became troublesome or offensive they were whipt from tything to tything, and stockt, punished and imprisoned. The enlightened commiseration of modern philanthropists has afforded them every protection, as the existing public and private asylums sufficiently evince. In these receptacles numbers are temporarily secluded who apparently recover, and afterwards form matrimonial alliances, or if already married, return to their families. The minute investigation of many hundred cases has fully satisfied my own mind that the offspring of a person who has laboured under insanity, is peculiarly liable to become similarly affected. Probably this occasional confinement and premature liberation, when the disease is only quiescent, but not eradicated, may in some degree explain the manner in which it is frequently transmitted. It is not my intention in this place to enter on a discussion of the subject, but leave the reader to form his own deductions.

37. John Haslam, *Restraint*

(Excerpt from *Considerations on the Moral Management of Insane Persons*, London: R. Hunter, 1817, pp. 26–9.)

The usual contrivance by which a maniac is restrained is the strait-waistcoat; this confines his arms and hands, which are crossed over the region of the stomach, and it is secured by being tied behind. This has been generally found a very convenient instrument of restraint, but it has been more convenient to the Keeper than advantageous to the Patient. As far as his hands are concerned, he is certainly prevented from doing mischief. But the disadvantages which result from the employment of this contrivance overbalance its conveniences. It will readily be seen, when a patient is compacted in this instrument of restraint, that he is unable to feed himself, and also prevented from wiping the mucus from his nose as it accumulates, and which, if long continued, would render him a driveller. He cannot assist himself in his necessary evacuations, and thereby is induced to acquire uncleanly habits. He is incapable of scratching to appease any irritation—If, in the warm season, flies annoy him, he cannot drive them away, and if, from the negligence of the keeper, his person should be infested with other insects, he must submit to their painful vexation: and it is always at the discretion of the keeper how tightly he may chuse to tie it. When several lunatics are confined in a room together, the strait-waistcoat is of little security, as it may be unloosed by any patient whose hands are at liberty, and I have known several ingenious maniacs who alone have been able to extricate themselves from it. It should also be kept in view that a single keeper will have the utmost difficulty in applying the strait-waistcoat if the patient be refractory, he will then be unable to effect his purpose without his most forcible efforts: and should his temper become exasperated in the contest, it is more than probable he will have recourse to undue advantages.

The other mode of restraining a furious maniac is by metallic manicles, which encompass the wrists, and prevent the hands from being separated when the patient may be disposed to strike. In my own opinion this mode of security is the most lenient, and subjects the person wearing them to none of the privations incurred by the strait-waistcoat. They are sooner and less difficultly applied, and cannot be removed by the assistance of another patient. Where the hands of the patient are in constant motion, which often occurs in the active state of the disorder, the friction of the skin against a polished metallic substance does not produce excoriation, which shortly takes place when it is rubbed against any linen or cotton materials. Considerable opposition has been made to the employment of metallic manacles, but the objectors have not condescended to adduce any reasons for their aversion to such mode of security. The sole object is to repress the efforts of a violent maniac with the least inconvenience to himself, and to allow him, under a restraint which shall be protecting to himself and others, a degree of liberty which enables him to assist himself, which exempts him from pressure, and is calculated to obviate those habits and infirmities which result from the fingers being muffled.

38. George Man Burrows, *Bleeding*

(Excerpt from *Commentaries on Insanity*, London: Underwood, 1828, pp. 583–95.)

Copious abstractions of blood are almost universally adopted in cases of insanity attended with symptoms of violence, and sometimes where the patient is tranquil. The practice has received the sanction of ancient authority, and is at present very universal. Many of eminent character among the moderns, however, have doubted its efficacy; and experience has convinced me, that, except in a very restricted sense, it is a practice fraught generally with mischief.

Following example rather than experience, I tried depletion by blood-letting for several years; but discovering my error, I became more cautious; and, I believe, that I have scarcely ordered venesection in six cases of simple mania or melancholia in as many years. My conclusion is, that since I changed my practice more have recovered, and certainly the cases have been less tedious and intractable.

I have premised that three disordered conditions in the circulating system exist in mental derangement. 1st, There may be too great a quantity of blood flowing to the brain at the expense of other parts, which suffer a diminution of it, thus producing a real determination. 2d, There may be an excessive momentum in the vascular system, indicative rather of morbid action than of excess in quantity. And, 3rd, there may be a deficiency in quantity, by which sufficient blood is not propelled to the brain, to give the intellectual organs their wonted energy. I may add, that mania, like gout, may be occasioned by a spontaneous effort to relieve general plethora, or to rectify a defective balance in the circulation.

Now it must be evident, that large abstractions of blood from the system in any of the three first conditions can never correct the error in the circulation.

In the young, or the gross and plethoric, the determination to the brain in mania may be so strong as to threaten sanguineous apoplexy. In this case, prompt and copious general depletion may save the patient's life. It may also, by producing syncope or mere exhaustion, procure quiescence, but it will not cure mania. The danger, however, of sanguineous apoplexy in mania is, as we have proved, less to be apprehended than, from the reported number of sudden deaths, has been hitherto inferred.

If any urgent necessity impells copious abstraction of blood in mania or melancholia, the more prudent practice is to effect the object with the greatest celerity.

Formerly, the practice was to abstract blood when the head was to be relieved, by a puncture in the frontal, nasal, or orbicular veins, or in the venæ raninæ under the tongue. The latter mode I have known practised in a case of insanity, where those veins were so distended as to hinder the flexible movements of the tongue, and protrude the point of it between the teeth. The relief of the engorgement was immediate. But Cælius Aurelianus, in whose time this operation was much resorted to, condemns it as a superstitious practice, founded on false principles, and, besides, objects to it from the difficulty of checking the flow of blood. For the same reason, it has been disapproved by the moderns. Bleeding from the feet or ankles has been a favourite remedy, with a view to derive blood from the head. But all these modes are very precarious in their effects, and should be abandoned for more direct means of detracting blood from the seat of mental disturbance, whenever such evacuation is deemed absolute.

Arteriotomy is often then the readiest and best course; and to divide either branch of the external carotid passing before or behind the ear, is more advantageous than dividing that of the temple. Bleeding from the jugular vein by a free orifice is seldom practicable, from the turbulence or position of the patient, or perhaps from obesity; and as the discharge by this mode is from the integuments of the head, and not immediately from the brain itself, it is less efficacious. If syncope be desired, the sooner it follows the less will be the deduction of blood and of the *vis vitæ* —two objects always to be cherished in the treatment of insanity. Hence, the making of one large, or even two, orifices, or bleeding from both arms at once, if it can be managed, has been advised.

It is only where a real state of plethora exists, or apoplexy is pending, that general blood-letting in mental derangement can, in my opinion, be justified.

Simple determination of blood by too great momentum, producing that state of congestion of the brain which originates cerebral irritation, and perhaps the maniacal action, is not relieved by venesection. Neither can that mode of abstraction of blood ever be admitted in the cachectic state, since that implies a deficiency of the vital fluid, and debility.

Topical Bleeding

The sudden diminution of vital energy frequently attendant on depletion of blood from the general system, can never be experienced in topical bleeding, except from some gross misconception or misapplication. Blood detracted by leeches, or cupping, will sometimes occasion faintness; but I never saw either, except when an excessive quantity has been unadvisedly or accidentally lost, produce any permanent bad effect, even though faintness have followed.

The primary symptoms in the commencement of insanity, whether mania or melancholia, denote increased vascular action or congestion of the vessels of the brain. The partial pains, tension, or throbbing in the head; extraordinary heat of the scalp, flushed face, blood-shot or glistening eyes, and general confusion of ideas, mark cerebral determination or congestion. It is true, there may also accompany these signs a white tongue and a very accelerated pulse; but neither of these in cases of insanity can be accepted as unequivocal proofs of general excitement: the white tongue is a common accompaniment of derangement of the alimentary canal, which usually attends insanity; and the pulse, which is influenced through the nervous system, will often be found amazingly rapid in cases of mental derangement where there is none of these symptoms of cerebral excitation.

From this view of the state of the intellectual organ in mental derangement, it may be inferred, that although venesection is not indicated, yet, that topical or local bleeding may be very useful.

In every case of recent insanity which I have seen, and I do not recollect an exception, local abstraction of blood from the head itself, or contiguous, as the nape of the neck, or between the shoulders, has been indicated. The mode has been by cupping or by leeches. Cupping on the occiput is to be preferred. Celsus says, this lessens the malady and brings on sleep. Sometimes the terror or prejudice against this operation is so very great that it cannot be performed with propriety; then leeches are the best substitute. Neither of these modes of abstracting blood weaken like general bleeding; for this reason, if for no other, they are preferable. Shaving the scalp is generally to be premised in the treatment of all recent attacks. Besides keeping the head cooler, it affords greater facility to the applying of cupping-glasses, or leeches, to such part of the cranium as may be requisite. If the patient describe a precise spot where pain or throbbing is felt, the glasses or leeches will afford much relief by being applied over it. If no particular part is referred to, I order them to be applied behind the ears, or across the occiput, and sometimes on the temples.

The quantity of blood to be taken away must be regulated by circumstances; the plethoric and the cachectic, the strong and the weak, difference of sex, constitutional varieties, the highly- and the moderately excited, all demand consideration, and require different measures. One case may require the loss of sixteen or twenty; another only ten, eight, or six ounces of blood, or even a smaller quantity.

Hallaran says, that the superficial heat is reduced by placing leeches behind each ear on a limited space, and afterwards by cupping-glasses applied over the orifices. Where more blood than the leeches take is wanted, this is a good mode. As, however, local determinations of blood either to the head or other parts do not depend upon fulness of the sanguiferous system, but may equally occur in the extenuated, so likewise may topical bleeding be called for in the one as well as in the other case, though of course in quantities relative to those respective conditions.

In the case detailed, perhaps depletion by cupping was prescribed where the patient was so extenuated and debilitated by continued disease that many would have deemed it imprudent. Nevertheless, it was successful, and is a good example how far the operation is admissible.

It is an excellent rule to observe in local abstractions of blood, that as many glasses or leeches should be applied at once, if possible, as are capable of abstracting as much blood as may be desired. The effect will be more certain, and the length of the operation be curtailed, which is an object of no small importance with impetuous and unruly patients.

Among those who admit the utility of local abstractions of blood from the head, or contiguous to it, in this malady, there is much diversity of opinion as to the propriety of its repetition, or if repeated, how long the practice should be pursued.

Some conceive that the object is attained by a single emptying of the surcharged vessels of the brain; others repeat it through exacerbation and remission, even into the continuous form. The latter course I hold to be dangerous, as likely to produce a permanent state of collapse of the brain. My practice is to repeat cupping or leeches so long as symptoms of great cerebral excitation prevail, especially while a preternatural heat of the scalp is felt; but when they remit, to desist from drawing away blood, and repeat it only with the renewal of these symptoms. If premonitory symptoms announce an attack, local depletion will often prevent it. Mere raving and fury must not be mistaken for cerebral excitation consequent on vascular excitement. They are probably the effect of that cerebral irritation which is produced by an opposite condition of the brain, and would inevitably be exasperated by any kind of depletion.

Patients are often so sensible of the relief of topical bleeding, that they will frequently solicit it as a boon.

When insanity has been relieved, and sometimes cured, by spontaneous hæmorrhages from the nose, uterine and hæmorrhoidal vessels, or varicose veins, I question whether such an effect may not have been produced more by change of determination than by the sanguineous evacuation. It is certain that the degree of mental anguish and disturbance which impels suicide, finds relief in the sudden loss of blood.

In cases of nymphomania, all the distressing symptoms whence this affection derives its name have been removed by the application of leeches to the vulva. In like manner, improvement of the mental faculties, dependant on menstrual obstruction, follows cupping on the sacrum. Sympathetic delirium from an affection of the liver, has subsided by local abstraction of blood from the hepatic region.

Local determination and congestion of the brain in mania, with other symptoms of excitation, may take place without flushing of the face. On the contrary, in mania, as well as sometimes in the apoplectic diathesis, a singular palor exists. Nay, cases occur where topical blood-letting has been required to relieve local congestion, and at the same time stimulants to support the general tone of the system. I have no hesitation in continuing abstractions of blood from the cerebral vessels by cupping or leeches, so often as the symptoms denote fresh excitation. It is advisable to pursue this plan even when tonics are indicated to support the patient's strength; for local determination is as frequent in the weak as in the strong. Of course, the quantity of blood detracted in such cases will be smaller. Should faintness or marks of exhaustion come on during the abstraction, the patient must be supported by good broths or a little wine.

The melancholic certainly hold life by a more precarious tenure than the maniacal. It is the natural effect of depressing passions. But in the commencement of melancholia, accompanied by uniform despondency, the symptoms of determination, or of congestion of the cerebral vessels, are as manifest often as in incipient mania. Sometimes, on the explosion taking place in melancholia, it is attended with great fury and excitation. Whether, however, accompanied by despondency or excitation, topical bleeding may be equally necessary and beneficial; and as the symptoms in this form of insanity persevere longer without remission, moderate local depletion may be repeated for a greater length of time than in an attack of mania. The ancients advised blood-letting in melancholia; and Willis says, 'Sanguinis emissio in omni ferè melancholiâ locum habet, et nonnunquam sæpiùs iteranda est.' He advises bleeding from the *vena salvatella*; adopting probably the popular opinion, that bleeding from this vessel was particularly useful in melancholy. It is the fact, however, which I wish to record, not the vessel whence the blood was taken; since many are afraid to detract blood in any way from a patient in melancholia. There is nothing in such practice inconsistent with the received pathology of insanity, since more authorities support the pretension of melancholia to be the original disease, of which mania is but a variety.

The practice so frequent on the continent of applying leeches to the anus, is founded, I conceive, on the obsolete doctrine of revulsion, and as a general principle should be declined. But where insanity may be reasonably suspected to arise from sympathy with some abdominal viscus morbidly affected, the loss of blood from that part may do good; and more especially if the patient has been accustomed to hæmorrhoidal flux, and that has been suppressed.

Dry Cupping

A few observations on this mode of operating may be here applicable as a corollary to the preceding. It is very desirable and useful in cases of insanity and transient delirium, where we have reason to suspect determination to the brain or congestion, to relieve the surcharged vessels; but the patient may be in such a state of emaciation and debility as to positively forbid the detracting of blood even in the smallest quantity. I have seen such cases; and have found sensible advantage, after shaving the scalp, from the repeated application of several glasses to the head, without scarification or loss of any blood. The blood is by this means derived from the surcharged internal vessels to those of the external, all of which will be seen greatly distended from the operation; and it is there retained awhile, without being absolutely withdrawn from the circulation, to the relief of the brain.

If a patient die soon after blood has been abstracted from the scalp by the usual process of cupping, and the head be immediately opened, all the exterior and interior anastamosing blood-vessels of the pericranium and the investing cerebral membranes, inclusive of those of the brain itself, will be found highly injected and distended with blood, to a circumference exactly correspondent with that of each glass which is applied on the surface. This appearance I saw remarkably displayed in the head of a patient who died in half an hour after he was bled by cupping, and whose head I examined six hours after he died. But where the examination takes place many hours after the operation, the internal evidence of this effect of cupping is nearly obliterated. This fact demonstrates the possibility of affording relief by simply attracting blood to the surface by the mere application of the glasses.

Friction on the pericranium after dry-cupping, and pediluvium, greatly tend to determine blood from the head to the general circulation.

Refrigeration

The utility of refrigeration where there exists a preternatural heat of the head, is confessed in all cases of cerebral disorder.

Divesting the scalp of all the hair by shaving, is not only a necessary preliminary to other applications, but deserves regard and adoption as in itself a refrigerating process. It is certain, that the simple denuding of the scalp produces a calming and even soporific effect, in violent mania.

Celsus sometimes advised clipping off the hair, sometimes shaving the head. In all diseases where the sensorium is affected, whether attended by pyrexia or without, the latter is an admirable auxiliary. Clipping the hair close does not suffice; for, besides that it does not produce the soothing effect of denuding, the process of evaporation, which abstracts caloric, never goes on so rapidly as when a naked surface like the shaven scalp presents itself; neither is the impression on the sensorium, the object desired by the operation, so effective. The abstraction of heat is much more rapid and complete by evaporation than by cold applications, such as ice, or any of the frigorific mixtures.

The head, when divested of the hair, should be kept so as long as symptoms of active cerebral excitation are manifested, and local applications to the surface are deemed necessary. When such symptoms subside, and the brain may be suspected to be in a state of collapse, refrigeration must cease, and the hair may be suffered to grow.

As a general rule, I recommend that the heads of all insane persons should be kept cool. For this reason, permitting them to have their heads covered when indoors is an injurious custom. In several public asylums I have visited, I observed this bad habit prevail, when, at the same time, the patients were crowded in apartments much too heated. This is very inconsiderate, and will produce in many cerebral excitement and sleepless nights, and consequent irritation to all the patients.

39. George Man Burrows, *Gyration and Swinging*

(Excerpt from *Commentaries on Insanity*, London: Underwood, 1828, pp. 599–603.)

Each of the preceding remedies, by diminishing cerebral excitation induces sleep in recent insanity, and hence greatly contributes to the cure of the malady.

Any remedy that invites sleep acts more beneficially on the disturbed functions of the brain than narcotics of any kind, though producing that effect.

One of the means recommended by Celsus and Aurelianus in mania, is motion in a suspended bed or movable seat, or by swinging.

The latter also speaks of the effect of the motion of a rotatory vehicle which produced vertigo and dimness, for the cure of epileptics.

Darwin advised gyration to procure sleep. He took the hint from the account of a man who extended himself across a large millstone while gently whirling round, and found that it lulled him to sleep before it acquired its full velocity. Hence, also, he inferred that death without pain might have been induced by an increase and continuation of this motion.

Probably the man alluded to by Darwin arrived at the knowledge of this effect from gyration by mere accident.

This appears also to be another common mode, among the aboriginal inhabitants of the Himālāya mountains, of obtaining rest. When the mother wishes her infant to go to sleep, she takes it by an arm, and, aided by her knees, gives it a violent whirling motion, till, in a few moments, sound sleep is the unerring result.

The effect of sea-sickness on the circulation and stomach is somewhat analogous to the action of the rotatory machine, and had been in olden times prescribed in cases of insanity.

From the influence of gyration and swinging also on the circulation, by producing vertigo and diminishing the velocity of the pulse, the late Dr. Carmichael Smyth recommended the latter in pulmonary consumption. It considerably lessens, likewise, the temperature of the surface of the body.

Darwin conceived that two objects were attained by the horizontal whirligig bed; first, the quieting of the violent action of the heart and arteries by gently compressing the brain, and that to accomplish this, the patient's head was to be distant from the centre of motion; and secondly, the forcing of the blood from the brain into the other circulating vessels, and this was to be done by reversing the position of the patient, and placing his head next the centre of motion.

Upon this theory, Darwin constructed a rotatory machine; but the late Dr. Joseph Mason Cox was the first who introduced it in the treatment of insanity. He prescribed the oscillatory as well as the circulating movement.

Dr. Hallaran very soon afterwards, on Cox's recommendation, adopted both modes in the Cork Lunatic Asylum; and these physicians, in their several publications, speak most confidently of its utility. The latter has given in his publication a graphic sketch of both apparatus, which he considers to be improvements on Cox's. The rotatory seat for the erect position is certainly better than a common Windsor chair; inasmuch as it supports the cervical column better, and guards against the possibility of the head in the vertiginous state from hanging over the side.

It is described as seldom failing to produce copious evacuations in the most obstinate cases, provided that, on increasing the velocity of the swing, the motion be suddenly reversed every six or eight minutes, pausing occasionally, and stopping its circulation suddenly: the consequence is, an instant discharge of the contents of the stomach, bowels, and bladder, in quick succession. Should the stomach only be acted upon, a purge should be afterwards given.

The erect machine is the best for procuring evacuations and producing moral repression, and the horizontal circular bed for inducing sleep. Clear evacuation of the bowels should precede the use of either; nor should they be used at the commencement of the disease until the violence of the paroxysm has subsided; nor in young plethoric persons, nor where there is a positive determination of blood to the head. Another caution is, to begin the motions gradually, till they are carried to the degree of velocity desired.

In the intermitting form of insanity, gyration has been found of particular benefit in checking the approaching paroxysm. When a great prostration of strength suddenly succeeds to the full motion of the swing, most advantage is expected. Its effect in lowering the circulation and temperature of the body is so immediate, that alarm for the consequences is generally created in those not accustomed to the use of it.

Where sleep is the wished-for object, a slow and long-continued action of the swing, if possible, without affecting the stomach to vomiting, is to be kept up.

Like every other antimaniacal remedy yet prescribed, it is acknowledged that this sometimes entirely fails in producing the desired effect. Possibly, as it always occasions great apprehensions, its ordinary operations on the system are thereby counteracted.

The operation of gyration, either vertically or horizontally, is strongly advised, as a moral as well as a medical agent in chronic cases; for where no expectation of cure has been entertained, a few trials have produced a wonderful improvement in manners and behaviour.

Where the degree of violence has been so great as to compel a rigid confinement, the patient has become tractable, and even kind and gentle, from its operation. The morbid association of ideas has been interrupted, and even the spell of the monomaniac's cherished delusion broken.

I remember, in the case I have mentioned (p. 293), seeing in the Military Asylum at Rochester, a marked instance of the good effects of the rotatory chair. It completely broke the catenation of morbid ideas; and the dread of being exposed to it again, made the patient alive to every thing around him.

Dr. Hallaran remarks, that patients of this description 'previously to any amendment, were invariably affected from the disturbance occasioned by the machine, with a smart fever of eight or ten days' duration, and from which the favourable occurrence here alluded to seems to have arisen;' but that he never saw any one instance, when the disease had assumed the chronic and uninterrupted form, of complete recovery having followed its use.

The works both of Drs. Cox and Hallaran contain many important observations on the application and effects of this powerful engine in the treatment of insanity, and to them I would refer the readers for more minute details.

The rotatory machine is met with now in most British public asylums; but its results are very differently reported;—some speaking most favourably of it, some dubiously; and with others it has fallen into disuse.

Without wishing to extol its merit more than is due, this diversity of opinion cannot be the fault of the remedy: it is reasonable to support, that the same degree of attention in selecting the cases to try it on, and the rules prescribed for applying it, have not been equally observed in different institutions; and hence these contradictions.

40. George Man Burrows, *Blistering*

(Excerpt from *Commentaries on Insanity*, London: Underwood, 1828, pp. 618–21.)

Blistering the head or nape of the neck is another very favourite remedy in insanity; but, like the exhibition of opiates, it is generally prescribed indiscriminately, without considering the nature of the case, whether symptoms of cerebral excitation or congestion are present or not, or the stage of the malady. As with opium, blistering appears to me too often prescribed at a venture, or as an experiment, and for want of knowing what better to do.

I have frequently had occasion, upon visiting an insane person, to order the removal of a blister from the patient's head or shoulders, and in a few minutes have seen his fury abate, or cease altogether.

Blistering can never be serviceable in mania any more than opium, where cerebral vascular excitement or congestion exists, till local or general depletion has preceded. The reason is obvious. Wherever too much vascular action is going on, any application which increases that action, such as vesication of the surface produces, must be injurious. Stimulation of the pericranium directly affects, through the anastamosing vessels and nerves, the encephalon; and if there be already cerebral excitement or coma, it does harm, unless the cerebral vessels are previously unloaded.

Perhaps vesication is so generally employed in mania upon the presumption of inflammation of some part of the encephalon; but as this pathological view of the malady is disproved, vesication on this principle cannot be justified.

Besides, it is well known that cantharides when applied to the skin are liable to be absorbed, and therefore may produce dreadful irritation of the meninges of the brain, as well as of the urinary organs in some persons. In fact, such effect often takes place when the blister is applied to the scalp. Soothing the action of the brain, whether by shaving, gentle friction, or abstraction of caloric, may do good in recent mania; but stimulation is adding fuel to fire.

Convalescent patients have complained that blisters to the head produce exactly the same sensation in the brain as when they were first attacked.

Where blistering is admissible at all, it is the more advanced stage of insanity, when vascular excitement is diminished and the nervous system requires stimulating.

Vesication is more beneficial in melancholia than in mania, because in the former the vital powers are more torpid. But it by no means applies as a general rule; for it must be recollected, that melancholia often commences and alternates with violence, and manifests strong marks of cerebral vascular action or congestion, which sometimes will persist as long as in mania.

When these symptoms, however, abate, blistering between the shoulders is sometimes useful. As derivatives, blisters do more good when applied to the thighs and legs; and then if the discharge be not kept up, they should be frequently renewed.

In some cases, when so applied, and benefit has accrued, I have thought it was more to be ascribed to the attention to himself which is forced upon the patient, in consequence of the pain and inconvenience suffered from the vesication, rather than to any other effect it produced. The association of morbid ideas in melancholia, or the fixed delusion in monomania, may be thus broken and dispersed.

Without the advantage to be expected is very apparent, vesication is on other accounts a dangerous remedy. The pain it occasions induces the patient to try all means to get rid of the blister. They have been known to eat them; and serious consequences, of course, have ensued; or, by accident, they slip and adhere to some other part, greatly to their annoyance. Besides, when the constitution has been much reduced, I have known troublesome sores, and even mortification, from blisters.

Mead, John Monro, Haslam, Hallaran, and the most experienced practitioners, attach little faith to blisters.

As derivatives or counter-irritants, however, there are other, and, in my opinion, better applications.

When this effect is required, the application of warm, stimulating cataplasmata on the soles of the feet, or to the legs, till the impatience of pain is expressed, is more efficacious.

But it is still preferable to excite vesication, where it is indicated in mania, by the application of a plaster composed of tartarised antimony and the common wax plaster. It soon occasions considerable heat, and a crop of pustules, from which a discharge may be kept up or checked at will. This application might judiciously supersede cantharides in mania; since it produces all their good, and none of their bad effects.

41. George Man Burrows, *Setons and Issues*

(Excerpt from *Commentaries on Insanity*, London: Underwood. 1828, pp. 621–2.)

Setons and issues inserted on the occiput, nape of the neck, &c. have been prescribed as derivants, to diminish cerebral irritation. I have rarely met with a case where I was quite satisfied that convalescence was the result of either of these applications. Recovery doubtless sometimes follows the introduction of them; but I have had reason for suspecting that other remedies have had an equal or greater share in the event. In two or three cases, however, in which the malady had continued some months, and there was still evident cerebral commotion, with throbbing in the head, I have certainly found these symptoms gradually decline after a discharge in this way had been established.

I think it probable, that where they have been reported to have effected a cure, the malady has originated in metastasis, by the retrocession of some cutaneous eruption or transfer of a morbid action of a remote part to the brain, or from the suppression of some long-continued or periodical discharge from the hæmorrhoidal vessels, gleet, or leucorrhœa. Drains of these kinds in such cases are decidedly useful.

Whenever any of these causes may be suspected of having influenced the mental disorder, a seton or issue should be introduced as near the head as is convenient.

Long-established setons and issues hastily dried up, have caused many cerebral affections, and insanity among them.

42. George Man Burrows, *Purging*

(Excerpt from *Commentaries on Insanity*, London: Underwood. 1828, pp. 632–5, 638–9.)

Keeping the bowels in free action is indispensable in all cases of insanity, but absolute purging in the incipient and active stages is especially necessary. The secretions at these periods of the disease are almost always bad; more morbid perhaps in melancholia than in mania.

Montanus inveighs against half purges, which tire nature and molest the body to no purpose. Thomas Willis seems to have been of the same opinion. His purging formula in melancholia was: calomel and extract of black hellebore, each a scruple, and extract of jalap, six grains. Either the human constitution was more vigorous, or these ingredients were not so potent as at present, for such a dose in these days would be dangerous.

I observe no stated days or periods for purging, but am governed by the circumstances of the case. And when the evacuations have become natural, I endeavour to keep them so by exercise, diet, and such means as are best calculated to preserve the functions of the body in health.

Drastic purgatives may be indicated in the first instance, not only to overcome the torpidity of the bowels common in incipient attacks, but also because there are often large quantities of morbid bile or scybala collected in the colon and large intestines, the evacuating of which will sometimes at once greatly diminish the cerebral irritation and delirium. And for this purpose very small doses (the sixth or fourth of a grain) of elaterium have proved very beneficial. Calomel, in conjunction with other cathartics, is very useful.

When the evacuations prove of this description, strong purges must be interposed; but the bowels in the interim should be kept regular by milder cathartics. If vomiting and purging are desired at the same time, I give a solution of Epsom salts, with one grain of emetic tartar to each ounce of the solution, and of this a table-spoonful or two every half hour, till both or one of the effects be produced. If great activity of the bowels be required, two grains of emetic tartar should be added to six ounces of the common senna mixture, and three or four table-spoonsful of it be repeated every two, three, or four hours, till it freely operates.

An impression prevails, that the bowels of all lunatics are difficult to move. This is a dangerous error that should be exploded, for they are often free to act, and sometimes are very irritable. Caution, therefore, at first ought to be observed. My practice has been to begin with moderate doses, and continue purging at intervals so long as the excretions bear an unhealthy appearance, and to remit it as they improve, always having regard to the constitution of the patient.

As men of studious and sedentary habits are often affected with melancholia and hypochondriasis, it should be remembered that they, especially, can never bear violent purging. Their intense application and abstraction generally brings on a cachectic habit. Hence, remedies which either strongly excite the nerves or produce large evacuations, induce in them debility—the one directly, the other indirectly.

Means of obviating Constipation

Where the system is much exhausted, either by long-continued violence, or for want of a proper quantum of nutrition, or disability of assimilation, all which conditions are frequently met with, drastic purges are out of the question. Glysters are then the only resource.

Very old and paralytic lunatics sometimes lose the power of evacuating the contents of the bowels, and an immense load accumulates in a hardened mass, forming, what is vulgarly called, a ball stool. This state is generally discovered by efforts to go to stool, and passing only a thin fæcal discharge, though with a great sense of forcing down of the rectum, and there is often an impediment to the passage of the urine from pressure of the ball on the neck of the bladder. As soon as this case is suspected, an examination *per anum* should take place; and if it prove so, the means advised . . . should be used.

Obstinate cases of constipation are most frequently seen in public lunatic asylums, among the lower orders, whose bowels, from habitual neglect, have become thus inactive. Such cases are much more rare in private practice.

I fear that the general impression of the difficulty in getting the bowels of insane people to act, must be imputed to that neglect of them which is consequent on a lunatic's indifference to the performing of all natural functions. This fact ought not to be forgotten. The bowels of some lunatics are disposed to act too much, and are not easy to restrain. We should therefore be careful, when the patient is a stranger and his history obscure, lest we rashly prescribe cathartics too drastic and powerful.

The determined resistance often met with to the taking of any medicines, or of submitting to any means of relieving the bowels, renders these cases very difficult to manage. It is of importance, then, to have recourse to such purgatives as from their bulk and insipidity can be best disguised. A dose of calomel mixed with a grain or two of tartar emetic to give it activity, is a convenient form. I have often succeeded, by putting this between two pieces of buttered bread, in getting it down. The croton oil may also be sometimes administered, rubbed down with a little sugar and mixed in a little beer. The elaterium, in point of bulk and certainty of effect, is an excellent medicine; but, unfortunately, it is so nauseous that it cannot be disguised except in a pill, and that is a form, if refused, very difficult to make them swallow. There is this objection, too, both to the croton oil and the elaterium, that intense nausea and vomiting sometimes follow.

When all other means have failed, and the necessity for evacuation has become urgent, surprise will occasion the sphincter muscle to relax, and expel copious dejections. In La Salpetrière I saw a strong arm-chair, like a night-chair, fixed to the ground, in which when the patient is firmly seated, a stream of cold water is suddenly propelled from a *douche ascendante*, full on the anus. The shock it occasions generally produces the wished-for effect. This, however, might fail on a second trial, with a cunning lunatic.

At the Glasgow Asylum I placed myself for a few minutes in a vibratory chair of great strength and power, in which when a patient is seated, he experiences a far more violent jolting than from the roughest-trotting horse. Such tremendous motion being given to all the viscera, I should think, would conduce most effectually to correct habitual costiveness; and if persevered in as a punishment, it must also soon break the resolution of constrained constipation.

Lunatics are but children of a larger growth. Their minds reason not, but they become the creatures of habit. Hence they may be led to do many things which neither reasoning nor persuasion can accomplish. We know that infants a few weeks old, if well managed, will, instinctively, have an evacuation upon being held in a certain position, and provided due regard be paid to a regular time. So I am persuaded will lunatics, generally, acquire a regular instinctive action of the bowels, whether they are perverse, indifferent, or fatuous, provided they be forced to go to the water-closet daily, at that stated time when nature in health makes the call. I have tried this plan with many where an opposition or disinclination has shewn itself, and have thus imperceptibly conquered it. I say imperceptibly, because the practice must be adopted as a matter of course, and not as a request or favour; for if the object desired be known, it would put the patient on his guard, and he would most likely purposely restrain the impulse.

If the movements of those who are unconscious of the calls of nature were carefully watched, the indication of their wants would soon be properly interpreted, and many filthy habits and much trouble be thereby avoided.

I have been consulted on cases of insane persons whose bowels, either from neglect or the difficulty of getting medicines taken, have been constipated an extraordinary time without apparent injury to the general health. Although the constitution possess the power of accommodating itself to the retention of the fæces for a length of time which seems incompatible even with life, as in the case, related by Dr. Baillie,* of Robert Hertsell, who, from a stricture in the rectum, lived nearly fifteen weeks without a stool, yet such instances should never influence us in the management of the insane.

Nature seeks and requires a daily evacuation of the bowels and bladder; and a deviation from that habit begets other functional derangements, and thus commences corporeal disease and mental disorder.

43. George Man Burrows, *Vomiting*

(Excerpt from *Commentaries on Insanity*, London: Underwood, 1828, pp. 639–42.)

There is no remedy for the cure of insanity that has been more generally or strongly recommended than vomiting.

Evacuation, says the elder Monro, is the best cure, and vomiting preferable to all others; and if not carried beyond the patient's strength, nor crowded too fast upon him, his health of body will visibly improve so long as vomits are continued. The prodigious quantity of phlegm which accumulates, he observes, is not otherwise to be got rid of; and he adds, that purges do not operate so well till after vomits. Hallaran, however, advises that purging should precede vomiting.

The opinions of Monro are certainly strengthened by the practice of many, before and since his day.

I am disposed, however, to think that the action of emetics

* Trans. Soc. Med. and Chir. Know. vol. iii.

when beneficial in cases of insanity, is not conducive to that end simply as an evacuant, but rather from the well-known effect vomiting produces on the circulation.

During the nausea first induced, the circulation is in a condition resembling the cold stage of fever; and when vomiting commences, the whole vascular system is in commotion, and an equality in the circulation ensues, which removes those local determinations to the brain which disturb its functions, and occasion delirium and mental derangement.

Dr. Bryan Robinson gave emetics daily for a whole year, and sometimes twice a day, with great success, in the cure of insanity; and Dr. John Monro gave a gentleman sixty-one emetics in six months, and also for eighteen successive nights, by which the patient was recovered.

Unfortunately, the question here recurs which is perpetually presenting itself when specific virtues are ascribed to remedies in the cure of diseases. Might not the efforts of nature, or the effects of diet, management, or other remedies, have restored these patients, and in less time than the emetics? The answer does not recommend the practice; for, twelve months which the cure of Robinson's patient occupied, and the six which it took Monro to cure his, are periods beyond the average which the majority of cases require to recover.

Influenced, however, by the strenuous recommendations of emetics for the cure of insanity, I gave them a fair trial; and in several cases relied upon their operation together only with purging. I used in turn every substance in the materia medica possessing emetic properties, and marked with attention the effect of each; but I must conscientiously declare, that, after several years' perseverance, my confidence in emetics alone in cases of insanity has been entirely dissipated.

Ferriar asserts, that he has known dangerous debility in this malady brought on by a single vomit of emetic tartar.

A vomit is sometimes given to refractory patients as a punishment. This is very inconsiderate, for no lunatic is at all times in such a state that vomiting may be excited without risk. Besides which, a prejudice against all medicines is raised, that nothing afterwards may be able to subdue.

Still, I have occasionally recourse to emetics, but only as I would in other diseases,—to free the stomach from troublesome ingesta, accumulated phlegm, or morbid bile; and sometimes to give activity to torpid viscera, and rouse and emulge the general system.

In melancholia, vomiting is decidedly more useful than in mania; for in the former the stomach is more apt to be loaded with saburra, and the viscera to perform their functions languidly. Then the action of an emetic, while it clears away the cause of offence, invigorates the powers of digestion and assimilation, and conduces to corporeal and mental health.

Emetics are occasionally useful, too, by interrupting intense abstrations, and morbid hallucinations, and capricious resolutions. Where the urine has been retained from obstinacy, the operation of an emetic will generally evacuate the bladder. In like manner, it sometimes will act on the rectum when the fæces are withheld.

In the apoplectic and hemiplegiac diatheses, it has been remarked, that powerful doses of emetic tartar are required to induce vomiting. The same may be generally observed in all diseases, as well as in insanity, where there is cerebral congestion. I have given to the extent of a scruple of it at a dose without the least nausea, in cases of mania where, as soon as the congestion was relieved by the abstraction of blood from the head, a grain or two has vomited.

So likewise, where the object has been merely to induce nausea to abate symptoms of great excitation. Till the vessels of the head are unloaded and the lower intestines well evacuated, a large dose is required; afterwards, a smaller will produce the effect.

These, however, are general remarks, not without exceptions; for sometimes, though rarely, the insane experience much gastric irritation, and then the slightest dose of any nauseating medicine cannot be borne on the stomach.

44. George Man Burrows, *Nausea*

(Excerpt from *Commentaries on Insanity*, London: Underwood, 1828, pp. 642–3.)

The action of nausea and vomiting is very opposite: the former diminishes the power of the heart, and retards the circulation; the latter increases the action, and determines the circulation to the surface. Emetics, therefore, exciting vomiting, or only nausea, may in the one event be of great service, in the other do infinite mischief. This observation especially applies in the treatment of insanity, and ought particularly to be regarded.

Nausea exercises a powerful control in mania. To the sensation it creates, the whole attention of a maniac is often directed. In this respect it acts like any thing that excites local pain. While nausea lasts, hallucinations of long adherence will be suspended, and sometimes be perfectly removed, or perhaps exchanged for others; and the most furious will become tranquil and obedient. In mania furibunda it is an excellent auxiliary, not only because it subdues violence, but because of its controlling power over the circulation.

Indeed, it is far safer to reduce the patient by nauseating than by depleting him. The effect of the former, when artificially produced, we can check and counteract when we please; the effect of the latter is not within our control, and often leaves lasting proof that it has been injudiciously practised.

Doses of emetic tartar at such intervals as will keep up the nausea, rarely fail to rescue the most stubborn to subjection. Sleep, also, which in these cases is so desirable, will sometimes occur while in this state. This plan should be continued so long as it is positively useful, and no longer. I have known it pursued for a fortnight, and the hallucinations by degrees dispersed, or so weakened that the cure has been quickly accomplished.

But in melancholia, nausea never ought to be excited intentionally as a remedy. The hallucinations in this case are generally full of suspicion, and especially of poison; therefore, any thing that disturbs the stomach the patients are apt to suspect is given with an evil intent, and it prejudices them against all other remedies, and, what is more material, against their food. The operation of an emetic they understand; and though very disagreeable to them, it excites no false alarms; but the terrors they endure in protracted nausea, is to many a realisation of their worst apprehensions.

Besides, in melancholia, where the vital powers are apt so suddenly and unaccountably to give way, exciting nausea, which is itself a state of collapse, and enfeebles the system, may have dangerous consequences.

45. George Man Burrows, *Separation and Seclusion*

(Excerpt from *Commentaries on Insanity*, London: Underwood, 1828, pp. 696–7.)

There is no general maxim in the treatment of insanity wherein medical practitioners, ancient or modern, foreign or domestic, are so unanimous as that of separating the patient from all customary associations, his family, and his home; and there is none wherein the advice of the faculty is so commonly and successfully opposed. Thus, cases which in the early stages are comparatively manageable, obedient to medical discipline, and commonly curable, are rendered obstinate, tedious, unnecessarily expensive, and too often incurable. The observant Dr. Heberden, perhaps, goes too far: he remarks, that if insane persons are taken away from their friends and servants at the beginning of the attack, and placed under the care of strangers, that in a short time they recover without any remedies.*

Few of the medical profession require arguments or proof to convince them of the great utility of separation. When the friends of any insane person have a doubt, and have not confidence in the advice or probity of their physician, they should consult the works of authors who have treated of insanity, and who can have no interest in the question. Such friends might then more readily and earlier yield their conviction, and consent to the separation and seclusion of the patient, whenever it is advised by those whom they consult, and think competent to judge.

I by no means imply that separation or insulation is indispensable in all cases of mental derangement. I have myself seen patients recover in their domicile; but, comparatively, those instances are rare indeed. The only case where it may be dispensed with, is when the affections are in no way perverted, nor the existing delusions associated with home, or any person or object about it. But even then there are other circumstances to be considered which may prevent recovery while in that situation.

Few persons when they become insane acknowledge being so: consequently, when they find themselves placed under control in their own houses, denied intercourse with their families, and their orders not only disobeyed, but their own servants concurring in controlling them,—they are naturally infuriated to a high degree,

* De Insaniâ, Comm. cap. 53.

or imbibe a plausible and strong suspicion that a conspiracy is formed against their life, liberty, or property. These are irresistible reasons why insane persons should be removed from home.

Reminiscences, whether agreeable or painful, may be associated with the most insignificant localities, which, when the feelings are morbidly sensitive, and reason cannot correct them, revive certain objects or ideas that powerfully excite or depress the passions. In whatever place an insane person is exposed to the danger of such mental associations, he ought to be removed from it.

In a strange place, attended by those equally strange, and whom he has never been accustomed to command, and confided to the direction of a competent medical attendant, a moral influence over the patient is thereby established, to which he usually readily submits; and a cure then may be expected, which never otherwise can be accomplished.

46. Andrew Wynter, *The Role of the General Practitioner*

(Excerpt from *The Borderlands of Insanity*, London, Robert Hardwicke, 1875, pp. 156–9.)

The insane action or idea as surely springs from a morbid derangement in the brain structure, as a bilious attack springs from a morbid condition of the liver. There is no mystery about it; it is a mental manifestation arising from a physical cause, and should form as necessary a branch of medical study as chest or heart disease. We believe ourselves that this separation of one organ, and that the highest, the brain, from general medical study, is the most fruitful cause of incipient insanity being suffered to degenerate into confirmed lunacy. The sentinel who is at every man's door, be he rich or poor—the general practitioner,—is the one who should be able to foresee the approach of an attack. But he has never studied, or has the slightest possible knowledge of, psychological medicine; the danger goes on from day to day, the chance of averting the evil is lost, and when the patient has become an outrageous lunatic, he is taken to a 'mad doctor,'—that is, if he has the means to pay his fees, if not he is allowed to linger on making his home miserable and sinking every day into deeper disease, when he is taken to the asylum.

The loss to the community by reason of this defect in the

knowledge of the general practitioner is not the only evil of this separation of psychological medicine from general medicine. The error which underlies all special study and experience, even if it makes the vision keener in a limited area, is far more serious where mental afflictions are concerned than in other diseases. A surgeon may with advantage devote himself to particular manipulative arts. A man who is drawing teeth all day makes a far better dentist than a general practitioner. The operation of lithotomy requires special skill, which practice alone can secure. But to treat mental disease properly, not only the condition of the brain but of the whole body must be taken into account, as in all cases madness arises from morbid bodily conditions, some of which the specialist overlooks, or rather he is so engaged in looking for one thing, that he overlooks another which may be of equal or greater importance. Of course, there will always be physicians eminent in mental disease, leading men whose genius in their own department overrides all other shortcomings, but these will necessarily be few. Otherwise we are convinced that, for the good of general medicine, this particular study, dealing as it does with so many complex problems, should be merged in the general routine of medical practice.

47. Charles Mercier, *Keeping the Public Informed*

(Excerpt from *Sanity and Insanity*, London: Walter Scott, 1890, pp. xii–xiv.)

Considering how common an affection insanity is; considering that there is scarcely a family in this country that has not had at least one of its members more or less insane; it is somewhat remarkable that so little should be generally known about insanity. It is not, indeed, remarkable that this malady is not discussed with the same freedom that bodily diseases are talked of, for its occurrence is still looked upon as almost a disgrace to the family in which it occurs, and he who introduces the subject never knows whose toes he may be treading on. Nor is it remarkable that it is not discussed with that fulness of knowledge with which the dyspeptic legislates on dietary, and the materfamilias on measles; for even amongst experts—the medical officers of asylums—the subject has hardly yet begun to be scientifically studied; so that there is no body of knowledge for the layman to draw upon beyond a mass of more or less authentic anecdotage. The eager interest with which these anecdotes are received and repeated, shows, however, that there is much curiosity alive upon the subject, and that systematic information with regard to it will be received with avidity. The dissemination of such information can scarcely fail to do good in several ways.

In the first place, it may tend to diminish the absurd and unreasoning horror with which insane people are regarded. I have known ladies, in other respects sensible and kind-hearted, refuse to sit at table with other ladies as well-bred and well-conducted as themselves, because the latter were unsound in mind. And if it were known, as I trust it never will be known, that scarcely a week passes in which I myself do not take a party of lunatics to one or other of the London theatres, it is very probable that those excellent places of entertainment would find a serious falling-off in their receipts. How often have I not watched an unsuspecting stranger chatting and exchanging criticisms between the acts with one of my companions, little thinking that for the last hour he had been sitting between a couple of lunatics, and was at that very moment talking to one of them.

In the second place, a little familiarity with the phenomena of insanity may prevent well-meaning people from making idiots of themselves by talking of insane people *in their presence*, as if the insane possessed neither hearing, understanding, nor memory. 'But does he *know* that he is in an asylum? or, 'He is not *dangerous*, is he?' a lady will ask (ladies are the chief offenders in this respect), in the hearing and in the presence of a courteous gentleman who has been doing his best to entertain her for the last half-hour. She appears to regard him as an automaton, who acts and speaks by machinery, has no feelings to be hurt, and is incapable of appreciating an insult.

Thirdly, a knowledge of the principles on which insanity should be regarded can scarcely fail to be of service to that large, and now much increased, section of the community who have to do officially, but as amateurs, with the insane. I refer to the magistrates under the new Lunacy Act, to barristers, and others. The want of knowledge of the rudiments of insanity among the general public is remarkable. I have heard a Queen's Counsel gravely tell a jury that it was against the law for a lunatic to be sent to an asylum unless he (the lunatic) was dangerous. That is, fortunately, not the law; but there are very many people who are strongly of opinion that it ought to be the law. A very little knowledge of lunacy would alter this opinion. Apart from the fact that it is desirable to cure the insanity, and that in many cases a cure can only be attempted within an asylum; apart from the necessity, that so often exists, of secluding a perfectly harmless lunatic in order to prevent him from squandering his means and ruining himself and his family; apart from the desirability of restraining him from performing acts which are not dangerous, but which are disgraceful, and which he himself would, on his recovery, be loudest in blaming his friends for not preventing; there remains the most important fact that the distinguishing feature of the insane is, not their dangerous aggressiveness, but their revolting indecency and obscenity. Of course, not all the insane are thus characterized, but a majority of them, probably a large majority, of both men and women are or would be if freed from restraint, more shameless and filthy in their conduct than so many monkeys. It is not merely that the public must be protected from such conduct as this. They have a right, also, to be prevented from witnessing it, to be protected from the danger of witnessing it; and it is for this reason, more than for any other, that the seclusion of the insane in asylums is necessary and right.

PART TWO

PSYCHIATRIC ROMANTICISM

Chapter IV

Moral Management

48. Bryan Crowther, *Medicine and Moral Management*

(Excerpt from *Practical Remarks on Insanity*, London: Underwood, 1811, p. 86.)

Management of the insane as a curative mean, can never be too highly estimated; but I do not agree with some, who think it supersedes the necessity of medicinal treatment.

It is true, that in many instances it has induced success, when the known medical means had certainly failed; yet judiciously combined, surely their mutual co-operation would encourage us to hope for a more favourable termination of the disorder, than when either is separately employed.

49. Samuel Tuke, *Moral Management*

(Excerpts from *A Description of the Retreat*, York: W. Alexander, 1813, pp. 131, 132, 133, 134, 138.)

If we adopt the opinion, that the disease originates in the mind, applications made immediately to it, are obviously the most natural; and the most likely to be attended with success. If, on the contrary, we conceive that mind is incapable of injury or destruction, and that, in all cases of apparent mental derangement, some bodily disease, though unseen and unknown, really exists, we shall still readily admit, from the reciprocal action of the two parts of our system upon each other, that the greatest attention is necessary, to whatever is calculated to affect the mind.

Insane persons generally possess a degree of control over their wayward propensities. Their intellectual, active, and moral powers, are usually rather perverted than obliterated; and it happens, not unfrequently, that one faculty only is affected. The disorder is sometimes still more partial, and can only be detected by erroneous views, on one particular subject. On all others, the mind appears to retain its wonted correctness.

The moral treatment of the insane, seems to divide itself into three parts; and under these, the practices of the Retreat may be arranged. We shall therefore inquire,

I. By what means the power of the patient to control the disorder, is strengthened and assisted.

II. What modes of coercion are employed, when restraint is absolutely necessary.

III. By what means the general comfort of the insane is promoted.

50. Samuel Tuke, *The Use of Fear*

(Excerpt from *A Description of the Retreat*, York: W. Alexander, 1813, pp. 141–4.)

The principle of fear, which is rarely decreased by insanity, is considered as of great importance in the management of the patients. But it is not allowed to be excited, beyond that degree which naturally arises from the necessary regulations of the family. Neither chains nor corporal punishments are tolerated, on any pretext, in this establishment. The patients, therefore, cannot be threatened with these severities; yet, in all houses established for the reception of the insane, the general comfort of the patients ought to be considered; and those who are violent, require to be separated from the more tranquil, and to be prevented by some means, from offensive conduct, towards their fellow-sufferers. Hence, the patients are arranged into classes, as much as may be, according to the degree in which they approach to rational or orderly conduct.

They quickly perceive, or if not, they are informed on the first occasion, that their treatment depends, in great measure, upon their conduct. Coercion thus flowing as a sort of necessary consequence, and being executed in a manner which marks the reluctance of the attendant, it seldom exasperates the violence of the patient, or produces that feverish and sometimes furious irritability, in which the maniacal character is completely developed; and under which all power of self-control is utterly lost.

There cannot be a doubt that the principle of fear, in the human mind, when moderately and judiciously excited, as it is by the operation of just and equal laws, has a salutary effect upon society. It is a principle also of great use in the education of children, whose imperfect knowledge and judgment, occasion them to be less influenced by other motives. But where fear is too much excited, and where it becomes the chief motive of action, it certainly tends to contract the understanding, to weaken the benevolent affections, and to debase the mind. As the poet of Liberty has well sung,

> ———————————— All constraint,
> Except what wisdom lays on evil man,
> Is evil; hurts the faculties, impedes
> Their progress in the road of science, blinds
> The eye-sight of discovery, and begets,
> In those that suffer it, a sordid mind,
> Bestial, a meagre intellect, unfit
> To be the tenant of man's noble form.
>
> COWPER'S TASK, BOOK V.

It is therefore wise to excite, as much as possible, the operation of superior motives; and fear ought only to be induced, when a *necessary* object cannot otherwise be obtained. If this is the true scale of estimating the degree in which this principle is, in general, to be employed, it is found, at the Retreat, equally applicable to the insane.

That the continual or frequent excitement of the sensations of fear, should 'bid Melancholy cease to mourn,' is an idea too obviously absurd in theory, to require the refutation of experience. There has, however, unhappily been too much experience on this subject; and hence we may perhaps, in great degree, explain, why melancholy has been considered so much less susceptible of cure than mania. To the mild system of treatment adopted at the Retreat, I have no doubt we may partly attribute, the happy recovery of so large a proportion of melancholy patients.

Is then the violent excitement of the principle of fear, better adapted to enable the maniac to control his wanderings, and to suppress his emotions? Is it not well known, that the passions of many maniacs, are extremely irritable? and, when once excited, are not all moral means to subdue them, as ineffectual as the attempt would be to quench, by artificial means, the fires of Etna?

If it be true, that oppression makes a *wise* man mad, is it to be supposed that stripes, and insults, and injuries, for which the receiver knows no cause, are calculated to make a *madman* wise? or would they not exasperate his disease, and excite his resentment? May we not hence most clearly perceive, why furious mania, is almost a stranger in the Retreat? why all the patients wear clothes, and are generally induced to adopt orderly habits?

51. John Haslam, *The Necessity of Restraint*

(Excerpt from *Considerations on the Moral Management of the Insane*, London: R. Hunter, 1817, pp. 30–2.)

Abundant experience teaches us that restraint is not only necessary as a protection to the patient and to those about him, but that it also contributes to the cure of insanity. It is not intended here to institute a physiological enquiry into the nature of madness, nor to investigate the history and constitution of its attendant passions: it will be sufficient to demonstrate that habits of self-control are established both in the sane and insane mind by the same agents. That the fear of punishment or degradation which deters a rational being, who exercises his reflection, from the commission of a crime, would in due time and properly administered check the outrageous sallies of the lunatic.

The fact is well established, that proper restraint on the conduct of an insane person will curb his propensity to precipitate his thoughts into immediate action, although the derangement of his intellect still continues. It should be the endeavour of the practitioner in those cases where malevolence forms a prominent feature, to ascertain how much appears to be derived from actual disease, and what part should be attributed to evil passions associated, but not actually depending on the morbid affection: and this enquiry will be considerably facilitated by a consideration of the natural character, education, and pursuits of the patient. The necessity of restraint, as a mean of cure, is most satisfactorily illustrated from the confession of those who have recovered, and who possess a recollection of their disordered state. When such persons have been asked, to what circumstances they especially attributed their recovery, they have in general deposed that when they found themselves effectually restrained from fulfilling the dictates of their will, they then became enlightened by a gleam of reflection, and ceased to obey the impulse which prompted them.

52. Alexander Morison, *Seclusion*

(Excerpt from *Outlines of Mental Diseases*, Edinburgh: MacLachlan & Stewart, 1824, pp. 79–80.)

The indications to be fulfilled by these (moral means), are the removal or diminution of moral causes—the separation of the patient from persons and objects tending to excite—the dissipation of delusions—the restraint of disorderly inclinations—and the encouragement of the timid and desponding, &c.

Domestic treatment is seldom admissible, from the patient being unconscious of disease, and the aversion to relatives which the necessary restraint imposed may create. It is more common in Russia than elsewhere, and is said to be there adopted with tolerable success.

Removal from objects which tend to keep up the disease, is effected by Seclusion. This is not hastily to be adopted. Persons in febrile delirium have been sent to a madhouse; therefore we ought to wait a reasonable time. Seclusion may be unnecessary where the patient has no aversion to the place, and to the persons about him; as his delusions may be dissipated by judicious intercourse with others; but when insanity is completely established, in most cases it is indispensably necessary.

53. George Man Burrows, *Patient Management*

(Excerpt from *Commentaries on Insanity*, London: Underwood, 1828, pp. 677–9.)

To reason with a lunatic is folly; to oppose or deny his hallucinations is worse, because it is sure to exasperate. If we wish to make an impression on him, it must be by talking *at*, not *to* him. Though he will not listen to what we address to him, yet he will notice what is said to others, and, if applicable at all, will apply the argument or point of your observation more forcibly to his own situation or delusions than we can.

To convince them, or break the catenation of their morbid ideas by fraud, trick, terror or surprise, is always attended with hazard. The chances are great that it will not succeed; and if it fail, the case is inevitably rendered more intractable; and perhaps the painful reflection is left, that our own imprudent and precipitate conduct prevented the recovery which patience might have insured.

Authors relate cases where this sort of hap-hazard practice has succeeded, and they justify it on the ground that desperate diseases require desperate remedies. But as I never could forgive myself were I frustrated in such an experiment; and as I think the proportion of cures in cases of insanity are as numerous, or more so, than in many active diseases, I shall proceed in that cautious course which experience has satisfied me is to be preferred.

The confidence of his patients is the sure basis of the physician's success; and among none is it more essential than with lunatics. A cheerful, encouraging, and friendly address; kind, but firm manners; to be patient to hear, but cautiously prudent in answering; never making a promise that cannot safely be performed, and when made never to break it; to be vigilant and decided; prompt to control when necessary, and willing, but cautious in removing it, when once imposed;—these are qualities which will always acquire the good-will and respect of lunatics, and a command over them that will accomplish what force can never attain.

The state of the insane in respect to moral management, has been rightly divided into active and passive. These opposite states necessarily require different treatment. In one state, moral remedies are almost useless; restraint and medical discipline must be applied till violence is subdued; in the other, restraint is never necessary except there be a propensity to suicide, or to habits which are injurious or improper.

Vigilance is necessary in all cases, for the passive state in a moment sometimes changes to the active; and therefore, unless always on the guard, mischief is done before it can be prevented.

Time displays all a patient's delusions and peculiarities: If he be subject to intermitting or periodical insanity, he requires the more caution, lest a paroxysm suddenly occur. In many, certain symptoms, or a peculiar cast of features, indicate the threatened attack; but in others it comes on without warning, and much confusion ensues before sufficient restraint can be imposed.

An unhappy solitary vice, to which I have referred as so frequently inducing mental derangement, requires peculiar and unwearied vigilance.

When this is a habit continued beyond the period of adolescence, it is extremely difficult to eradicate. Numerous, indeed, are the cases of insanity arising from this cause. However strong the mental powers of the patients may originally have been, or however forcible reflection on the consequences, yet few can ever be broken of the practice. Sexual intercourse, as a preventive, does not always cure the propensity. Often, the virile powers are too enfeebled to be exercised in this way; but even when there is sufficient vigour, and the act has been completed and repeated, it does not always stop a recurrence to this odious vice. If it be a habit contracted only during the continuance of insanity, it ceases generally with a return to reason.

To prevent the commission of the act by restraint, is extremely difficult, and yet it is imperative to impose it. A thousand subtle expedients will be resorted to, to accomplish the purpose. To prevent it effectually, the patient must never be left alone one instant; and even though a strait waistcoat be worn, and the hands be secured, such confinement only will be unavailing when in bed. Constraint, so that he cannot turn himself, is necessary; and some mechanical contrivance must be applied to guard against friction. The ancients were supposed to employ infibulation, as much with a view to prevent this practice in youth as too early intercourse.

54. Robert Gardiner Hill, *The Abandonment of Restraint*

(Excerpt from *Total Abolition of Personal Restraint in the Treatment of the Insane*, London: Simpkin, Marshall & Co., 1839, p. 21.)

I wish to complete that which Pinel began. I assert then in plain and distinct terms, *that in a properly constructed building, with a sufficient number of suitable attendants, restraint is never necessary, never justifiable, and always injurious, in all cases of Lunacy whatever.* I assert the possibility of the total banishment of instruments of restraint, and all other cruelties whatsoever. I assert that the Asylum of your own City, when completed, may be conducted without a single instance of restraint occurring from one year's end to another.

55. Robert Gardiner Hill, *The Nature of Moral Management*

(Excerpt from *Total Abolition of Personal Restraint in the Treatment of the Insane*, London: Simpkin, Marshall & Co., 1839, pp. 37–42, 45–7.)

But, it may be demanded, 'What mode of treatment do you adopt, in place of restraint? How do you guard against accidents? How do you provide for the safety of the attendants?' In short, what is the substitute for coercion? The answer may be summed up in a few words, viz.—*classification—watchfulness—vigilant and unceasing attendance by day and by night—kindness, occupation, and attention to health, cleanliness, and comfort, and the total absence of every description of other occupation of the attendants.* This treatment, in a properly constructed and suitable building, with a sufficient number of strong and active attendants always at their post, is best calculated to restore the patient; and all instruments of coercion and torture are rendered absolutely and in every case unnecessary.

In order, however, that this plan may be undeviatingly pursued, several essential requisites must unite:—

1. A suitable building must be provided, in an airy and open situation, with ground sufficient for several court-yards, gardens, and pleasure-grounds, commanding (if possible) a pleasing and extensive prospect.

2. There must be a proper classification of the patients, more *especially by night.**

3. There must be also a sufficient number of strong, tall, and active attendants whose remuneration must be such as to

* Suicide under this system must be obviated by the constant attention of the House-Surgeon to the proper Classification of the Patients *by night.* Those disposed to suicide should always be placed in an Open Dormitory under watch. *Nothing else can prevent Suicide under any system whatever.*

secure persons of good character, and steady principle, to undertake their arduous duties. And

4. The House-Surgeon must exercise an unremitting control and inspection, in order that the plan may never, under any circumstances whatever, be deviated from in the slightest degree.

1 & 2. The nature of the Building required will be best understood from a view of the Classification, which renders a proper number of Apartments, Dormitories, Galleries, and Court-yards, unavoidably necessary. The following is a view of the Classification adopted in our Asylum.

Degrees of Rank—Three,—according to the payments made;—viz., *First, Second, Third.*

Classes of Insanity—Three;—viz., *Convalescent and Orderly, Moderate, Disorderly.*

The Day apartments consist of fourteen sitting-rooms, six galleries, and six dining-rooms.

The Convalescent and Orderly, and the Moderate of the first Rank have front rooms in the centre part of the House.

The Convalescent and Orderly of the second and third Ranks have front rooms at the extremities of the east and west Wings.

The Moderate Patients of the second and third Ranks have the use of Galleries and Sitting-rooms in the front on the ground and first floors;—these Galleries and Sitting-rooms have a southern aspect.

The Disorderly of the Three Ranks have the use of Galleries and Sitting-rooms which project northward from the back of the Wings, and have eastern and western aspects respectively.

The patients of the Three Ranks have at all times access to the Courts, and the Convalescent and Orderly, and the Moderate are allowed for many hours during the day to take exercise on the lawn in front of the Establishment. As an indulgence, the quieter patients are allowed occasionally to accompany the porter and attendants into the town;—i.e. one or two at a time:—occasionally as many as six females have gone out together into the fields.

The night apartments consist of two Open Galleries or Dormitories, containing eighteen beds each;—two Watch-rooms adjoining the Dormitories, with eight beds each;—also four rooms, with two beds each;—four rooms, with three beds each;—and forty-eight rooms, with one bed each:—besides the above there are two Infirmaries for the first and second Rank Patients, each containing three beds.

The long Dormitories are used for the patients disposed to self-destruction:—the beds in the Watch-rooms to those who destroy bed-clothing, and to the epileptics;—the rooms containing two and three beds each, to the harmless and convalescent and the single bedded rooms to the harmless, the noisy, the violent, or the insensible.

In the treatment of the insane, medicine is of little avail,* except (of course) when they are suffering also from other diseases, to which lunatics as well as sane persons are liable. *Moral treatment with a view to induce habits of self-control, is all and every thing.* I have spoken of classification and watchfulness: but these things are done by their guardians, and have little or no reference to their feelings; for they should if possible be watched without leading them to suppose that they are suspected of any thing improper or injurious.† But occupation and kindness have especial reference to the patient; and their object is (as I have stated) to induce habits of self-control and cleanliness, which qualities are both essential to recovery, and yet cannot possibly be attained unto by a patient under restraint. Out-door employments with moderate exercise—cheerful society—the occasional presence of friends and even of visitors—healthy recreations and amusements—the enjoyment of the sweet music of spring, of a calm summer evening—the care of a garden, or a shrubbery, or the cultivation of rare and choice flowers—all unite in producing a healthy tone, and giving nerve and vigour to the shattered mind. No patient should be *compelled* to work in any way; but many of them, both males and females, will voluntarily make themselves useful and be industrious; and in many cases their services are very valuable. Sedentary employments are not good. The offices of religion have a soothing and favourable effect on many:—I have found the use of evening service, and the calm and sober strain of piety which pervades the Liturgy, to be well adapted to these unfortunate beings. Religious excitement of the feelings is

* The use of the lancet, leeches, cupping-glasses, blisters, drastic purgatives, and the practice of shaving the head are totally proscribed in this Asylum as at Gloucester. The patients' bowels are kept open, their general health is attended to, and they are allowed a generous diet but no fermented liquor. The daily allowance of meat, bread, milk, &c., will be seen on reference to the Diet Table which is appended to this lecture.

† It is essential, however, that the patient should be aware that he is *observed* though not *suspected of wrong*: and aware also that the person who observes him is powerful enough to control him.

always bad and has brought a great number of patients to this, as well as to every other Asylum. A patient should never be terrified.

56. Daniel Noble, *The Therapeutic Environment*

(Excerpt from *Elements of Psychological Medicine*, London: John Churchill, 1853, pp. 311–12, 314–15.)

The moral management of the insane is, in principle, precisely the same as that which obtains in the treatment of ordinary disease; it comprises negative requirements in removal of *lædentia*, and positive indications in furnishing *juvantia*. Every circumstance that is prejudicial to the disordered mind must be counteracted; and agreeable diversion of thought, with grateful impressions on the feelings, must, so far as practicable, be brought about. In more purely physical maladies, we adopt an analogous proceeding—removing causes of irritation, and seeking by direct remedies to restore healthy action. This idea kept steadily in view, may always render itself the guiding-thread in our moral management of insanity.

I would here observe that, in any general account of treatment, it is *principles*, for the most part, that must be laid down. Modifications of management demanded by individual cases, can be stated only when the circumstances in detail come before us. Nevertheless, I will proceed to explain, somewhat more particularly, the method of dealing with some of the more prominent varieties of mental disorder, commencing with what has been denominated emotional insanity.

In those instances in which there is melancholic depression of spirits, or in which there is exaltation or depravation of any of the feelings, one aim must always be maintained. Everything that is calculated to excite or provoke the particular emotion which is under morbid influence, should be avoided or withdrawn; and everything that is fitted to counteract the circumstances of the disordered sensibility, should be practised. When the patient is overwhelmed or prostrated by sorrow, the train of ideas associaated with it should be broken; and allusions to the real or supposed causes should never be made, but with unusual care and delicacy. The thoughts should be directed into other channels, and with uncommon care and skill,—not by ill-judged attempts of a bold and direct character. Such a proceeding would inevitably fail.

When a patient begins to recover the natural control over his ideas, he should be reminded of the power which every person possesses, and should exercise, over his own current of thought; and how, by voluntary efforts, he should direct his attention to objects and pursuits calculated to establish states of mind antagonistic to his melancholy. The extent, indeed, to which an individual may modify his own sensibility by exerting a directing power over his thoughts, has a great deal to do with final and complete restoration to mental soundness, and still more with warding off threatened attacks of insanity. It is the *constant brooding* over depressing ideas, that gives them such a hold upon the mind as to destroy its balance. Some people notoriously *nurse* their sorrow, as if it were some pet child. The application of these principles in the actual management of the melancholic, will, of course, vary according to the varying circumstances of individual cases.

57. John Conolly, *The Treatment of the Insane before and after the Advent of Moral Management*

(Excerpt from *The Treatment of the Insane without Mechanical Restraints*, London: Smith, Elder & Co., 1856, pp. 12–16, 36–9, 43–5, 58–60.)

Indeed it would almost seem as if, at the period from the middle to near the end of the last century, the superintendents of the insane had become frantic in cruelty, from the impunity with which their despotism was attended. Some of the German physicians meditated even romantic modes of alarm and torture; wished for machinery by which a patient, just arriving at an asylum, and after being drawn with frightful clangour over a metal bridge across a moat, could be suddenly raised to the top of a tower, and as suddenly lowered into a dark and subterranean cavern; and they avowed that if the patient could be made to alight among snakes and serpents it would be better still. People not naturally cruel became habituated to severity until all feelings of humanity were forgotten. I used to be astonished, even seventeen years ago, to see humane physicians going daily round the wards of asylums, mere spectators of every form of distressing coercion, without a word of sympathy, or any order for its mitigation. But men's hearts had on this subject become gradually hardened. In medical works of authority the first principle in the treatment of lunatics was laid down to be fear, and the best means of producing fear was said to be punishment, and the best mode of punishment was defined to be stripes. The great authority of Dr. Cullen, certainly one of the most enlightened physicians of his time, was given to this practice, although his theory of madness was that it depended upon an increased excitement of the brain.

Thus, by degrees, restraints became more and more severe, and torture more and more ingenious. Among many cruel devices, an unsuspecting patient was sometimes induced to walk across a treacherous floor; it gave way, and the patient fell into a bath of surprise, and was there half drowned and half frightened to death.

In some continental asylums the patients were chained in a well, and the water was allowed gradually to ascend, in order to terrify the patient with the prospect of inevitable death. Other methods adopted, even within the last sixty years, for controlling the phenomena of insanity, can only be regarded as tacit acknowledgments of the general inefficiency of medicine, and of the coarse determination of vain or ignorant men to effect by force what they could not accomplish by science. We read with almost as much amusement as wonder the respectful acknowledgment of Dr. Hallaran, that Dr. Cox made known to the profession the 'safe and effectual remedy' of the circulating swing, the invention of which Dr. Cox 'generously gives the credit of' to Dr. Darwin; this invention being one by means of which the maniacal or melancholic patient, fast bound on a sort of couch, or in a chair, was rotated at various rates up to one hundred gyrations in a minute. This machine was used with two indications; the horizontal position being adopted when the object was to procure sleep; and the erect posture, the other failing in cases of excitement, to procure intestinal action. It is acknowledged that patients once subjected to the swing were ever afterward terrified at the mention of it; that it lowered the pulse and the temperature to such a degree as to alarm the physician; that it occasioned a 'disagreeable suffusion of the countenance,' frequently leaving an ecchymosis of the eyes; that it acted as an emetic, and as a hypercathertic;

but still it was lauded as reducing the unmanageable, and, stranger still, as causing the melancholy to take 'a natural interest in the affairs of life.' It is curious to be told, also, that the inconvenient effects mentioned were induced more certainly when the patient was in the erect position. Worse consequences occasionally resulted, I believe, from this barbarous invention; which probably rendered Dr. Hallaran's recommendation, that no 'well regulated institution intended for the reception and relief of insane persons' should be unprovided with a machine of that description, ineffectual. Allusion is made to the practice in Esquirol's work (vol. i, page 156), in which he describes 'la machine de Darwin' as resembling the *jeu de bague:* and he speaks of it as having passed from the arts into medicine. It found some temporary favour on the continent; but the violent evacuations produced by its employment, followed by fainting and excessive debility, led to its disuse. Dr. Cox had advised its being used in some 'hopeless' cases, in the dark; with the addition of unusual noises, smells, &c.; that every sense might be assailed; but I do not think this advice was ever acted upon.

With the same simple intention of subduing violent symptoms, all the forms of mechanical restraint that ingenuity could devise seem successively to have been adopted, many of which have been from time to time reluctantly abandoned, whilst several are even now retained as essential to the control of the insane. The principal object of all such contrivances is to limit the movements of the patient, and this has been variously effected in different asylums and countries. The simplest and cheapest means was by the use of chains, to which, as more lenient, succeeded strong waistcoats confining the arms to the trunk, the legs being secured by hobbles. Handcuffs, and leather muffs and straps, have been much relied upon, with complications, in difficult cases, investing the patient with a kind of heavy circular collar and harness. Patients were seen standing by a wall to which their hands were chained, or sitting on a bench, to which they were strongly secured. Others were fastened in a sort of chair resembling the ancient watchman's box, and many were chained or strapped down in bed. The methods of restraint varied according to the ingenuity of the superintendents; but the object of all the methods was the same —to restrain the movements of the patient. The vagrant action of the limbs was suppressed, but the source of irritation in the brain left out of consideration.

But I must be permitted to suppose a case admitted at Hanwell; a place which I know the best, and can speak of the most positively. The case may be that of a man who for a week or two has been violently maniacal; who, becoming first, perhaps, idle and intemperate, has terrified his family, broken the furniture of his house, or attacked his neighbours; or harangued the public and disturbed the streets, and resisted all control until overcome by the police. He comes to the asylum bound very tightly, sometimes hand and foot, or fastened in a strait-waistcoat. He is still violent but exhausted; he is flushed, feverish, thirsty; in appearance haggard, and in manner fierce, or sullen. His voice is hoarse with shouting. He is unwashed, unshaved, and half starved. His clothes are torn and dirty. He has often many bruises or injuries, which he has incurred in his furious condition. His violence is still dreaded, and he exhibits capricious proofs of remaining strength; so that those who have brought him to the asylum are afraid to stay, and unfeignedly rejoice to get rid of him; wondering that any people should be found to take charge of him, and earnestly warning them to take care of themselves.

Or the case may be that of a female patient, equally violent, but whose frantic exertions proceed from a dread she entertains that some fearful punishment is impending over her; that she is to be cut to pieces, or to be burned alive; and this for crimes of which she believes herself to be accused. With these impressions, her thoughts are probably bent on suicide, as an expiation, or as a means of escape from sufferings. Cases of infinite variety may be imagined; in all of which confusion, and bewilderment, and terror under all surrounding circumstances, for a time disturb the mind. In all these cases, the first difficulties appear so great, and the dangers so pressing, that the idea of mere security naturally predominates in the bystanders; and this would seem to be most readily obtained by continuing the restraints, and superadding seclusion and darkness. These ready means were formerly wholly relied upon; and starvation, dirt, and severities of many kinds as naturally followed in their train. But it is a part of the non-restraint system to remember, whatever the state and circumstances of a newly admitted patient may be, that he comes to the asylum to be cured, or, if incurable, to be protected and taken care of, and kept out of mischief, and tranquillized; and that the strait-waistcoat effects none of these objects. Therefore, although the patients may arrive bound so securely as scarcely to be able to move, they are at once released from every ligature and bond and fetter that may have been imposed upon them. They appear generally to be themselves surprised at this proceeding; and for a time are tranquil, yet often distrustful, and uncertain in their movements. Now and then the tranquillising effect of this unexpected liberty is permanent: more frequently it is but temporary. But every newly admitted patient is as soon as possible visited by the medical officers of the asylum. They assure the stranger, by a few kind words, that no ill-treatment is any longer to be feared. This assurance sometimes gains the confidence of the patient at once, and is ever afterward remembered: but in many cases the patient is too much confused to be able to comprehend it. Few or none, however, are quite insensible to the measures immediately adopted in conformity to it.

The wretched clothes are removed; the patient is taken gently to the bath-room, and has, probably for the first time, the comfort of a warm-bath; which often occasions expressions of remarkable satisfaction. The refreshed patient is taken out of the bath, carefully dried, and has clean and comfortable clothing put on: he is then led of the day-room, and offered good and well prepared food. The very plates, and knife and fork, and all the simple furniture of the table, are cleaner by far then what he has lately been accustomed to, or perhaps such as in his miserable struggling life he never knew before. A patient seen after these preliminary parts of treatment is scarcely to be recognised as the same patient who was admitted only an hour before. The non-restraint treatment has commenced; and some of its effects already appear.

Many English superintendents speak of seclusion as something worse than mechanical restraint; seeming to forget that it is as much adapted to secure an irritable brain from causes of increased irritability as a quiet chamber and the exclusion of glare, and of many visitors, is adapted to the same state of brain in a fever. The patient needs repose, and every object, or every person seen, irritates him. No physician of experience in cases of insanity can be unacquainted with the tendency to exhaustion and death in all recent cases of violent insanity—a tendency which struggling with restraints, or the continued excitements unavoidable in a crowd of lunatics, greatly increases, and which silence and rest can alone obviate. It is often seen that the mere moving of the cover of the inspection-plate in the door of a patient's room, if not cautiously done, rouses the patient from tranquillity, and causes him to start up and rush violently to the door. When let alone he lies down again. Seclusion gives him the benefit of continued tranquillity, by removing at once every cause of excitement. He sits in his own bed-room instead of sitting exposed to a crowd of patients. The superintendents who condemn seclusion as if it were a mere punishment would find, I believe, if they passed more hours in their wards, that by many an afflicted patient, silence and retirement are the blessings most anxiously desired.

The great advantage of a padded room in all these cases, is that it renders both mechanical restraints and muscular force unnecessary for the control of even the most violent patients. Such an apartment, at Hanwell, is prepared by a thick soft padding of coir (cocoa-nut fibre), enclosed in ticken, fastened to wooden frames, and affixed to the four walls of the room—the padding extending from the floor to a height above the ordinary reach of a patient. The whole floor of the room is padded also, or covered with a thick mattress, of the same material as the padded walls, so that it makes a complete bed. In general, the room contains no furniture except bolsters or pillows, also covered with strong ticken. The window is guarded by a close wire-blind, which admits light and air, but prevents access on the part of the patient to the glass or window frames. If the patient is disposed to suicide, the clothing he wears is of a strength and consistence resisting his efforts to tear it into strings to effect his purpose, and the blankets are enclosed in strong ticken cases. In a room so arranged the patient cannot easily injure himself, or receive accidental injury. Nor is he left to chance. The seclusion, and the reasons for it, are always immediately reported to the superintendent or physician, and, in the case of female patients, to the matron also. The ward is visited from time to time by these officers, and an accurate knowledge of the state of the secluded patient is obtained by means of an inspection-plate or covered opening in the door of the room. The patient is not left to suffer from thirst or hunger, nor are his personal state and cleanliness unattended to; nor is he allowed to remain in seclusion longer than his excited state requires. A written report of each instance of seclusion, and of its duration, is sent to the physician at the close of each day, and copied by him into a book, which is inspected at every meeting of the Committee.

Wherever they go they meet kind people, and hear kind words; they are never passed without some recognition, and the face of every officer is the face of a friend. In the evening, the domestic meal of tea refreshes them. Their supper and their bed are not negligently prepared. Day after day these influences operate, and day by day mental irritation subsides, and suspicions die, and gloomy thoughts gradually disperse, and confidence grows and strengthens, and natural affections re-awake, and reason returns.

In short, in an asylum conducted on just principles, and where not only mechanical restraints, but all kinds of neglect and severity are abolished, patients of every rank appreciate and benefit by the change. Those who have been well educated express themselves in warm terms of satisfaction, and the poorer classes often convey their simple gratitude in the most affecting terms. They refer to their former treatment with horror, and recall, again and again, the first kind words which they say they had heard for many years, and which some sympathizing officer or attendant uttered soon after their arrival.

A newly received patient, being brought to a condition of comparative comfort by the mode of reception described, is now capable of deriving benefit from the conversation of the medical superintendent, and generally, from the cheerful aspect of a well governed asylum. Hope, which had abandoned him, begins to return. He sees no wretched patients hobbling about in leg-locks, or, although dressed in strait-waistcoates, which confine their arms, running a-muck at all they meet. He sees no blows inflicted, and hears no taunting and unkind words. The fearful images which lately possessed his mind, of a prison, of punishment, or a cruel death, gradually depart; and sometimes, even at this early period, his recovery seems to commence. Harsh treatment would have confirmed his apprehensions, and have prolonged his violence; so as to have made a resort to mechanical restraints appear excusable. But in a well regulated asylum such modes of restraint are never thought excusable. Each case is studied as soon as the interval of calmness ensues; and means are provided which cause every return of excitement, and every accident or change of the malady, to be met without serious difficulty, and without a danger. All this, however, supposes a complete establishment, humane attendants, faithful officers, and a chief physician resolved to allow no excuse for cruelty, or for the indolence which so often leads to cruelty. It demands the constant supervision of efficient officers over attendants, whose duty is positively to obey the physician. If the attendants are not sufficiently numerous, or if the officers have not sufficient authority, or if the discipline required to be daily and hourly observed is relaxed, or can possibly be relaxed by a capricious board or committee, vain of their own power, and not unwilling to humiliate their own officers, the non-restraint system, in pureness and integrity, cannot be maintained. There can be no security for its continuance. The asylum may now and then be dressed up as a place of show; but the condition of the patients, day by day, night by night, hour by hour, may still be rendered unhappy, and many concealed severities practised upon them.

58. Daniel Hack Tuke, *The Founding of the Retreat*

(Excerpt from *Reform in the Treatment of the Insane*, London: John Churchill, 1892, pp. 34–8.)

Now, what were the primary objects in view in the foundation of this Institution?

First, the revulsion from the inhumanity which had come to light rendered it necessary that the fundamental principles of moral treatment should be those of kindness and consideration for the patients. They were the basis of the proceedings which were taken; in fact, as we have seen, they were carved upon the very foundation stone of the building.

A *second* object undoubtedly was to provide an atmosphere of religious sentiment and moral feeling congenial to the accustomed habits and principles of those for whom the institution was primarily intended.

Thirdly, it is a significant fact when the Retreat was instituted, it was laid down that there should be 'a few acres for keeping cows and for garden ground for the family, which will afford scope for the patients to take exercise when that may be considered prudent and suitable.' Recreation and employment were put prominently forward directly the Institution was opened, and were carried out into practice much to the surprise of those who visited the house. The Swiss physician (Dr. de la Rive), who in 1798 visited the Retreat, as I have related already, reported thus:—'As soon as the patients are well enough to be employed, they endeavour to make them work. The women are employed in the usual female occupations; and the men are engaged in straw and basket work, etc. The Institution is surrounded by some acres of land which belong to it. The superintendent had undertaken to make the patients cultivate this land, giving each a task proportioned to his strength. He found that they were fond of this exercise, and that they were much better after a day spent in this work than when they had remained in the house, or even when they had taken a walk.'

Fourthly, the moral treatment must no doubt be emphasized as characteristic of the early practice of the Retreat. The physician just mentioned writes:—'You see that in the moral treatment they do not consider the insane as absolutely deprived of reason, that is to say, as inaccessible to the motives of hope, feeling, and honour; rather they are regarded, it would seem, as children who have an excess of force and who make a dangerous employment of it.' In the first Annual Report (written by W. Tuke) occurs the following:—'They who think the object worthy of their attention may be encouraged to promote it, not only on the principle of charity to the poor, but even from compassion to those in easy and affluent circumstances, who will, doubtless, think themselves benefited, though they may pay amply for it.' It is pointed out that 'those who have embarked in this undertaking have not been influenced by interested views, nor are they requesting or desiring any favours for themselves. A malady, in many instances, the most deplorable that human nature is subject to, hath excited their sympathy and attention.' Lastly, an appeal is made for 'co-operation in an Establishment which hath for its object the mitigation of human misery, and the restoration of those who are lost to civil and religious society, in the prosecution of which they humbly rely on the favour of Him whose tender mercies are over all His works.' I may add that the title page of this Report bore the words: *'The State of an Institution near York, called the Retreat, for persons afflicted with Disorders of the Mind;'* certainly a very sufficient description of the object for which it was established, and this title page remained undisturbed until 1869, when, unhappily, as I think, it was discarded for another.

Fifthly, that which from the first has been regarded as a most important feature of the Institution, is its *homishness*—the desire to make it a family as much as under the peculiar circumstances of the case is possible. However desirable the scientific study of insanity may be, and I hope we shall never underrate it, it would be a fatal mistake to allow it to interfere with or in the slightest degree take the place of the social and domestic element, and the personal relationship between the physician and his patient, which tend to mitigate the distress which may be occasioned by the loss of many home comforts and associations, along with the residence amongst strangers.

59. Andrew Wynter, *The Demise of Moral Management*

(Excerpt from *The Borderlands of Insanity*, London: Robert Hardwicke, 1875, pp. 124–6.)

The time has at length arrived when it is obvious that if our asylums are to resume the true position from which they should never have been allowed to depart—that of hospitals for the treatment of the insane—a thorough revolution must be made in their management; and in order to bring about new measures, we must pray for the advent of entirely new men. There are epochs in all institutions at which a paralysis seems to seize upon those conducting them. With regard to our present superintendents as a body, with a few noble exceptions, we unhesitatingly assert the spirit of Conolly is dead. A miserable spirit of routine, without resources, spring, or energy, is sapping and destroying asylum life. The gross fallacy of supposing that no man without experience in pauper, lunatic asylums is capable of taking charge of such establishments, is the cause of an infinity of mischief. Our own belief is, that wholly fresh blood is imperatively demanded. Who have been the great reformers—the leaders in the onward, ever onward course of non-restraint? Not physicians trained in all the bad traditions of asylums, but general physicians, who have come to the task with fresh minds and habits untainted by an unhappy experience. Pinel, before he took charge of the Bicêtre, was a general physician. Conolly, happily, was innocent of the ways of asylums before he became superintendent of Hanwell; and the far-famed Retreat at York received its inspiration from an intelligent Quaker layman, William Tuke, of York. It is the same with all other professions and arts; improvements come, as a rule, from without; from a class of thinkers, who have not to unlearn habits of mind instilled into them by a kind of Chinese practice and a reverence for old authority.

Chapter V

Moral Force and Responsibility

60. John Abercrombie, *Moral Discipline*

(Excerpt from *Culture and Discipline of the Mind*, Edinburgh: William Whyte & Co., 1837, pp. 12–18.)

But life presents another aspect, when we view it as a scene of moral discipline;—when we look not at its pains and its pleasures, but its high duties and its solemn responsibilities,—and at the discipline of the heart, from which springs a true and solid happiness which external circumstances cannot destroy. All then is defined and clear. The object is definite, and the way to it is marked as by a light from heaven. Each step that is gained is felt to be a real and solid acquirement; and each imparts a sense of moral health, which strengthens every principle within, for farther progress. I know that I carry your best feelings along with me, when I thus call your attention to that course of life, which alone is adapted to its real and solemn importance,—which alone is worthy of those powers of our intellectual and moral nature, with which we have been endowed by Him who formed us. In the culture of these is involved not only a duty and a responsibility, but a source of the purest and the most refined enjoyment. For there is a power which is calculated to carry a man through life, without being the sport and the victim of every change that flits across the scene;—this power resides in a sound moral discipline, and a well-regulated mind.

The foundation of all mental discipline consists in the 'power of mastering the mind.' It is in having the intellectual processes under due regulation and control,—and being thus able to direct them, upon sound and steady principles, to the acquisition of useful knowledge, and the discovery of truth. Here we are, in the first place, reminded of that remarkable power which we possess over the succession of our thoughts. We can direct the thoughts to any subject we please, and can keep them directed to it with steady and continuous attention. In the due culture of this power consists a point in mental discipline, of primary and essential importance. By the neglect of such culture, the mind is allowed to run to waste amid the trifles of the passing hour, or is left the sport of waking dreams and vain delusions entirely unworthy of its high destiny. There is not a greater source of difference between one man and another, than in the manner in which they exercise this power over the succession of the thoughts, and in the subjects to which these are habitually directed. It is a mental exercise which lies at the foundation of the whole moral condition. He who, in early life, seriously enters upon it, under a sense of its supreme importance;—who trains himself to habits of close and connected thinking,—and exerts a strict control over the subjects to which his thoughts are habitually directed, —leading them to such as are really worthy of his regard, and banishing all such as are of a frivolous, impure, or degrading character,—this is he who is pursuing the highest of all earthly acquirements, the culture of the understanding, and the discipline of the heart. This due regulation, and stern control of the processes of the mind, is, indeed, the foundation of all that is high and excellent in the formation of character. He who does not earnestly exercise it,—but who allows his mind to wander, as it may be led by its own incidental images or casual associations, or by the influence of external things to which he is continually exposed, endangers his highest interests both as an intellectual and a moral being. 'Keep thy heart with all diligence,' says the sacred writer, 'for out of it are the issues of life.'

Now, it cannot be too anxiously borne in mind, that this great attainment is, in a remarkable degree, under the influence of habit. Each step that we take in the prosecution of it will facilitate our farther progress,—and, every day that passes over us, without making it the object of earnest attention, the acquirement becomes the more difficult and the more uncertain;—and a period at length arrives, when no power exists in the mind capable of correcting the disorder which habit has fixed in the mental economy. The frivolous mind may then continue frivolous to the last, amusing itself with trifles, or creating for itself fictions of the fancy, no better than dreams, and as unprofitable: The distorted mind may continue to the last eagerly pursuing some favourite dogma, while it is departing farther and farther from truth: And the vitiated and corrupted mind may continue to the last the slave of its impure and degrading passions. Such is the power and such the result of mental habits;—and let us ever bear in mind how such habits are formed. They arise out of individual acts of the mind, and we have not the means of determining what number of such acts are necessary for forming the habits,—and at what period these may acquire a mastery which shall peril the highest interests of the mind. We cannot determine how many instances of frivolity may constitute the permanently frivolous mind;—how many trains of impurity may constitute the permanently corrupted mind; or what degree of inattention to the diligent culture of the powers within, may be fatal to the best interests of the man, both as an intellectual and a moral being. Hence the supreme importance of cultivating in early life the mastery of the mind,—and of watching with earnest attention the trains of thought which we encourage there, as we cannot determine at what period a habit may be formed, the influence of which shall be permanent and irremediable.

61. John Abercrombie, *The Cultivation of Genius*

(Excerpt from *Culture and Discipline of the Mind*, Edinburgh: William Whyte & Co., 1837, pp. 37–8.)

According to a loose, though common mode of expression, we speak of *genius*, as an original quality of particular minds. But what is of greater value, than that which often receives the name of genius, is not to be considered as an original quality, but a habit of the mind. It is nothing more than intense mental activity, steadily directed to some leading pursuit. This important principle was well illustrated by Sir Charles Bell, in his introductory address to his first course of lectures in Edinburgh, when he took occasion to allude to that distinguished physiologist and surgeon, Mr. John Hunter. Mr. Hunter, he said, had been called a man of genius, but he was disposed to take a different view of his character, from that which is commonly expressed by that term. The great and leading feature in Mr. Hunter's character, he added, was,—that he was steadily and eagerly devoted to his object,—and that no change of external circumstances had the power, for one moment, of turning him aside from it. Was he in his study, or in his dissecting room, or mingling with men in the common occupations of life;—was he at sea, shut up in a crowded transport,—or was he in the field of battle with bullets flying and men dropping around him,—one great object was steadily and habitually before him, and he never lost an opportunity of seizing upon every thing that could, in any way, be made to bear upon it. This is true genius,—or, call it by what name you will, this is the source of all distinction. It is greatly assisted by education, —but what I am anxious to impress upon you is, that it is not an original quality, but an acquired habit of mind,—and a habit which may be cultivated by every one who determinedly devotes himself to the high attainment.

62. John Barlow, *Self-Control*

(Excerpt from *Man's Power over Himself to Prevent or Control Insanity*, London: William Pickering, 1843, pp. 1–8.)

Now it is the property of all scientific views, if true, that they announce a few simple principles which admit of an extensive practical application; and I endeavoured to apply this test to the theory I then brought forward as to the dual nature of man. I asked myself how it bore on that most terrible of all diseases connected with the brain—madness; and I found that wise and good men, even without thinking of the theory, had practically applied it in the treatment of maniacs; whose intelligent will they had roused to a certain degree of self-control by a system of kind and rational treatment, instead of the chains and whips of former times.

4. In the human species a portion of the brain, which begins to develope itself in the higher order of animals, assumes a preponderance over the rest. I mean the hemispheres—which fill the upper part of the skull. Less immediately connected with the nerves of sense, this part has its own peculiar function: and I formerly brought examples to prove that this function is that of thought.* I then took occasion to notice a peculiar force found in

* Vide No. II. of Small Books on Great Subjects.

man, which is capable of assuming a control over this portion of the brain; and, through it, over the greater part of the bodily functions—a force whose agency, as Professor Liebig has well observed, is 'entirely distinct from the vital force, with which it has nothing in common,' but in so far as it is viewed in connection with matter, manifests itself as an acceleration, a retarding, or a disturbance of the 'processes of life.' We find therefore, as this acute observer goes on to state, two forces in activity together, namely the mechanical-vital force—or, as he terms it, *vegetative life*, and the source of the higher phænomena of mental existence, which is of a perfectly distinct, and so far a superior nature, that it is able sometimes to exercise a dominion over the vital force which nullifies its action, and at all times controls and modifies it.

I have placed side by side the two great forces which manifest themselves in the phænomena of man's nature. The VITAL FORCE by virtue of which he is an animal—and the INTELLECTUAL FORCE by virtue of which he is something more. Throughout nature we find the advance to a higher grade of being, made by addition rather than by change. The power of assimilation is added to chemical affinity, and we have organized life, as in vegetables; but set in motion by external causes: nervous matter is added in the animal; and vegetative life proceeds still unconsciously, but by means of a main-spring within the body; and this lowest kind of life is found, as I formerly observed, in the rooted zoophyte no less than in man. It forms the first subdivision of the Table. Nerves of sensation and of movement are added, and the animal becomes locomotive, and is impelled by a feeling of pain or of pleasure to the acts needful for the maintenance of vegetative life: and this state of being is marked in the second division. Then the hemispheres of the brain are developed in addition, as in the class mammalia, and the animal seeks its object by contrivance, and by suiting the means to the end. Finally, as in the great step from inorganized to organized matter, a fresh *force* is added, not superseding, but availing itself of the other; and man steps forth a denizen of two worlds, and capable of an advance which we can set no limit to.

7. Such is the constitution of man. When in healthy action, we cannot easily figure to ourselves anything better calculated to produce the most admirable results than the reciprocal influence of the different parts and forces of this complex being:

but in proportion to the variety of parts is the danger of derangement: and our business to-night is not to consider man in his normal, but in his abnormal state. I shall therefore now endeavour to apply the theory, which I have just given a brief abstract of, to practical use, first by giving a classification of the different kinds of mental derangement, and next by considering how far the immense power of the Intellectual force can in any case be applied to their prevention or cure. I prefer the term *mental derangement* to that of *Insanity*, because it will embrace all departures from the normal condition of man, as far as the functions of the brain are concerned: and I conceive (herein following the great authority of Dr. Conolly*) that a certain degree of mental derangement may exist without constituting insanity in the usual sense of that word; that is,—the patient retains so much of the reasoning faculty that the delusions of the senses are recognized by him as such, and he remains capable of exercising so much control over himself as either to resist wholly the impulses consequent on these delusions, or to seek the aid of others to do so, when he finds the effort too great for his unassisted fortitude.

63. John Barlow, *An Example of Self-Government by the Insane*

(Excerpt from *Man's Power over Himself to Prevent or Control Insanity*, London: William Pickering, 1843, pp. 10–11.)

Another case is that of a maniac confined in the Bicêtre before the use of chains as a mode of discipline had been abolished in that hospital. He was subject to periodical returns of insanity during six months of the year, and could himself judge when the fury of his attack was over. Sometimes, notwithstanding the discomfort of his confinement, he would himself ask to have the period of his liberation delayed, because he did not yet feel his reason strong enough to curb the blind impulse of his disordered senses, which led him to acts of violence. In commenting on this kind of insanity, which he more properly terms delirium, M. Pinel observes, 'I can assert with the utmost truth, that in

* Vide An Enquiry concerning the Indications of Insanity. By John Conolly, M.D.

most of the cases which I have observed of delirium which either became incurable, or were terminated in some other fatal malady, all the results of the *post mortem* examination, no less than the symptoms themselves, prove that this sort of insanity is of a purely nervous character, and is not produced by any organic disease in the substance of the brain. It is no wonder, therefore, that a moral as well as physical regimen should sometimes suffice to produce a complete cure.' Thus there is every reason to suppose that where the habit of self-government is strong, this kind of nervous affection is not likely to occur, and that many of the most frightful instances of crimes committed under the influence of the kind of delirium above mentioned, might have been avoided by an early attention to the moral training of the individual.

64. John Barlow, *Responsibility in Insanity*

(Excerpt from *Man's Power over Himself to Prevent or Control Insanity*, London: William Pickering, 1843, pp. 27–8, 31–6.)

The affection of the brain which causes these delusions, *is not* madness, but *the want of power or resolution to examine them, is.* Nothing then but an extent of disease which destroys at once all possibility of reasoning, by annihilating, or entirely changing the structure of the organ, can make a man necessarily mad. In all other cases, the being sane or otherwise, notwithstanding considerable disease of brain, depends on the individual himself. He who has given a proper direction to the intellectual force, and thus obtained an early command over the bodily organ by habituating it to processes of calm reasoning, remains sane amid all the vagaries of sense; while he who has been the slave, rather than the master of his animal nature, listens to its dictates without question even when distorted by disease,—and is mad. A fearful result of an uncultivated childhood, or of a manhood too much devoted to the active, money getting employments of this world, which so often form the chief pursuit of life. These, instead of strengthening the mind to bear the reverses of fortune which all are liable to, but render it more acutely sensible of the disappointments incident to such pursuits, and form too often one of the proximate causes of this terrible affliction.

If I am right in what I have advanced, a man may labour under a mental delusion, and yet be a responsible agent: and if sanity or insanity be in a great many instances the consequences of a greater or less resolution in exerting the power of reasoning still possessed, the same kind of motives which influence a man in common life, are still available, though they may require to be somewhat heightened. It is on this principle that the treatment of lunatics has been generally conducted. Fear, one of the lowest, but also one of the most general of instinctive emotions, has been called in to balance the delusions of sense, and, excepting in cases where the structural disease is so extensive as to deprive the man of all power of connecting cause and effect, it has been found sufficient to curb violence, and enforce a certain degree of peaceable demeanour towards the attendants. And in this the insane person differs not from the cultivated man who is left at liberty, whose self-control rarely amounts to more than the avoiding actions which would have unpleasant consequences to himself. Suppose an irascible man, incensed by a false report; which, however, he believes to be true; he seeks his supposed enemy, and horsewhips or knocks him down: he does not assassinate, because he fears for his own life if he does; for it is clear that no feeling of duty has held his hand, or he would not have transgressed the laws both of God and man by thus revenging himself.

The madman has the false report from his own senses; wherein do the two differ? Neither has employed means within his power to ascertain the truth, and both are aware that such vengeance is forbidden. I can see no distinction between them, save that the delusion of sense has, as a chemist would say, decomposed the character, and shown how much of the individual's previous conduct was rational, and how much the result of mere animal instinct. It would be well for the world if the soi-disant sane were sometimes to ask themselves how far their sanity would bear this test; and endeavour to acquire that rational self-command which nothing but the last extremity of cerebral disease could unseat. We do not descend from our high rank with impunity;—and as, when matter has become organized, in the process of change, occasioned by the vital force, be impeded or arrested, the plant pines away and perishes:—as, after the organs of locomotion have been superadded, the animal debarred from the use of them, languishes and becomes diseased; so man, if he gives not full scope to the intellectual force, becomes subject to evils greater than animals ever know, because his nature is of a higher order.

65. John Barlow, *Differences in Types of Insanity between Social Classes*

(Excerpts from *Man's Power over Himself to Prevent or Control Insanity*, London: William Pickering, 1843, pp. 53–7.)

The poor and the uneducated are the classes which most usually suffer from the *inefficiency* of the intellectual force: it is among the higher ranks usually that its *misdirection* is a source of insanity. Among these, more distant objects of pursuit keep the thoughts longer upon the stretch towards one point; the organs of mechanical memory are strengthened, nay, even strained by the habit of learning much by rote, while the constant supply of learning ready-made leaves no necessity for the more laborious processes of reasoning and comparison. Hence we not unfrequently find an elegant scholar, who can readily quote the words and opinions of others, unable himself to carry on a course of close argument, or to *prove* the truth of what he advances. Whoever has moved in society, knows that it is rare to meet with any one who can command his thoughts in conversation sufficiently to reject all that is not relevant to the subject, so as to keep on the chain of reasoning unbroken.

When the mind is thus exercised in remembering the opinions of others, thus unaccustomed accurately to examine its own, what wonder is it if it should become prepossessed with some irrational notion which cannot be removed by reasoning, because the individual man in his healthiest state had never chosen so to exercise his mind; or if, when a delusion of sense occurs, he should choose rather to act upon it as truth, than to examine into the grounds he has for believing it to be such. It is a melancholy fact, that a great number of mankind are in this state as regards the faculties most requisite to self-control, and depend far more on the accident of good health, than the exertion of their own intellectual power, for their sanity.

Insanity from *misdirection* of the intellectual force is so various in its forms, that it would be impossible to give instances of all;

but it has one very general character—namely, that at first there are very few symptoms, if any, of structural disease. Some derangement of general health may be observed, but even this is not constant, or, at least, not sufficient in many instances to excite attention: it seems therefore not unreasonable to conclude, that the evil originates rather in the misuse than in the impairment of the organ. Thoughts too long and too intensely fixed on one object, weary the part of the brain so employed, and we usually then seek relief by varying our occupation: if this is not done, the weariness may end in disease.

I remember being told by a friend, that having determined to commit to memory a certain number of Greek primitives every day, after persisting some time, he found that though competent to other study, *this* wearied him. Resolved not to be thus mastered, he persevered in spite of weariness, but in a short time delirium came on. He took the hint, laid aside the Greek primitives, and recovered himself very quickly. Here the misuse of the organ had produced temporary disease: had the subject been one not so easy to lay aside, the temporary disease might have become permanent; especially if the engrossing thought were one originating in instinctive emotion, which always influences the circulation largely, and thus is likely to induce an unnatural rush of blood through the brain.

66. John Barlow, *Importance of Education*

(Excerpt from *Man's Power over Himself to Prevent or Control Insanity*, London: William Pickering, 1843, pp. 59–61.)

Education is the training and exercise of the mind: and as when we recommend bodily exercise we do not mean the unnatural postures of the ballet, or the violent exercises of the gymnasium, neither by education do we mean an intemperate straining of the mental faculties. To educate a man, in the full and proper sense of the word, is to supply him with the power of controlling his feelings, and his thoughts, and his actions; between doing which, and becoming insane, or unable to control his feelings, his thoughts, and his actions there is no very visible connexion. The best way of deciding the matter is by an appeal to facts. Whoever will converse with lunatics, with a view to its elucidation, will soon be satisfied, that a very small proportion of them consists of those whose talents have been regularly and judiciously cultivated. If I may trust to my own observation, I should say that a well educated man or woman is an exception to the rest; that the majority is made up of weak or ignorant persons; even those who seem to have acquired some little knowledge, being commonly those who have picked it up as they could, with many disadvantages, and without the method which what alone deserves the name of a good education would have imparted to their application. The registers of the Bicêtre, for a series of years, show that even when madness affects those who belong to the educated classes, it is chiefly seen in those whose education has been imperfect or irregular, and very rarely indeed in those whose minds have been fully, equally, and systematically exercised. Priests, artists, painters, sculptors, poets and musicians, whose professions so often appear marked in that register, are often persons of very limited or exclusive education; their faculties have been unequally exercised; they have commonly given themselves up too much to imagination, and have neglected comparison, and have not habitually exercised the judgment. Even of this class it is to be remembered that it is commonly those of the lowest order of the class, in point of talent, who become thus affected: whilst of naturalists, physicians, chemists and geometricians, it is said not one instance occurs in these registers.* If one go from individual to individual in any lunatic establishment, and investigate the character and origin of the madness of each, we shall find for every one who has become insane from the exercise of his mind, at least a hundred have become insane from the undue indulgence of their feelings. Those men who really most exercise the faculties of their minds, meaning thereby all their faculties, their attention, reflection, or comparison, as well as their imagination and memory, are least liable to insanity. An irregular and injudicious cultivation of poetry and painting has often concurred to produce madness, but nothing is rarer than to find a mad mathematician: for, as no study demands more attention than mathematics, so it secures the student during a great part of his time, from the recurrence of feelings which are always the most imperious in those who are the least occupied.

* Conolly's Inquiry concerning the Indications of Insanity, p. 191.

67. John Barlow, *Increase in Insanity*

(Excerpt from *Man's Power over Himself to Prevent or Control Insanity*, London: William Pickering, 1843, pp. 76.)

The cases of insanity, we are told, have nearly tripled within the last twenty years!—a fearful increase, even after allowing to the utmost for a larger population!—of these cases it is calculated that less than three hundred in one thousand are the result of disease, or of unavoidable circumstances, thus leaving above seven hundred resulting from bodily excess or mental misgovernment.—On the heads, then, of legislators, of teachers, and of parents, lies the heavy charge of having, in all these instances, left those godlike faculties uncultivated, which, if duly used, might make earth the ante-room of heaven, and man the fit Vicegerent of the Deity in this fair world. What man *is* generally, and what the world is in consequence, I need not detail.—We all know and feel it. Would to heaven we all knew what man *could* be, and had felt what the world might be were he such!

68. James Sheppard, *Control of Blood*

(Excerpt from *Observations on the Proximate Causes of Insanity*, London: Longman, Brown, Green & Longmans, 1844, pp. 62–3.)

Now, whether mental emotions are capable of *immediately* altering the constitution of the blood, or whether the blood is altered only *secondarily*, does not *materially* affect any position; inasmuch, as though the alteration may possibly be only secondary, still it is *almost* instantaneous; for, when the mind experiences any adequate emotion, the impression on the nervous system is instantaneous, and, consequently, the impression made on the secreting organs is instantaneous; therefore the blood is altered in its character *almost* instantaneously, and circulates, so altered, *almost* instantaneously through the brain; but, I apprehend, that mental emotions act, not only on the secreting organs, but that they are also equal to the arrest of *universal nutrition*; and, if so, the time that elapses between the original emotion, and the moment when vitiated blood commences to circulate through the brain, cannot be long.

69. James Cowles Prichard, *Monomania*

(Excerpt from *On the Different Forms of Insanity in Relation to Jurisprudence*, London: Hippolyte Ballière, 1847, pp. 67–9.)

Monomania is the name by which physicians now designate the disorder which English jurists after Lord Hale termed partial insanity. This is, as we have already observed, generally conceived to be a disorder of the mind in which a single false notion is impressed upon the understanding, which is otherwise unclouded, so that the insane person is capable of reasoning correctly on all subjects unconnected with a particular train of thought, and even on topics connected with his illusion, if the erroneous conviction be conceded as truth and matter of fact. This is the form of mental disorder on which Mr. Locke's definition of insanity, and almost all definitions are founded; and such a notice being established it is not to be wondered at, that much discussion should have arisen on the question, whether lunatics are capable of exercising their personal rights and retain their responsibility in relation to acts with which the particular insane illusion is unconnected. All these doubts have been raised without reason or necessity. They depend upon a very erroneous notion as to the real nature of monomania.

Nothing, indeed, can be more remote from the truth than the opinion that madmen of this description have their whole disorder centered in, and restricted, to one delusive idea. The false impression which occasions the disorder to be termed monomania is generally a particular symptom which supervenes on a previously existing affection of that kind, which I have already described as constituting in itself a particular form of insanity, and consisting in a total perversion of the moral character, feelings, affections and habits of the individual who is the subject of it. One illusive notion or set of notions is to be traced in his mind, which for the most part occupies his attention to the exclusion of almost all other subjects, and is ever uppermost in his thoughts; but a careful inquiry will generally shew that his whole mind is diseased. There are indeed, cases on record, which answer to the psychological definition of monomania. It is said, that persons have continued to exercise their profession and to conduct themselves with propriety to the relations of life who have yet been known to labour under one illusion. But if these examples are faithfully recorded, they must be regarded as extremely rare phenomena. The real history of monomania is very different. It is well known to those who are conversant with the insane, that in persons who are considered as labouring under monomania, the mind is otherwise disordered and weakened, though the characteristic illusion is the most striking phenomenon. The social affections are either obliterated or perverted; some ruling passion seems to have entire possession of the mind, and the hallucination is in harmony with it, and seems to have had its origin in the intense excitement of the predominant feeling; this is always a selfish desire or apprehension, and the illusory ideas relate to the personal state, and circumstances of the individual.

70. Daniel Noble, *The Connection between Sanity and Moral Liberty*

(Excerpt from *Elements of Psychological Medicine*, London: John Churchill, 1853, pp. 11–12.)

If I venture to propose a definition of my own, it certainly is not in the expectation of succeeding in an attempt wherein so many others have failed; I will, nevertheless, for convenience, and with regard to ensuing descriptions, state insanity to consist in *apyrexial disorder of the brain, perverting thought or feeling, to the destruction or impairment of moral liberty.*

I have said, disorder of the brain that is *apyrexial*, to distinguish it from the delirium of inflammation, fever, and some other morbid conditions attended with the kind of excitement: I have qualified it as that sort of disorder which *perverts thought or feeling*, in contra-distinction to certain morbid states of the encephalon,—simple congestion, tuberculosis, ramollissement, and some forms of hydrocephalus,—in which there is sometimes no very obvious derangement either of the intelligence or the moral sensibility: and I have stated another of its characteristics to be the *destruction or impairment of moral liberty*, or a notable diminution of that controlling power over self which belongs to every soundly-constituted person, since this last-mentioned feature separates insanity from those slighter perversions of the temper and those diminished facilities of thinking, which obtain in disease very generally.

When disordered thought or feeling exists, what proof have we that the *cerebral* functions are disturbed? The reply to this inquiry introduces a topic of considerable importance.

Writers upon diseases of the mind have not always been agreed as to their site in the organism. Various structures have been fixed upon. Some have referred them to the abdominal viscera, others to the heart, and others, again, to the sympathetic nervous system. These several allocations have all been maintained with some plausibility. In the present advanced state of physiology, however, we must reject these doctrines as untenable. It is true enough that serious mischief in the structures referred to may coexist with mental derangement, and may constitute the source of many of the symptoms preceding an attack, or may form, indeed, the principal cause of disordered cerebral action; when, however, there is manifestation of actual insanity, the brain is undoubtedly more or less affected.

71. Daniel Noble, *The Importance of Energetically Exercising the Will*

(Excerpt from *Elements of Psychological Medicine*, London: John Churchill, 1853, pp. 334–5.)

Before quitting this branch of the subject, I would say a word concerning the importance of energetically exercising the will, in resistance to unwonted ideas that present themselves so often to a morbid fancy, when disorder of the digestive organs depresses the emotional sensibility. If this were well-understood and acted-upon, there is no doubt that many cases of melancholia and notional delusion would be prevented. I have at this time as a patient a gentleman who frequently suffers from nervous dyspepsia, and who during his attacks is decidedly hypochondriacal. He tells me that, on these occasions, ideas the most outrageous and bizarre will generally haunt his disordered imagination; that, for example, the notion of cutting off the nose of one of his servants is particularly vivid. There is not in this gentleman's family the slightest tendency to insanity, so far as I can learn; and he is himself a strong-minded man, with a firm and resolute will; and, moreover, he thoroughly appreciates the actual circumstances of his own case. He has often told me that, but for strong volitional efforts, he believes that he should have been insane.

72. Anonymous, *Madness: the Universal Presence*

(Excerpt from *The Times*, 22 July 1853.)

Nothing can be more slightly defined than the line of demarcation between sanity and insanity. Physicians and lawyers have vexed themselves with attempts at definition in a case where definition is impossible. There has never yet been given to the world anything in the shape of a formula upon this subject, which may not be torn to shreds in five minutes by any ordinary logician. Make the definition too narrow, it becomes meaningless; make it too wide, the whole human race are involved in the drag-net. In strictness, we are all mad when we give way to passion, to prejudice, to vice, to vanity; but if all the passionate, prejudiced, vicious, and vain people in this world are to be locked up as lunatics, who is to keep the key of the asylum? As was very fairly observed, however, by a learned Baron of the Exchequer, when he was pressed by this argument, if we are all mad, being all madmen, we must do the best we can under such untoward circumstances. There must be a kind of rough understanding as to the forms of lunacy which can't be tolerated. We will not interfere with the spendthrift, who is flinging his patrimony away upon swindlers, harlots, and blacklegs, until he has denuded himself of his possessions and incurred debt. We have nothing to say to his brother madman, the miser, who pinches his belly to swell the balance at his banker's—being 73 years of age, and without family,—but, if he refuse to pay taxes, society will not accept his monomania as pleadable in bar.

73. John Charles Bucknill, *The Measurement of Responsibility*

(Excerpt from *Unsoundness of Mind in Relation to Criminal Insanity*, London: Longman, Brown, Green & Longmans, 1854, pp. 2–6.)

There is no quality of anything cognizable to our senses or to our understanding, more variable in its degrees or its combinations than insanity. But legal responsibility is strictly defined. It is bounded by a line, a Rubicon, on one side of which Cæsar is the servant of the state, on the other a traitor and a rebel. It is also uniform, it admits not of degrees of greater or smaller, of more or less. If this uniformity is unreal and inconsistent with the actualities to be found in nature, and if the boundary line is capable of being moved to and fro, these circumstances will increase the difficulty of making the characteristics of insanity correspond with the common law essence of irresponsibility. It is no doubt of importance that under all possible circumstances the administrators of our laws should have landmarks erected for their guidance; for the smaller the latitude of private opinion which is permitted to the executive, the surer will be the guarantees of liberty and of the impartial administration of justice. Fixed points therefore are rightly decided upon whenever it is possible to do so.

But how can responsibility be measured? Extension in time and place can be measured by duration and by substance; gravitation can be measured by weight, and power of various kinds by its effect on gravitation; even color and such like qualities can be measured by comparison with a standard: but in what practical balance shall the responsibility of man for his actions be estimated? As the weight of a body is measured by the power it overcomes, so degrees of responsibility must be measured by the degrees of mental disorder, and by the amount of inflection they produce from the standard of health.

A man having the knowledge of right and wrong, and in the possession of the power of choosing the one and refusing the other, is rightly held to be responsible for his conduct to his God, to his neighbours, and to himself. A man knowing and capable of discharging his duties to his God, to his neighbours, and to himself, is a sane man. A man who from any mental imperfection or infirmity is incapable of discharging these duties cannot be considered to be in a state of mental sanity, and cannot with justice be held responsible to do that which he is morally unable to do.

It will be hereafter seen, that the neglect of this distinction between *knowledge* and *power* forms one of the fundamental difficulties of the question.

74. John Charles Bucknill, *The Supremacy of the Will*

(Excerpt from *Unsoundness of Mind in Relation to Criminal Insanity*, London: Longman, Brown, Green & Longmans, 1854, pp. 27–8.)

What is the condition to which insanity, mental alienation, unsoundness, derangement, is opposed? It is that condition of the mind in which the emotions and the instincts are in such a state of subordination to the will, that the latter can direct and control their manifestations; in which moreover the intellectual faculties are capable of submitting to the will sound reasons for its actions. Such co-ordinate action of the faculties is termed sanity; a condition in which that is lost is termed insanity, or derangement, or alienation, or unsoundness, all terms having reference to the deprivation of the power of the will so directed.

It is evident that in this definition of sanity there are three terms, the subjected emotions, the directing intellect, and the middle term of free will. Supposing our nature to be fallible throughout its composition, it is evident that erroneous action may originate at any of these points: the mutinous emotions may be indomitable, the power of the will may be abortive, or the intellect may mislead by false guidance. Insanity may thus be Intellectual, Emotional, or Volitional, and though in the concrete it is not easy to find pure and unmixed cases under either of these heads, such cases do occasionally subject themselves to observation. The experienced psychopathist will also find little difficulty in apportioning a vast number of the other cases according to their predominant character, under one or other of these headings.

Insanity therefore may be defined as, A condition of the mind in which a false action of conception or judgment, a defective power of the will, or an uncontrollable violence of the emotions and instincts, have separately or conjointly been produced by disease.

75. John Charles Bucknill, *Psychological Power*

(Excerpt from *Unsoundness of Mind in Relation to Criminal Insanity*, London: Longman, Brown, Green & Longmans, 1854, pp. 58–60.)

The sense of duty, the feeling of right and wrong, is an innate principle of the human mind implanted by the Almighty, and serving as a sure foundation for the responsibility of man for his actions; which is thus not left to chance development, but is rendered an essential and necessary part of human nature. It seems needful to enquire to what extent this absolute and necessary part of human nature becomes capable of being perverted or destroyed under the influence of cerebro-mental disease. It may be taken as an axiom, that *the innate and essential principles of mind are ever present where mind exists.* It may also be asserted as the result of observation and experience, that in all lunatics, and even in the most degraded idiots, whenever manifestations of any mental action can be educed, the feeling of right and wrong may be proved to exist. The education of idiots and cretins has proved that there is no zero in the human mind; and the success of the *moral treatment* prevailing in lunatic asylums has demonstrated, that insanity does not neutralize the influences by which the moral government of the world is effected. But if insanity does not remove these innate principles, does it on that account leave persons under their influence wholly responsible for their actions? Certainly not: *Responsibility depends upon power, not upon knowledge, still less upon feeling. A man is responsible to do that which he can do, not that which he feels or knows it right to do.* If a man is reduced under thraldom to passion by disease of the brain, he loses moral freedom and responsibility, although his knowledge of right and wrong may remain intact.

76. Daniel Hack Tuke, *The Importance of Arousing the Patient's Will*

(Excerpt from *The Influence of the Mind on the Body*, London: John Churchill, 1872, pp. 384–7.)

The power of the Will in resisting disease, apart from the influence of the Imagination or the concentration of the Attention, is unquestionable. 'Oh, if I could once make a resolution, and determine to be well!' exclaimed the German physician Walderstein.

The poet Churchill said—

> The surest road to health, say what they will,
> Is never to suppose we shall be ill;
> Most of those evils we poor mortals know
> From doctors and *imagination* flow.

It is a pity, however, that we have to confess that the poet died at the early age of thirty-four (of fever). We must conclude that his dissipated life neutralized the good effects likely to result from supposing that he should not be ill.

At a *séance* of the Royal Academy of Medicine of Paris, Dr. Barthélemy expressed his conviction that the symptoms of hydrophobia in man were mainly due to the imagination and irritability of the patient. In proof of this he adduced his own case. He had introduced his finger into the throat of a mad dog, and drew it out covered with frothy saliva; in drying it he observed that he had a slight excoriation on his finger. He lightly cauterized it, but ten days after, he experienced a sense of constriction about the throat. He felt alarmed; the difficulty of swallowing increased until he could not drink anything, and the sight of water caused spasms. The Will, however, was strongly exercised, and at last gained the day; the symptoms gradually abated, and in about a week he was well (lx, p. 140).

An event in the life of Andrew Crosse, the electrician, illustrates, in a striking manner, the power of the Will over threatened disease, the symptoms in his case being those of hydrophobia. It would seem to illustrate the force of this influence, not only directly over the incipient irregular action of certain motor nerves and muscles, by forcing them into healthy exercise, but over the automatic action of the cerebrum itself, by resolutely arresting the train of ideas which have been excited. If 'an act of the Will frequently excites such changes in the brain as to arrest an incipient paroxysm of angina pectoris or epilepsy, (Laycock), there seems no reason why it should not exert the same influence over the symptoms present in this case.

Mr. Crosse was severely bitten by a cat, which died the same day hydrophobic. He appears to have thought little of the circumstance, and was certainly not nervous or imaginative in regard to it. Three months, however, after he had received the wound, he felt one morning great pain in his arm, accompanied by extreme thirst. He called for a glass of water. The sequel will be best told in his own words:—'At the instant that I was about to raise the tumbler to my lips, a strong spasm shot across my throat; immediately the terrible conviction came to my mind that I was about to fall a victim to hydrophobia, the consequence of the bite that I had received from the cat. The agony of mind I endured for one hour is indescribable; the contemplation of such a horrible death—death from hydrophobia—was almost insupportable; the torments of hell itself could not have surpassed what I suffered. The pain, which had first commenced in my hand, passed up to the elbow, and from thence to the shoulder, threatening to extend. I felt all human aid was useless, and I believed that I must die. At length I began to reflect upon my condition. I said to myself, either I shall die or I shall not; if I do, it will only be a similar fate which many have suffered, and many more must suffer, and I must bear it like a man; if, on the other hand, there is any hope of my life, my only chance is in summoning my utmost resolution, defying the attack, and exerting every effort of my mind. Accordingly, feeling that physical as well as mental exertion was necessary, I took my gun, shouldered it, and went out for the purpose of shooting, my arm aching the while intolerably. I met with no sport, but *I walked the whole afternoon, exerting, at every step I went, a strong mental effort against the disease*. When I returned to the house I was decidedly better; I was able to eat some dinner, and drank water as usual. The next morning the aching pain had gone down to my elbow, the following it went down to the wrist, and the third day left me altogether. I mentioned the circumstance to Dr. Kinglake, and he said he certainly considered that I had had an attack of hydrophobia, which would possibly have proved fatal had I not struggled against it by a strong effort of mind.' ('Memoirs of Andrew Crosse,' p. 125.)

In hysteria, the influence of the Will *versus* the reflex action of voluntary muscles is constantly seen. Mr. Skey records the case of a young lady of sixteen, who for many months had been suffering from inversion of the left foot, which was twisted at right angles with the other, and was treated by orthopœdic surgeons with an elaborate apparatus of splints. Neither they nor Mr. Skey (though he recognised the nature of the affection) succeeded in curing it. Psychical agents, however, effected a cure in a few minutes. She willed to use her foot like other people, and she did. 'She accompanied her family to a ball, her foot, as she entered the ball-room, being not yet restored to its normal position. She was invited to dance, and under this novel excitement she stood up, and to the astonishment of her family, she danced the whole evening, having almost suddenly recovered the healthy, muscular action of the limb. She came to see me,' adds Mr. Skey, 'two days afterwards. She walked perfectly well into my room, and paced the room backwards and forwards with great delight. The actions of the limb were thoroughly restored, and all trace of previous malady had disappeared' (xlv, October 13th, 1866). Fortunately no quack medicine or doctor aroused the Will in this case; fortunately, not only because they would have had the credit of the cure, but because the reality of the disorder would have been denied by those who have still to learn that such recoveries are possible, and that it is one thing to admit the virtue of inert remedies, and another thing to recognise the secret of their frequent success.

The influence of the Will in controlling disease has already been incidentally referred to in the case of Irving. His own account of an attack of cholera may be made use of advantageously here.* During the invasion of the cholera in 1832 he was 'seized with what was in all appearance, and to the conviction of medical men when described to them, that disease which has proved fatal to so many of our fellow creatures.' He had risen in perfect health at his usual early hour. By breakfast time he had become very cold and was labouring under severe pain. His appearance shocked his friends. Vomiting succeeded, and wringing or gnawing pains,† and being so weak that he could not sit up, he lay on the bed wrapped in blankets till he had to set out to preach at half-past eleven. It appears that he had a little brandy and arrowroot, but felt no better. With sunken eyes, pallid cheeks, and an altogether ghastly appearance, he tottered to the church, a quarter of a mile distant, and found another minister officiating for him. He was tempted to shrink back, but summoned resolution to tell his beadle to go into the pulpit and inform him that he would shortly take his place. In the meantime he stretched himself on three chairs in the vestry before the fire. 'Even as I shifted my position I endured much suffering, and was almost involuntarily impelled to draw up my limbs in order to keep the pain under. Nevertheless, when I stood up to attire myself for the pulpit, and went forward to ascend the pulpit stairs, the pains seemed to leave me.' His sight was dim, his

* It should be observed that he held and preached that disease is sin, and that no one with faith need or ought to yield to it.

† A medical friend informs me that to his knowledge, Irving laboured under severe diarrhœa, and that his state at one time was that of dangerous collapse.

head swam, he breathed with difficulty, he laid hold on the pulpit sides and looked wistfully about, wondering what would befall him. The crisis came. 'That instant a cold sweat, chill as the hand of death, broke out all over my body, and stood in large drops upon my forehead and hands. From that moment I seemed to be strengthened.' He preached upwards of an hour with more unction than he had ever done before. After the service he walked home, eating little or nothing. . . .

Chapter VI

Moral Insanity

77. James Cowles Prichard, *The Inadequacy of Locke's View of Insanity*

(Excerpt from *A Treatise on Insanity*, London: Marchant, 1833, pp. 4–7.)

It is generally supposed that the intellect or the reasoning faculty is principally disordered in persons labouring under mental derangement. Mr. Locke made a remark, that 'madmen do not appear to have lost the faculty of reasoning; but having joined together some ideas very wrongly, they mistake them for truths, and they err as men do that argue right from wrong principles.' From Mr. Locke's time it has been customary to observe that insane persons reason correctly from erroneous premises; and some instances of hallucination, or some particular erroneous impression, have been looked for as the characteristic of the disease, or an essential circumstance in it. Dr. Cullen seems to have had Mr. Locke's observation in his mind when he had laid down the definition of madness which occurs in his First Lines. He describes this disease to be 'in a person awake a false or mistaken judgment of those relations of things which, as occurring most frequently in life, are those about which the generality of men form the same judgment; and particularly when the judgment is very different from what the person himself had before usually formed.' Cullen attempted to draw even this description within narrower limits, by observing that 'there is generally some false perception of external objects, and that such false perception necessarily occasions a *delirium or erroneous judgment*, which is to be considered as *the disease*.' That this is by far too limited an account of madness, and only comprises one, and that by no means the most frequent form of mental derangement, every person must be aware who has had opportunities of extensive observation.

Of those lunatics whose intellectual faculties are manifestly disordered, there is always a considerable proportion in whose minds it is impossible to trace any particular hallucination or erroneous perception or recollection. The rapid succession of thoughts, the hurried and confused manner in which ideas crowd themselves into the mind in a state of incoherence, or without order and connection, is in very many instances among the most striking phenomena of madness. There are, likewise, cases of a different description, in which the intellectual faculties appear to have sustained but little injury, while the feelings and affections, the moral and active principles of the mind, are strangely perverted and depraved; the power of self-government is lost or greatly impaired; and the individual is found to be incapable, not of talking and reasoning upon any subject proposed to him, for this he will often do with great shrewdness and volubility, but of conducting himself with decency and propriety in the business of life. His wishes and inclinations, his attachments, his likings and dislikings, have all undergone a morbid change, and this change appears to be the originating cause, or to lie at the foundation of any disturbance which the understanding itself may have sustained, and even in some instances to form throughout the chief character or constituent feature of the disease. The older nosologists, Sauvages, Sagar, and Linnæus, were not wholly unaware of these distinctions; for in their distributions of mental diseases we find (besides an order of *Vesaniæ* or *Hallucinationes*, in which erroneous impressions were supposed to affect the understanding) another department styled '*Morositates*' or '*Morbi Pathetici*,' consisting of depraved appetites and other morbid changes in the feelings and propensities. The disorders, however, which are classed under these heads, are not, all of them at least, strictly forms of insanity; and Pinel appears to have been the first writer who, with a clear conception of the subject, distinguished a class of maniacal affections under the term of 'madness without delirium or hallucination.' Pinel, who was an acute and original observer, and whose opinions carry much weight on account of his extensive opportunities of investigating the history of madness, has made the following remark in reference to the sentiments of Mr. Locke. 'We may justly admire,' he says, 'the writings of this philosopher, without admitting his authority upon subjects not necessarily connected with his inquiries. On resuming at the Bicêtre my researches into this disorder, I thought, with the above author, that it was inseparable from delirium,' (meaning what is termed by English writers hallucination;) 'and I was not a little surprised to find many maniacs who *at no period gave evidence of any lesion of the understanding*, but who were under the dominion of instinctive and abstract fury, as if the active faculties alone had sustained injury.'

78. James Cowles Prichard, *Moral Insanity*

(Excerpt from A *Treatise on Insanity*, London: Marchant, 1833, pp. 14–16, 18, 25–7.)

Moral insanity.—This form of mental disease has been said above to consist of a morbid perversion of the feelings, affections, habits, without any hallucination or erroneous conviction impressed upon the understanding; it sometimes co-exists with an apparently unimpaired state of the intellectual faculties.

There are many individuals living at large, and not entirely separated from society, who are affected in a certain degree by this modification of insanity. They are reputed persons of singular, wayward, and eccentric character. An attentive observer may often recognise something remarkable in their manner of existence, which leads him to entertain doubts as to their entire sanity, and circumstances are sometimes discovered on inquiry which assist in determining his opinion. In many instances it is found that there is an hereditary tendency to madness in the family, or that several relatives of the person affected have laboured under other diseases of the brain. The individual himself is discovered in a former period of life to have sustained an attack of madness of a decided character. His temper and dispositions are found on inquiry to have undergone a change; to be not what they were previously to a certain time; he has become an altered man, and this difference has perhaps been noted from the period when he sustained some reverse of fortune, which deeply affected him, or since the loss of some beloved relative. In other instances the alteration in his character has ensued immediately on some severe shock which his bodily constitution has undergone. This has been either a disorder affecting the head, a slight attack of paralysis, a fit of epilepsy, or some fever or inflammatory disorder which has produced a perceptible change in the habitual state of the constitution. In some cases the alteration in temper and habits has been gradual and imperceptible, and it seems only to have consisted in an exaltation or increase of peculiarities which were always more or less natural or habitual.

In a state such as that above described many persons have continued for years to be the sources of apprehension and solicitude to their friends and relatives. The latter in many instances cannot bring themselves to admit the real nature of the case. The individual follows the bent of his inclinations; he is continually engaging in new pursuits, and again relinquishing them without any other motive than mere caprice and fickleness. At length the total perversion of his affections, the dislike and even enmity manifested towards his dearest friends excite greater alarm.

Individuals labouring under this disorder are capable of reasoning or supporting an argument on any subject within their sphere of knowledge that may be presented to them, and they often display great ingenuity in giving reasons for their eccentric conduct, and in accounting for and justifying the state of moral feeling under which they appear to exist. In one sense, indeed, their intellectual faculties may be termed unsound, but it is the same sense in which persons under the influence of strong passions may generally be said to have their judgment warped, and the same or healthy exercise of their understandings impeded. They think and act under the influence of strongly excited feelings, and a person accounted sane is under such circumstances proverbially liable to error in judgment and conduct.

The following cases will afford some observations illustrative of the history of moral insanity.

J.K.—, a farmer, several of whose relatives had been the subjects of mental derangement, was a man of sober and domestic habits, and frugal and steady in his conduct, until about his forty-fifth year, when his disposition appeared to have become suddenly changed in a manner which excited the surprise of his friends and neighbours, and occasioned grief and vexation in his family. He became wild, excitable, thoughtless, full of schemes and absurd projects. He would set out and make long journeys into distant parts of the country to purchase cattle and farming-stock, of which he had no means of disposing; he bought a number of carriages, hired an expensive house ready furnished, which had been inhabited by a person much above his rank, and was unsuitable to his condition; he was irascible and impetuous, quarrelled with his neighbours, and committed an assault upon the clergyman of the parish, for which he was indicted and bound to take his trial. At length his wife became convinced that he was mad, and made application for his confinement in a lunatic asylum, which was consequently effected. The medical practitioners who examined him were convinced of his insanity by comparing his late wild habits and unaccountable conduct with the former tenor of his life, taking into account consideration the tendency to disease which was known to prevail in his family. The change in his character alone had produced a full conviction of his madness in his friends and relatives. When questioned as to the motives which had induced him to some of his late proceedings, he gave clear and distinct replies, and assigned with great ingenuity some plausible reason for almost every part of his conduct. After a period of time passed in great seclusion, his mind became gradually tranquillized; the morbed excitement of his temper and feelings disappeared; he was set at liberty, and has since conducted himself with propriety.

79. James Cowles Prichard, *Features of Moral Insanity*

(Excerpt from *On the Different Forms of Insanity in Relation to Jurisprudence*, London: Hippolyte Ballière, 1847, pp. 30–5.)

Moral insanity is a disorder of which the symptoms are only displayed in the state of the feelings, affections, temper, and in the habits and conduct of the individual, or in the exercise of those mental faculties which are termed the active and moral powers of the mind. There is in this disorder no discoverable *illusion* or *hallucination* or false conviction impressed upon the belief similar to the delusive or erroneous impressions which characterise monomania. It is often very difficult to pronounce, with certainty, as to the presence or absence of moral insanity, or to determine whether the appearances which are supposed to indicate its existence do not proceed from natural peculiarity or eccentricity of character. The existence of moral insanity is palpable and easily recognised only in those instances to which it comes on, as it often does, after some strongly marked disorder affecting the brain and the general state of health, such as a slight attack of paralysis, and when it displays a state of mind strikingly different from the previous, and habitual or natural character of the individual. If a person of quiet and sedate temper, little subject to strong emotions, becomes excitable, violent, impetuous, thoughtless, and extravagant to such a degree as to surprise his friends and relatives, a suspicion is often produced that this change may depend upon a disordered state of mind. There are many individuals who are subject to alternate fits of excitement and depression; the contrast renders the peculiarities of such persons apparent. The fact that they are so affected is always known to their families, but they are not suspected of insanity, unless the affection is very strongly marked. A gentleman who had been for many years a county magistrate and a person of great talents and great influence, had been several times, during his life, subject to such alternate depression and excitement. During the former state, he was low spirited, and dejected, timid and apprehensive, and even kept his bed for weeks; gradually this state was changed; he became then boisterous, irascible, extravagant, and given to intoxication; he would wander about the country in the dress of a horse-jockey, frequented fairs and markets, was followed by horse dealers, and made the most extravagant purchases of horses and dogs, and associated with people of the lowest class. During these times he was overbearing and impetuous; has been known to horse-whip his female domestics. His countenance bore a different aspect from that which was natural to it, so that his servants and relations immediately recognised the peculiarity. This person displayed in conversation no trace of a cloud on the understanding; he was under no illusion or hallucination. His extravagance and absurd conduct were thought to be ruinous and disgraceful to his family, and on application, a writ 'de lunatico inquirendo' was obtained for the purpose of keeping him for a time in confinement and taking care of his property. When brought before a jury, he displayed the greatest sagacity in accounting for all the odd actions that were alleged of him. He passed some months in a lunatic asylum, where he was treated judiciously, and is now perfectly recovered.

A tolerably full account of this form of mental disease is to be found in my Treatise on Insanity, where it was first named and defined as a particular form of mental disorder. In that work it is thus described:

'There are many individuals living at large and not entirely separated from society, who are affected, in a certain degree, with his modification of insanity. They are reputed persons of a singular, wayward, and eccentric character. An attentive observer will often recognise something remarkable in their manners and habits, which may lead him to entertain doubts as to their entire sanity, and circumstances are sometimes discovered on inquiry, which add strength to this suspicion. In many instances, it has been found that an hereditary tendency to madness has existed in the family, or that several relatives of the person affected have laboured under other diseases of the brain. The individual himself has been discovered to have suffered, in a former period of life, an attack of madness of a decided character. His temper and disposition are found to have undergone a change; to be not what they were previously to a certain time; he has become an altered man, and the difference has, perhaps, been noted from the period when he sustained some reverse of fortune, which deeply affected him, or the loss of some beloved relative. In other instances an alteration in the character of the individual has ensued immediately on some severe shock which his bodily constitution has undergone. This has been either a disorder affecting the head, a slight attack of paralysis, or some febrile or inflammatory complaint, which has produced a perceptible change in the habitual state of his constitution. In some cases, the alteration in temper and habits has been gradual and imperceptible, and it seems only to have consisted in an exaltation and increase of peculiarities, which were always more or less natural and habitual.'

In a state like that above described, many persons have continued for years to be sources of apprehension and solicitude to their friends and relatives; the latter, in many instances, cannot bring themselves to admit the real nature of the case.

80. Henry Maudsley, *Moral Sense*

(Excerpt from *Body and Mind*, London: Macmillan & Co., 1873, pp. 59–60.)

If the moral sense (which is derived, then, insomuch as it has been acquired in the process of human development through the ages) were not more or less innate in the well-born individual of this age,—if he were obliged to go, as the generations of his forefathers have gone, through the elementary process of acquiring it,—he would be very much in the position of a person who, on each occasion of writing his name, had to go through the elementary steps of learning to do so. The progressive evolution of the human brain is a proof that we do inherit as a natural endowment the laboured acquisitions of our ancestors; the added structure represents, as it were, the embodied experience and memories of the race; and there is no greater difficulty in believing that the moral sense may have been so formed, than in believing, what has long been known and is admitted on all hands, that the young fox or young dog inherits as an instinct the special cunning which the foxes and the dogs that have gone before it have had to win by hard experience.

These remarks are not an unnecessary digression. Nor will they have been made in vain if they serve to fix in our minds the conviction that the law of progressive evolution and specialization of nerve-centres, which may be traced generally from the first appearance of nerve tissue in the lowest animals to the complex structure of the nervous system of man, and specially from the rudimentary appearance of serebral convolutions in the lower vertebrata to the numerous and complex convolutions of the human brain, does not abruptly cease its action at the vesicular neurine of the hemispheres, but continues in force within the intimate recesses of the mental organization. Moreover, they are specially to the purpose, seeing that they enable us to understand in some sort how it is that a perversion or destruction of the moral sense is often one of the earliest symptoms of mental derangement: as the latest and most exquisite product of mental organization, the highest bloom of culture, it is the first to testify to disorder of the mind-centres. Not that we can detect any structural change in such case; it is far too delicate for that. The wonder would, indeed, be if we could discover such more than microscopical changes with the instruments of research which we yet possess. We might almost as well look to discover the anatomy of a gnat with a telescope.

I purposely selected for consideration the defective brain of the idiot, because it exhibits an undeniable fault of structure, which is often plainly traceable to evil ancestral influences. When we duly consider this, and reflect that we might, if we chose, arrange a series of human brains which should present a regular gradation from the brain of an ape to that of a well-developed European, are we not fully justified in supposing that like unfavourable ancestral influences may occasion defects in the constitution or composition of the mind-centres which we are yet quite unable to detect?

81. Henry Maudsley, *Moral Degeneracy*

(Excerpt from *Body and Mind*, London: Macmillan & Co., 1873, pp. 125–7.)

Let me come to the particular problem which we have to face—namely, whether there is the same essential connection between moral sense and brain which there is between thought and brain, or between any of our special senses and its special ganglionic centre in the brain? Is conscience a function of organization? I will ask you to look without prejudice at the facts of observation, and to consider if they admit of any other scientific interpretation. For the medical psychologist, whose duty brings him into constant intercourse with facts, cannot rest satisfied with vague speculations; he is bound to investigate the phenomena as they present themselves to observation, and to form conclusions from them, without regard to accepted theories of faith or knowledge; and if he arrives at sound conclusions from such observation of facts not before observed, these will not contradict old faiths unless in that wherein old faiths are wrong, and it is right they should be contradicted. His generalizations, like the generalizations of astronomy, chemistry, or any other branch of science, must rest on their own merits; they cannot justly be tested by any preconceived standard of truth, however much hallowed by antiquity or sanctioned by authority.

When we come to deal with examples of moral degeneracy, whether among the insane or among criminals, we perceive at once that it is not sufficient to ascribe immorality to the devil; that we must, if we would not leave the matter a mystery, go on to discover the cause of it in the individual. The effect defective comes by cause, we are constrained to believe; what is the cause and what are the laws of moral degeneracy? As society is constituted, certain forms of evil-doing are certainly not profitable in the long run; how comes it, then, that an individual, capable of looking before and after, remembering the retribution of past sin, and foreseeing the Nemesis that waits on future wrong-doing, is so forgetful of true self-interest as to yield to evil impulses? And whence do those impulses come? One thing is certain, that moral philosophy cannot penetrate the hidden springs of feeling and impulse; they lie deeper than it can reach, for they lie in the physical constitution of the individual, and, going still further back, perhaps in his organic antecedents. Because the fathers have eaten sour grapes, therefore it often is that the children's teeth are set on edge. Because the fathers had stoned the prophets, therefore it was that the children rejected Him who was sent unto them. Assuredly of some criminals, as of some insane persons, it may be truly said that they are born, not made; they go criminal, as the insane go mad, because they cannot help it; a stronger power than they can counteract has given the bias of their being. Those who doubt this when it is put in this positive form, will hardly continue to do so when they consider that between the drivelling idiot, equally destitute of intellect and moral feeling, whom no labour of training can raise to a human level, and the highest example of intellect and moral feeling, there are beings marking every step of the long gradation; that we may mount from entire absence of moral sense through every grade of deficiency up to its highest state of development. I do not dispute that much may sometimes be done by education and training to counteract in this respect the ills of a bad inheritence, but it is still true that the foundations upon which the acquisitions of education must rest are inherited, and that in many instances they are too weak to bear a good moral superstructure.

82. Henry Maudsley, *Morals and Constitution*

(Excerpt from *Body and Mind*, London: Macmillan & Co., 1873, pp. 136–7.)

Moral peculiarities are constitutional; they are marks of one variety of the insane temperament, and, as such, are of interest to us in our present inquiry. For the facts which I have thus far mentioned seem to me to prove the essential connection of the moral sense with organization, and to admit of interpretation only on that supposition. It, or the potentiality of it, is inherited by most persons, though some appear to be born without it; it is developed by culture; decays from disuse; and is perverted or destroyed by disease. The last acquired faculty in the progress of human evolution, it is the first to suffer when disease invades the mental organization. One of the first symptoms of insanity—one which declares itself before there is any intellectual derangement, before the person's friends suspect even that he is becoming insane—is a deadening or complete perversion of the moral sense. In extreme cases it is observed that the modest man becomes presumptuous and exacting, the chaste man lewd and obscene, the honest man a thief, and the truthful man an unblushing liar. Short of this, however, there is an observable impairment of the finer moral feelings—a something different, which the nearest friends do not fail to feel, although they cannot always describe it. Now, these signs of moral perversion are really the first symptoms of a mental derangement which may, in its further course, go through all degrees of intellectual disorder, and end in destruction of mind, with visible destruction of the nerve-cells which minister to mind. Is the end then dependent on organization, or rather disorganization, and is the beginning not? This course of degeneracy is but a summary in the individual of what we have already seen to take place through generations, and in both cases we are constrained to believe that the moral changes are as closely dependent upon physical causes as are the intellectual changes which accompany or follow them. If it be not so, we may bid farewell to all investigation of mental function by a scientific method.

83. Henry Maudsley, *Moral Sense and Disordered Brain*

(Excerpt from *Responsibility in Mental Disease*, London: Henry S. King & Co., 1874, pp. 13–16.)

In many quarters there is the strongest desire evinced, and the most strenuous efforts are made, to exempt from physical researches the highest functions of mind, and particularly the so-called moral sense and the will; while the old metaphysical spirit still inspires the criterion of responsibility which is sanctioned and acted upon by courts of justice in cases of insanity. If a madman be supposed to know he is doing wrong, or doing that which is contrary to law, when he does some act of violence, he is held to be not less responsible than a sane person. The conclusions reached by the observations of self-consciousness in a sane mind are strictly applied to the phenomena of diseased mind; not otherwise than as if it were solemnly enacted that the disorder and violence of convulsions should be measured by the order and method of voluntary movements, and that whosoever, being seized with convulsions, and knowing that he was convulsed, transgressed that measure, should be punished as a criminal. The unfortunate sufferer, or others on his behalf, might, it is true, innocently argue that the very nature of convulsions excluded the idea of full voluntary control; but the metaphysical intuitionist would rejoin that it was certain from experience that man has a power of control over his movements; that the convulsive movements were a clear proof to all the world that he had not exercised that power; and that his convulsions, therefore, were justly punishable as crime. This pathological comparison is scientifically just, and its justness has oftentimes received terribly striking illustration in the effects of the legal criterion of responsibility; for it is certain that in conformity with it many persons unquestionably insane, who have done homicide, not because they *would* not, but because they *could* not, exercise efficient, control, have been, and still from time to time are, executed as simple criminals. Harsh and exaggerated as this statement might seem, there is not, I believe, in this or any other civilized country a physician, practically acquainted with the insane, who would not unhesitatingly endorse it.

No one now-a-days who is engaged in the treatment of mental disease doubts that he has to do with the disordered function of a bodily organ—of the brain. Whatever opinion may be held concerning the essential nature of mind, and its independence of matter, it is admitted on all sides that its manifestations take place through the nervous system, and are affected by the condition of the nervous parts which minister to them. If these are healthy, they are sound; if these are diseased, they are unsound. Insanity is, in fact, disorder of brain producing disorder of mind; or, to define its nature in greater detail, it is a disorder of the supreme nerve-centres of the brain—the special organs of mind—producing derangement of thought, feeling, and action, together or separately, of such degree or kind as to incapacitate the individual for the relations of life.*

The opinion that insanity is a disease of the so-called immaterial part of our nature we may look upon as exploded even in its last retreat. The arguments that have been adduced in favour of it —first, that madness is produced sometimes by moral causes, and, secondly, that it is cured sometimes by moral means—are entirely consistent with the theory of material disease, while the

* Mind may be defined physiologically as a general term denoting the sum total of those functions of the brain which are known as thought, feeling, and will. By disorder of mind is meant disorder of those functions.

arguments in favour of the materialistic theory are quite inconsistent with the spiritualistic hypothesis, which has the further disadvantage of not being within the range of rational human conception.

84. Henry Maudsley, *Conscience and Organization*

(Excerpt from *Responsibility in Mental Disease*, London: Henry S. King & Co., 1874, pp. 62–4.)

If other arguments were needed in support of the opinion that conscience is a function or organization—the highest and most delicate function of the highest and most complete development thereof—they might be drawn from observation of conditions of moral degeneracy. Let it be noted how it is perverted or destroyed sometimes by disease or injury of brain. The last acquired faculty in the progress of human evolution, it is the first to suffer when disease invades the mental organization. One of the first symptoms of insanity—one which declares itself before there is any intellectual derangement, before the person's friends suspect even that he is becoming insane—is a deadening or complete perversion of the moral sense. In extreme cases it is observed that the modest man becomes presumptuous and exacting, the chaste man lewd and obscene, the honest man a thief, and the truthful man an unblushing liar. Short of this, however, there is an observable impairment of the finer moral feelings—a something different, which the nearest friends do not fail to feel, although they cannot always describe it. Now, these signs of moral perversion are really the first symptoms of a mental derangement which may, in its further course, go through all degrees of intellectual disorder, and end in destruction of mind, with visible destruction of the nerve-cells which minister to mind. Is the end, then, dependent on organization, or rather disorganization, and is the beginning not? This course of degeneracy is but a summary in the individual of what may be traced through generations; and in both cases we are constrained to believe that the moral changes are as closely dependent upon physical causes as are the intellectual changes which accompany or follow them. If it be not so we may bid farewell to all investigation of mental function by a scientific method.

Note, again, the effect which a severe attack of insanity sometimes produces upon the moral nature of the individual. The person entirely recovers his reason; his intellectual faculties are as acute as ever, but his moral character is changed; he is no longer the moral man that he was; the shock has destroyed the finest part if his mental organization. Henceforth his life may be as different from his former life as, in an opposite direction, was the life of Saul of Tarsus from the life of Paul the Apostle to the Gentiles. An attack of epilepsy has produced the same effect, effacing the moral sense as it effaces the memory sometimes; and one of the most striking phenomena observed in asylums is the extreme change in moral character in the epileptic which precedes and heralds the approach of his fits. A fever or an injury to the head has in like manner transformed the moral character. Many instances from different quarters might be brought forward in illustration of such physical effect upon moral being, but one mentioned by Dr. Prichard, which lies to hand, may suffice. In a large and well-regulated family all the members save one boy were of quiet and sober habits, of excellent disposition, and regular and industrious. This boy met with a severe accident, which injured his head. As he grew up he was quite different from the other children; he was utterly unmanageable, dissipated, wild, addicted to all kinds of excesses,—was on the verge of madness, though not intellectually deranged. Dr. Wigan puts the matter in a way that may seem more extravagant than it really is when he says:—'I firmly believe that I have more than once changed the moral character of a boy by leeches to the inside of the nose.'

85. Henry Maudsley, *Moral Insanity versus Will*

(Excerpt from *Responsibility in Mental Disease*, London: Henry S. King & Co., 1874, pp. 170–6.)

This is a form of mental alienation which has so much the look of vice or crime that many persons regard it as an unfounded medical invention. Much indignation therefore has been stirred up when it has been pleaded to shelter a supposed criminal from the penal consequences of his offences; and judges have repeatedly denounced it from the bench as a 'a most dangerous medical doctrine,' 'a dangerous innovation,' which in the interests of society should be reprobated. The doctrine has no doubt been sometimes used improperly to shelter an atrocious criminal, but of the actual existence of such a form of disease no one who has made a practical study of insanity entertains a doubt. To the angry declamation of the vexed judge, the sufferer from it might fairly answer in the words of Imogen:

> I beseech you, sir,
> Harm you not yourself with your vexation.
> I'm senseless of your wrath. A touch more rare
> Subdues all griefs, all fears.

Notwithstanding prejudices to the contrary, there is a disorder of mind in which, without illusion, delusion, or hallucination, the symptoms are mainly exhibited in a perversion of those mental faculties which are usually called the active and moral powers—the feelings, affections, propensities, temper, habits, and conduct. The affective life of the individual is profoundly deranged, and his derangement shows itself in what he feels, desires, and does. He has no capacity of true moral feeling; all his impulses and desires, to which he yields without check, are egoistic; his conduct appears to be governed by immoral motives, which are cherished and obeyed without any evident desire to resist them. There is an amazing moral insensibility. The intelligence is often acute enough, being not affected otherwise than in being tainted by the morbid feelings under the influence of which the persons think and act; indeed they often display an extraordinary ingenuity in explaining, excusing, or justifying their behaviour, exaggerating this, ignoring that, and so colouring the whole as to make themselves appear the victims of misrepresentation and persecution. Their mental resources seem to be greater sometimes than when they were well, and they reason most acutely, apparently because all their intellectual faculties are applied to the justification and gratification of their selfish desires. One cannot truly say, however, that the intellect is quite clear and sound in any of these cases, while in some it is manifestly weak. A sane person who is under the influence of excited feelings is notably liable to error of judgment and conduct; and in like manner the judgment and conduct of an insane person who is under the dominion of morbid feelings are infected. Moreover, the reason has lost control over the passions and actions, so that the person can neither subdue the former nor abstain from the latter, however inconsistent they may be with the duties and obligations of his relations in life, however disastrous to himself, and however much wrong they may inflict upon those who are the nearest and should be the dearest to him. He is incapable of following a regular pursuit in life, of recognising the ordinary rules of prudence and self-interest, of appreciating the injury to himself which his conduct is. He is as distrustful of others as he is untrustworthy himself. He cannot be brought to see the culpability of his conduct, which he persistently denies, excuses, or justifies; has no sincere wish to do better; his affective nature is profoundly deranged, and its affinities are for such evil gratifications as must lead to further degeneration, and finally render him a diseased element which must either be got rid of out of the social organization, or be sequestrated and made harmless in it. He has lost the deepest instinct of organic nature, that by which an organism assimilates that which is suited to promote its growth and well-being, and his displays in lieu thereof perverted desires, the ways of which are ways of destruction. His alienated desires betoken a real alienation of nature.

It may be said that this description is simply the description of a very wicked person, and that to accept it as a description of insanity would be to confound all distinction between vice or crime and madness. No doubt, so far as symptoms only are concerned, they are much the same whether they are the result of vice or of disease; but there is considerable difference when we go on to inquire into the person's previous history—when we pass from psychological to medical observation. This vicious act or crime is not itself proof of insanity; it must, in order to establish moral insanity, be traced from disease through a proper train of symptoms, just as the acts of a sane man are deduced from his motives; and the evidence of disease will be found in the entire history of the case. What we shall often observe is this—that after some great moral shock, or some severe physical disturbance, in a person who has a distinct hereditary predisposition to insanity, there has been a marked change of character; he becomes 'much different from the man he was' in feelings, temper, habits, and conduct. We observe, in fact, that after a sufficient and well-recognised cause of mental derangement—a combination of predisposing and exciting causes which are daily producing it—a person exhibits symptoms which are strangely inconsistent with his previous character, but which are consistent with moral insanity. Or it may appear that there has been an attack of paralysis or epilepsy, or a severe fever, and that the change of character and the symptoms of moral alienation have followed one of these physical causes. In all cases, as Dr. Prichard, who was the first to describe the disease, has remarked, there has been an alteration in the temper and habits in consequence of disease or of a sufficient cause of disease.

Perhaps the strongest evidence of the nature of moral insanity as a disease of brain is furnished by the fact that its symptoms sometimes precede for a time the symptoms of intellectual derangement in a severe case of undoubted insanity, as, for example, a case of acute mania, or of general paralysis, or of senile dementia. It is interesting, indeed, to notice that at least one of Dr. Prichard's cases, on which he founded his description of the disease, was really a case of general paralysis—a disease not specially recognized in his day, but the best known now of all the forms of mental derangement. Surely, then, when a person is subject to a sufficient cause of insanity, exhibits thereupon a great change of character, and finally passes into acute mania or general paralysis, we cannot fairly be asked to recognize the adequate cause of the disease and the intellectual disorder as disease, and at the same to deny the character of disease to the intermediate symptoms.

Not only may moral derangement thus go before intellectual derangement for some time and itself constitute the disease, but it constantly accompanies the latter; so much so that Esquirol declared 'moral alienation,' not delusion, 'to be the proper characteristic of mental derangement.' 'There are,' he says, 'madmen in whom it is difficult to find any trace of hallucination, but there are none in whom the passions and moral affections are not disordered, perverted, or destroyed. I have in this particular met with no exceptions.' So true is this that disappearance of hallucination or delusion only becomes a trustworthy sign of convalescence after an attack of mental derangement when the person begins to return at the same time to his natural way of feeling. It is hardly to be expected that medical science will, in order not to vex the souls of judges, dissociate the moral from the intellectual phenomena in a downright case of madness, and regard the former, because they look like vice, as vice, the latter only as disease, or deem it right to excuse the man for his insane thinking but to punish him for his insane feeling and acts, so far at any rate as these acts are not the direct unqualified offspring of his insane thought.

Again, moral insanity may occur in a person who has at one time laboured under another form of madness, being, as it were, a recurrent attack under a different guise: an attack of mania or melancholia comes on and in due time passes off favourably, but on some subsequent occasion he has a genuine moral insanity, which may terminate again in mania or melancholia. There are intervals of what looks for all the world like badness, alternating with attacks of what all the world sees to be madness. In the most typical case of moral insanity which has come under my observation there had been previous attacks of melancholia, and it was upon one of these that the moral derangement directly followed. Such cases commonly end in dementia, the disease of mind passing into destruction thereof.

86. Henry Maudsley, *A Traitor in one's Nature*

(Excerpt from *The Pathology of Mind*, London: Macmillan & Co., 1879, pp. 102–3.)

Good moral feeling is to be looked upon as an essential part of a sound and rightly developed character in the present state of human evolution in civilised lands; its acquisition is the condition of development in the progress of *humanization*. Whosoever is destitute of it is to that extent a defective being; he marks the beginning of race-degeneracy; and if propitious influences do not chance to check or to neutralize the morbid tendency, his children will exhibit a further degree of degeneracy and be actual morbid varieties. Whether the particular outcome of the morbid strain shall be vice, or madness, or crime, will depend much on the circumstances of life, but there is no doubt in my mind that one way in which insanity is generated *de novo* is through the deterioration of nature which is shown in the absence of moral sense. It was the last acquisition in the progress of *humanization*, and its decay is the first sign of the commencement of human degeneracy. And as absence of moral sense in one generation may be followed by insanity in the next, so I have observed that, conversely, insanity in one generation sometimes leaves the evil legacy of a defective moral sense to the next. Any course of life then which persistently ignores the altruistic relations of an individual as a social unit, which is in truth a systematic negation of the moral law of human progress, deteriorates his higher nature, and so initiates a degeneracy which may issue in actual mental derangement in his posterity.

When we make a scientific study of the fundamental meaning

of those deviations from the sound type which issue in insanity and in crime, by searching inquiry into the laws of their genesis, it appears that these forms of human degeneracy do not lie so far asunder as they are commonly supposed to do. Moreover, theory is here confirmed by observation; for it has been pointed out by those who have made criminals their study that they oftentimes spring from families in which insanity, epilepsy, or some allied neurosis exists, that many of them are weak-minded, epileptic, or actually insane, and that they are apt to die from diseases of the nervous system and from tubercular diseases. One might venture to describe, and to place side by side as having near relations to one another, three neuroses—the epileptic, the insane, and the criminal neurosis—each of which has its corresponding psychosis or natural mental character. In like manner as the form of every living creature answers to its habits, it desiring only what it can attain by means of its organs, constructed as they are, and its organs never urging it to that which it has not a desire for, so it is with the particular neurosis of that congeries of nerve-centres which constitute specially the organ of mind; it inspires a desire for and determines a tendency to that form of mental activity, in other words, to that development of the psychosis, which is the fullest expression of its function. The sufferer from any one of these neuroses represents an initial form of degeneracy, or a commencing morbid variety, of the human kind, and life to him will be a hard struggle against the radical bias of his nature, unless he minds not to struggle and leaves it to the free course of a morbid development. He is sadly weighted in running the race that is set before him, since he has an enemy in his camp, a traitor in his own nature, which is ever ready to conspire with external adversities, and often lends them a secret help, without which they would be powerless to overcome him.

87. Furneaux Jordan, *Moral Nerve*

(Excerpt from *Character as Seen in Body and Parentage*, London: Kegan Paul, Trench, Trubner & Co., 1886, pp. 121–2.)

Probably the most significant characteristics of moral nerve are its mobility, pliancy, and greater facility for change as well as its perhaps narrower range of action. Intellectual nerve power wanders over vast and illimitable and diverse fields; moral nerve power, less wandering, less vague, lights up a more restricted area. It has been pointed out in a preceding note that the intellectual endowments permit of only limited increase or diminution. It is otherwise with the moral endowments. Intellectual nerve is more or less stable; moral nerve is more or less unstable. Intellectual nerve is capable of great and prolonged effort; moral nerve, well-doing nerve, temptation-resisting nerve, is more easily exhausted. Well-inherited, well-nourished, well-trained, massive moral nerve will it is true tire slowly if at all. It is the reverse with poorly-inherited or scanty or ill-nourished or ill-trained nerve. A clerk of, perhaps, congenitally inadequate moral nerve, or nerve already in some degree spoiled by, say, alcohol, can still, through the instrumentality of his intellectual nerve deal with complex figures for some hours consecutively. When he goes home in the evening he passes through one, it may be two, streets of drink-shops; in the third street his moral nerve, in spite perhaps of much help from intellectual and emotional nerve, is exhausted and he passes through the tempting door.

88. General William Booth, *Asylums for Moral Lunatics*

(Excerpt from *In Darkest England and the Way Out*, London: The Salvation Army, 1890, pp. 204–5.)

There will remain, after all has been said and done, one problem that has yet to be faced. You may minimise the difficulty every way, and it is your duty to do so, but no amount of hopefulness can make us blink the fact that when all has been done and every chance has been offered, when you have forgiven your brother not only seven times but seventy times seven, when you have fished him up from the mire and put him on firm ground only to see him relapse and again relapse until you have no strength left to pull him out once more, there will still remain a residuum of men and women who have, whether from heredity or custom, or hopeless demoralisation, become reprobates. After a certain time, some men of science hold that persistence in habits tends to convert a man from a being with freedom of action and will into a mere automaton. There are some cases within our knowledge which seem to confirm the somewhat dreadful verdict by which a man appears to be a lost soul on this side of the grave.

There are men so incorrigibly lazy that no inducement that you can offer will tempt them to work; so eaten up by vice that virtue is abhorrent to them, and so inveterately dishonest that theft is to them a master passion. When a human being has reached that stage, there is only one course that can be rationally pursued. Sorrowfully, but remorselessly, it must be recognised that he has become lunatic, morally demented, incapable of self-government, and that upon him, therefore, must be passed the sentence of permanent seclusion from a world in which he is not fit to be at large. The ultimate destiny of these poor wretches should be a penal settlement where they could be confined during Her Majesty's pleasure as are the criminal lunatics at Broadmoor. It is a crime against the race to allow those who are so inveterately depraved the freedom to wander abroad, infect their fellows, prey upon Society, and to multiply their kind. Whatever else Society may do, and suffer to be done, this thing it ought not to allow, any more than it should allow the free perambulation of a mad dog. But before we come to this I would have every possible means tried to effect their reclamation. Let Justice punish them, and Mercy put her arms around them; let them be appealed to by penalty and by reason, and by every influence, human and Divine, that can possibly be brought to bear upon them. Then, if all alike failed, their ability to further curse their fellows and themselves should be stayed.

They will still remain objects worthy of infinite compassion. They should lead as human a life as is possible to those who have fallen under so terrible a judgment. They should have their own little cottages in their own little gardens, under the blue sky, and, if possible, amid the green fields. I would deny them none of the advantages, moral, mental, and religious which might minister to their diseased minds, and tend to restore them to a better state. Not until the breath leaves their bodies should we cease to labour and wrestle for their salvation. But when they have reached a certain point access to their fellow men should be forbidden. Between them and the wide world there should be reared an impassable barrier, which once passed should be recrossed no more for ever. Such a course must be wiser than allowing them to go in and out among their fellows, carrying with them the contagion of moral leprosy, and multiplying a progeny doomed before its birth to inherit the vices and diseased cravings of their unhappy parents.

PART THREE

PSYCHIATRIC DARWINISM

Chapter VII

Heredity and Character

89. George Man Burrows, *Hereditary Predisposition*

(Excerpt from *Commentaries on Insanity*, London: Underwood, 1828, pp. 100–3.)

Hereditary Predisposition

In certain constitutions peculiar modifications exist, which are termed idiosyncrasies. Thus, ipecacuanha is sometimes obnoxious to the Schneiderian and the mucous membranes; shell-fish, drupaceous and other fruits, to the stomach; the odour of different flowers and particular substances, to the olfactory nerves; and these idiosyncrasies may descend through successive generations. The gout is the inheritance of one, phthisis of another, apoplexy of a third, scrofula of a fourth, and so on; and these likewise may be propagated. All these peculiarities are predispositions. Peculiarities of form, features, or complexion, also, are transmitted to our offspring. Every disease that assumes a constitutional character can, John Hunter said, be given to a child; and then it becomes what is called hereditary. There is, however, he adds, no such thing as an hereditary disease; but there is an hereditary disposition for a disease.

If the external figure, features, and colour, be propagated—if certain perversions and peculiarities of our external senses and bodily functions, descend to our progeny—if particular diatheses are transmitted through generations, no doubt ought ever to have been raised that the brain may be imprinted with an hereditary disposition to insanity, and be, like any other constitutional characters, propagated *ad perpetuum*.

The doctrine of constitutional predispositions to specific diseases being propagated, is not new; and we have, in the instance of syphilis, a disease propagating itself. Why insanity should have been supposed to be exempt from this general law of nature, it is difficult to conceive, except on the mystic ground of its immaterial origin.

The liability of mania, demency, epilepsy, leprosy, &c., to extend through future generations, is an opinion confirmed by the experience of all ages. Some have imagined that insanity moves *per saltum*, and appears in every other, or every third individual, in lineal descent. Such was the opinion of Ludovicus Mercatus, a Spanish physician, who wrote a work on hereditary diseases. This, however, is incorrect. The development of insanity may escape one generation, and appear in another; but no rule in this respect obtains.

It is of little real importance whether it be a predisposition, or the malady itself, which descends and becomes hereditary; but no fact is more incontrovertibly established than that insanity is susceptible of being propagated; or, in other words, that a specific morbid condition sometimes exists in the human constitution, which, by intermarriage, or according to the vulgar but expressive language of cattle breeders, by breeding *in and in*, may be perpetuated *ad infinitum*.

Hereditary predisposition, therefore, is a prominent cause of mental derangement.

Mania and melancholia do not propagate their respective types: a maniac may beget a melancholic, and *vice versâ*.

Sometimes, in a large family, we find all the forms and relations of insanity developed in a remarkable manner. Mania, melancholia, hypochondriasis, apoplexy, paralysis, epilepsy, convulsions, chorea, hysteria, &c., or high nervous irritability, are often found to pervade one or the other of the same progeny. Nay, even the degrees of comparison are marked in the capacities of some families. This I have seen exemplified in a respectable family—one son has transcendent talents, the second is inferior, the third has been for years in a state of fatuity, and the fourth is an idiot. That great wit and madness are nearly allied, is not a poetical fiction; but there is this dissimilarity,—the one is rarely ever, the other is generally an inheritance.

Few, I believe, are more particular than myself in endeavouring to trace every case of insanity to its source. It is a duty which

I conceive every physician owes to his patient, as well as to himself, to ascertain whether there be an hereditary predisposition; because the correctness of his prognostic greatly depends on a knowledge of the truth.

Hereditary insanity may be as successfully treated as when it arises from an accidental cause; but when we know that a predisposition exists, we can decide with more accuracy the degree of excitement necessary to produce the effect, and the probability of a recurrence of the attack.

Common sense, if not a regard to the welfare of the patient and happiness of his family, one would think to be sufficient to induce the relations of an insane person to give the physician whom they consult every information required on this point. What can be a motive sufficiently strong in such case not only to conceal, but often to deny, an hereditary predisposition, is to me quite incomprehensible; yet nothing is more common. I will quote a strong instance: A young lady, of good family and fortune, was placed under my care, in whom mental derangement had been some time developed, till at length she was too violent to be kept at home. I made the usual inquiry into the probable causes of the malady, and whether hereditary predisposition might be suspected. This was positively denied; but it was suggested, that being very fond of hunting, she had several times experienced severe falls from her horse, and might have injured her head. Upon examining the cranium, I actually found a very singular depression of a part of the skull; but whether it was natural or accidental, no one could inform me. I stated to my patient's friends my suspicion that this depression might operate mechanically as a cause of the insanity; and, with their consent, an eminent surgeon was consulted upon the propriĕty of applying the trephine, with a view of removing such cause. Before any decision upon this question, I learnt from another quarter that several of this young lady's nearest relations had been insane, and that two had died in that state. The operation was, therefore, declined; and she recovered. I believe few cases can occur where the inducements to a candid avowal of hereditary predisposition to insanity were more powerful, yet they were not of sufficient force to elicit the truth. This perverse concealment has often a very baneful effect.

It is very remarkable, that when the desire of concealing hereditary insanity is so great as to run every hazard rather than confess it, yet no care is taken to correct such predisposition; and although a person knows that it is inherent in himself, he is the least careful in betraying proofs of it to the world.

90. Alfred Beaumont Maddock, *Conception and Inheritance*

(Excerpt from *On Mental and Nervous Diseases*, London: Simpkin, Marshall & Co., 1854, pp. 4–5.)

Children too, are often brought into the world with sickly constitutions, and with predisposition to disease, arising from antecedent circumstances, connected with the union of their parents. Marriages contracted too early, or too late in life, or those entered into between parties too nearly allied by blood, or by those in whom there exists too great a disparity in years, are peculiarly open to this objection. Not alone the habitual state of health of the parents, but even also the condition of their mental, as well as bodily powers at the period of conception, may determine the future constitution of their descendants. Numerous instances in corroboration of this opinion may be met with in most physiological works, in which abundant evidence exists, illustrative of the low condition of mental power in those children who have dated their origin from the drunken orgies of their parents; and the frequent and oft-remarked deficiency in mental calibre of the eldest child of a family to the rest, has been shrewdly attributed to the more sensual conditions under which its existence was commenced.

That the opposite condition of things is referrible to a similar mode of argument, is shown by the fact that the rudiments of the intellectual frame, may, by error of education, or a too early and violent impulse towards what is sublime and beautiful in morals and in mind, be fostered into madness.

91. Henry Maudsley, *The Tyranny of Organization*

(Excerpt from *Body and Mind*, London: Macmillan & Co., 1873, pp. 75–6.)

The insane neurosis which the child inherits in consequence of its parent's insanity is as surely a defect of physical nature as is the epileptic neurosis to which it is so closely allied. It is an indisputable though extreme fact that certain human beings are born with such a native deficiency of mind that all the training and education in the world will not raise them to the height of brutes; and I believe it to be not less true that, in consequence of evil ancestral influences, individuals are born with such a flaw or warp of nature that all the care in the world will not prevent them from being vicious or criminal, or becoming insane. Education, it is true, may do much; and the circumstances of life may do much; but we cannot forget that the foundations on which the acquisitions of education must rest are not acquired, but inherited. No one can escape the tyranny of his organization; no one can elude the destiny that is innate in him, and which unconsciously and irrestibly shapes his ends, even when he believes that he is determining them with consummate foresight and skill. A well-grounded and comprehensive theory of mind must recognize and embrace these facts.

92. Henry Maudsley, *The Ineffectiveness of Education*

(Excerpt from *Responsibility in Mental Disease*, London: Henry S. King & Co., 1874, pp. 20–1.)

So much in human development being due to education, it is evident that the training which a person undergoes must have a great influence on the growth of his intellect and the formation of his character. What he shall be and what he shall do will be determined in great measure by what has been done to bring into full activity the capabilities of his nature. But great as is the power of education, it is yet a sternly limited power; it is limited by the capacity of the individual nature, and can only work within this larger or smaller circle of necessity. No training in the world will avail to elicit grapes from thorns or figs from thistles; in like manner, no mortal can transcend his nature; and it will ever be impossible to raise a stable superstructure of intellect and character on bad natural foundations. Education can plainly act only, first, within the conditions imposed by the species, and, secondly, within the conditions imposed by the individual organization: can only, in the former case, determine what is predetermined in the organization of the nervous system and of the bodily machinery in connection with it—cannot, for example, ever teach a man to fly like a bird, or see like an eagle, or run like an antelope; can only again, in the latter case, make actual the potentialities of the individual nature—cannot make a Socrates or a Shakespeare of every being born into the world.

There was a foundation of fact, though not the fact of which he dreamed, in the speculations of the astrologer who believed that by observation of the star in the ascendant at the time of a mortal's birth he might predict his destiny. He was conscious of a fate in human life, but he failed to see that it was the fate made for a man by his inheritance.

93. Henry Maudsley, *Deterioration of Race*

(Excerpt from *Responsibility in Mental Disease*, London: Henry S. King & Co., 1874, pp. 46–8.)

When the insane temperament has been developed in its most marked form, we must acknowledge that the hereditary predisposition has assumed the character of deterioration of race, and that the individual represents the beginning of a degeneracy which, if not checked by favourable circumstances, will go on increasing from generation to generation and end finally in the extreme degeneracy of idiocy. With the occurrence of idiocy there is happily the extinction of the degenerate variety, for with it come impotence and sterility. Beneath and beyond the little span of nature which lies within the reach of our faculties, with which our senses bring us into relation, there is a power which inspires evolution on earth, taking good care that its work is done, no matter at what cost in time, in prodigality of life, in individual suffering, animal or human.

Let it be observed now that in its less marked forms the insane neurosis is by no means the unmixed evil which it might on a superficial consideration appear to be. When we look into the matter it is truly remarkable how much mankind has been indebted for its originating impulses and for special displays of talent, if not of génius, to individuals who themselves or whose parents have sprung from families in which there has been some predisposition to insanity. Such persons are apt to seize on and pursue the bypaths of thought which have been overlooked by more stable intellects, and so, by throwing a side light upon things, to discover unthought of relations. One observes this tendency of mind even in those of them who have no particular genius or talent; for they have a novel way of looking at things, do not run in the common groove of action or follow the ordinary routine of thought and feeling, but discover in their remarks a certain originality and perhaps singularity, sometimes at a very early period of life. This is illustrated now and then by a remarkable aptitude for punning and by strange quirks and cranks of fancy, such as a person not so peculiarly gifted might die before he could invent. Notable again is the emancipated way in which some of them discuss, as if they were problems of mechanics, objects or events round which the associations of ideas and feelings have thrown a glamour of conventional sentiment. In regard to most beliefs they are usually more or less heterodox or heretical, though often not constant, being apt to swing round suddenly from one point to a quite opposite point of the compass of belief. It is a fact too that they frequently display remarkable æsthetic feeling and special artistic talents and aptitudes. An intensity of feeling and energy characterizes them: inspired with strong faith in the opinions which they adopt, they exhibit much zeal and energy in the propagation of them, and so become useful as reformers; they are possessed with a degree of fanaticism which bears them on to their end, reckless of the most formidable obstacles.

94. Henry Maudsley, *Evolution and Inheritance*

(Excerpt from *Responsibility in Mental Disease*, London: Henry S. King & Co., 1874, pp. 108–10.)

No doubt, from the evolutionist's point of view, circumstance has very materially controlled human and all other character because it has, under the physiological law of infinitesimally slight steps of change, controlled all bodily and nerve organisation. But what does this imply? Not the fallacious idea that circumstance has at any time impressed itself upon and changed organisation and character: but that, during incalculable time, *the* organisation and therefore *the* character which was best fitted* for its environ-

* The most felicitous phrase of our epoch, 'survival of the fittest,' we owe to Herbert Spencer. It applies as much to the world of morals as to the world of intellect and feeling and action.

ment ultimately survived—a wholly different matter. The Bushman, as Mr. Spencer argues, has stronger eye-sight than the European; but circumstance, that is, distant danger to be shunned, or food to be secured, did not strengthen his vision; he, and such progeny as took after him, survived because they had stronger vision than their fellows. The trees on which the giraffe feeds do not elongate its neck and tongue; the giraffe which had the longest neck and longest tongue was fittest to survive. Now change of circumstance, I venture to say, could no more change human 'nerve' and character in one, or many, generations than, during one or many generations, short trees could shorten a giraff's neck or tall trees lengthen it. The evolution argument is altogether in favour of the dominant potency of organisation and heredity; for it is improbable that the 'nerve' and character of many millions of years admit of material change in a single generation. Speaking broadly, and keeping aloof from detail and from psychological refinements, we may look on character as compounded mainly of endowments and propensities. The endowments or natural gifts of nerve lie at the foundation of character: circumstance and volition can add but little to these and can take but little from them. The propensities comprise the uses, including methods and aims, to which the endowments are put; undoubtedly these are much under the influence of circumstance and volition, but they are based on the endowments which lie behind them. Village Hampdens, mute inglorious Miltons, and bloodless Cromwells do *not* sleep in the graves of the rude forefathers of the hamlet. Burns was not a peasant; his father was a reading contemplative recluse; increasing knowledge shows that his ancestors filled high and responsible positions. The burial-place of Thomas Carlyle contains numerous heraldic evidences of distinguished forerunners.

We may with advantage draw illustrations from bodily organisation and actions. Of two men, apparently similar in physical conformation and size, one is capable of great athletic feats, the other is not. Circumstance, even in the form of training, has comparatively little to do with the adequacy of the one and the inadequacy of the other. The explanation is, that the two men possess by inheritance two wholly different skeletons; their bones are differently formed and are differently put together. In one man, as in women generally, the bones are more or less smooth, consequently the muscles are attached to them with less firmness, and act on them with less power. In the other man's rougher bones numerous projections spring out, as it were, to meet their appropriate muscles, and so give to them an efficiency which normal circumstances might modify but which it cannot materially add to or take away. The brain and its powers and properties are not less determined by inheritance than are bone and muscle. It is with man as with animals: no circumstance could give marked swiftness to the hereditary cart-horse and its progeny, or slowness and strength to the hereditary racer.

95. Henry Maudsley, *Character and Will*

(Excerpt from *Responsibility in Mental Disease*, London: Henry S. King & Co., 1874, pp. 272–5.)

It would be quite useless to inculcate rules for self-formation upon one whose character had taken a certain mould of development; for character is a slow and gradual growth through action in relation to the circumstances of life; it cannot be fashioned suddenly and through reflection only. A man can no more will than he can speak without having learned to do so, nor can he be taught volition any more than he can be taught speech except by practice. It was a pregnant saying, that the history of a man is his character; to which one might add that whosoever would transform a character must undo a life history. The fixed and unchanging laws by which events come to pass hold sway in the domain of mind as in every other domain of nature.

A striking illustration of the difficulty of realising the reign of law in the development of character and in the events of human life is afforded by the criticisms of those who have blamed Goethe because he made Werter commit suicide, instead of making him attain to clearer insight, calmer feeling, and a tranquil life after his sorrows; had they reflected well they must have perceived that suicide was the natural and inevitable termination of the morbid sorrows of such a nature. It was the final explosion of a train of antecedent preparations, an event which was as certain to come as the death of the flower with a canker at its heart. Suicide or madness is the natural end of a morbidly sensitive nature, with a feeble will, unable to contend with the hard experiences of life. You might as well, in truth, preach moderation to the hurricane as talk philosophy to one whose antecedent life has conducted him to the edge of madness.

I cannot but think that moral philosophers have sometimes exaggerated greatly the direct power of the will, as an abstract entity, over the thoughts and feelings, without at the same time having taken sufficient account of the slow and gradual way in which the concrete will itself must be formed. The culminating effort of mental development, the final blossom of human evolution, it betokens a physiological development as real, though not as apparent, as that which distinguishes the nervous system of man from that of one of the lower animals. Time and systematic exercise are necessary to the gradual organisation of the structure which shall manifest it in full function. No one can resolve successfully by a mere effort of will to think in a certain way, or to feel in a certain way, or even, which is easier, to act always in accordance with certain rules; but he can, by acting upon the circumstances which will in turn act upon him, imperceptibly modify his character: he can thus, by calling external circumstances to his aid, learn to withdraw his mind from one train of thought and feeling, the activity of which will thereupon subside, and can direct it to another train of thought and feeling, which will thereupon become active, and so by constant watchfulness over himself and by habitual exercise of will in the required direction, bring about insensibly the formation of such a habit of thought, feeling and action as he may wish to attain unto. He can make his character grow by degrees to the ideal which he sets before himself.

The development of the power of co-ordinating in complex action various distinct muscles for the accomplishment of a special end is truly the development of the volitional power of such purposive movements; in like manner the development of the power of co-ordinating ideas and feelings for the achievement of a special life-aim is the development of the volitional power to achieve it. There is a multitude of concrete volitions, but there is no abstract will apart from the particular volitions. Just in fact as an individual gains by practice a particular power over the muscles of his body, associating them in action for the performance of complicated acts, which, without previous training, he could no more perform than he could fly, and rendering his muscles in this regard habitually obedient to the dictates of his will; so can he gain by practice a particular power over the thoughts and feelings of his mind, associating them in action for the accomplishment of a definite purpose in life, and rendering them in this regard habitually obedient to the dictates of the will in the pursuit of its ideal. Striking examples of the gradual development of the power of will over both movements and ideas under most unfavourable conditions are witnessed in our idiot asylums; the records of these establishments showing that there is hardly an idiot so low that he cannot be so far improved by patient and laborious culture as to acquire some power of self-government both in regard to his body and his mind. Great then as the power of will unquestionably is, when rightly developed, we ought not to lose sight of the fact that its development is effected only by the gradual education of a continued exercise in relation to the circumstances of life.

96. Henry Maudsley, *Prudent and Imprudent Marriage*

(Excerpt from *Responsibility in Mental Disease*, London: Henry S. King & Co., 1874, pp. 276–7.)

It would scarcely be an exaggeration to say that few persons go mad, save from palpable physical causes, who do not show more or less plainly by their gait, manner, gestures, habits of thought, feeling and action, that they have a sort of predestination to madness. The inherited liability may be strong or weak; it may be so weak as hardly to peril sanity amidst the most adverse circumstances of life, or so strong as to issue in an outbreak of madness amidst the most favourable external circumstances. Now it is certain that if we were interested in the breeding of a variety of animals, we should not think of breeding from a stock which was wanting in those qualities that were the highest characteristics of the species: we should not willingly select for breeding purposes a hound that was deficient in scent, or a greyhound that was deficient in speed, or a racehorse that could neither stay well nor gallop fast. Is it right then to sanction propagation of his kind by an individual who is wanting in that which is the highest attribute of man—a sound and stable mental constitution? I note this as a question to be seriously faced and sincerely answered, although not expecting that mankind, in the present state of their development, will either seriously face it or sincerely answer it.

When one considers the reckless way in which persons, whatever the defects of their mental and bodily constitution, often get married, without sense of responsibility for the miseries which they entail upon those who will be the heirs of their infirmities, without regard, in fact, to anything but their own present gratification, one is driven to think either that man is not the preeminently reasoning and moral animal which he claims to be, or that there is in him an instinct which is deeper than knowledge. He has persuaded himself, rightly or wrongly, that in his case there is in the feeling of love between the sexes something of so sacred and mysterious a character as to justify disregard to consequences in marriage. We have only to look at the large part which love fills in novels, poetry and painting, and to consider what a justification of unreason in life it is held to be, to realise what a hold it has on him in his present state of development, and what a repugnance there would be to quench its glow by cold words of reason. At bottom, however, there is nothing particularly holy about it; on the contrary, it is a passion which man shares with other animals; and when its essential nature and function are regarded, we shall nowhere find stronger evidence of a community of nature between man and animals.

97. Andrew Wynter, *Eccentricity and Latent Insanity*

(Excerpt from *The Borderlands of Insanity*, London: Robert Hardwicke, 1875, pp. 45–6.)

When we remember the number of persons in the country whose insanity is undoubted, it will be admitted that there must be a very large number of individuals who inherit either the disease direct, or are saturated with the seeds of nervous disorders, which only require some exciting cause to force them into vigorous growth. It is this class of incipient lunatics with whom we wish to deal in these following pages—persons whose unsoundness of mind is mistaken by the world either for mere eccentricity or for moral perversity. Going about the world with a clean mental bill of health, as it were, these unfortunate individuals are the cause of more misery to themselves and to the world than the proclaimed lunatic, for the reason that society cannot restrain them from acts as destructive to the well-being of others as to themselves.

98. Henry Maudsley, *Inheritance and Destiny*

(Excerpt from *The Pathology of Mind*, London: Macmillan & Co., 1879, p. 88.)

Whence comes this individuality of nature? Without doubt it comes from the same source as the individuality of bodily conformation, of gait, of features—that is to say, from ancestors. There is a destiny made for each one by his inheritance; he is the necessary organic consequent of certain organic antecedents; and it is impossible he should escape the tyranny of his organization. All nations in all ages have virtually confessed this truth, which has affected in an important manner systems of religion, and social and political institutions. The institution of caste among the Hindoos owed its origin to it; and there can be little doubt that the philosophy of that large sect among them which taught the perpetual re-birth of mortals and the development in this life of the deeds done in a former state of being, holding the antecedent life of a being to be his destiny, was founded on a recognition of hereditary action—of the fact that the present nature has descended from the past by regular laws of development or of degeneration. The dread, inexorable destiny which plays so grand and terrible a part in Grecian tragedy, and which Grecian heroes are represented as struggling manfully against, knowing all the while that their struggles were foredoomed to be futile, embodied an instinctive perception of the law by which the sins of the father are visited upon the children unto the third and fourth generations. Deep in his inmost heart everybody has an instinctive feeling that he has been predestined from all eternity to be what he is, and could not, antecedent conditions having been what they were, have been different. It was a proverb in Israel that when the fathers had eaten sour grapes the children's teeth were set on edge; and Solomon justly proclaimed it to be one of the virtues of a good man that he left an inheritance to his children's children. In village communities, where the people remain stationary, and where the characters of fathers and grandfathers are remembered or are handed down by tradition, peculiarities of character in an individual are often attributed to some hereditary bias, and so accounted for: he got it from his fore-elders, it is said, and the aberration has allowance made for it.

99. Henry Maudsley, *The Formation of Character*

(Excerpt from *The Pathology of Mind*, London: Macmillan & Co., 1879, pp. 86–7.

Thoughts, feelings, and actions leave behind them residua which are organized in the nerve-centres, and thenceforth so modify their manner of development as to constitute an acquired nature, wherefore what we habitually feel, think, and do foreordains in great part what we shall feel, think, and do; and as moral manifestations throughout life thus determine corresponding physical organization, it is evident that a steadily acting moral cause of insanity is all the while producing its physical changes in the occult recesses of the supreme nerve-centres of mind. In fact the brain that is exercised so regularly in a given manner as to acquire during health a strong peculiarity or bias of action is sometimes more liable to disorder in effect of this bias; and when the disorder is produced by an independent cause, the bias or habit will, according to its good or evil character, help to overcome or to aggravate its effect. When, for example, insanity is the consummate exaggeration of a particular vice of character, the morbid symptoms mark a definite habit of morbid nutrition in the supreme nerve-centres—a gradually effected modification of the mental organization along a morbid line. On the other hand, the brain that is exercised habitually in the best way acquires a strong and healthy habit of thought, feeling, and volition, which counteracts the effects of a morbid strain. On the whole, perhaps, a man had more need to practise good habits than to meditate sound principles, if it were a question between the two; but it is not, forasmuch as meditation on sound principles is a preparation for the formation of good habits that have not been taught.

100. Henry Maudsley, *The Germs of Insanity*

(Excerpt from *The Pathology of Mind*, London: Macmillan & Co., 1879, pp. 83–4.)

No man knoweth his own character, which is ever under his inspection: how then can he know that of his neighbour, when he has only brief and passing glimpses into it?

Great mistakes are oftentimes made in fixing upon the supposed causes of the disease in particular cases; some single prominent event, which was perhaps one in a train of events, being selected as fitted by itself to explain the catastrophe. The truth is that in the great majority of cases there has been a concurrence of steadily operating conditions within and without, not a single effective cause. All the conditions, whether they are called passive or active, which conspire to the production of an effect are alike causes, alike agents; all the conditions, therefore, which co-operate in a given case in the production of disease, whether they lie in the individual or in his surroundings, must be regarded as alike causes. When we are told that a man has become mentally deranged from sorrow, need, sickness, or any other adversity, we have not learned much if we are content to stay there: how is it that another man who undergoes an exactly similar adversity does not go mad? The entire causes could not have been the same where the effects were so different. What we want to have laid bare is the conspiracy of conditions, in the individual and outside him, by which a mental pressure, inoperative in the one case, has weighed so disastrously in the other; and that is information which a complete and exact biography of him, such as never yet has been written of any person, not neglecting the consideration of his hereditary antecedents, could alone give us. Were all the circumstances, internal and external, scanned closely and weighed accurately it would be seen that there is no accident in madness; the disease, whatever form it had, and however many the concurrent conditions or successive links of its causation, would be traced as the inevitable consequence of its antecedents, just as the explosion of a train of gunpowder may be traced to its causes, whether the train of events of which it is the issue be long or short. The germs of insanity are most often latent in the foundations of the character, and the final outbreak is the explosion of a long train of antecedent preparations.

101. Henry Maudsley, *Eccentricity*

(Excerpt from *Natural Causes and Supernatural Seemings*, London: Kegan Paul, Trench, Trubner & Co., 1886, pp. 152–3.)

There is a large class of peculiar persons, much differing from one another, who, agreeing in being unlike the majority of people of their age and country in their modes of thought, feeling, and action, have their several tendencies to deviation from the common nature described as eccentricity; instead of moving in the common orbit of human thought and feeling, they manifest impulses to start from it—are eccentric. All insane persons are necessarily eccentric, but not all eccentric persons are insane. From a practical point of view, any one may be permitted to be as eccentric as he pleases, to go as much as he likes off the customary track of thinking, feeling, and doing, so long as his deviations or vagaries do not compromise social order; but there is a point of nonconformity at which the body social must interfere to protect itself, if it is to continue in well-being. Unlimited licence for the erratic individual to do as he likes would be incompatible with the holding together of the framework of society. From another point of view, eccentricities of thought and conduct have a special philosophic interest, inasmuch as from time to time they turn out to be valuable mental variations that initiate new and useful developments; rarely and exceptionally, no doubt, but still here and there, and now and then.

It is a matter of curious observation that remarkable special sensibilities and brilliant ability of thought or performance in particular departments of knowledge or art go along sometimes with signal eccentricity; an extraordinary development of one part of the mind being by no means incompatible with an irregular and unstable condition of other parts of the mind.

102. Furneaux Jordan, *Body and Character*

(Excerpt from *Character as Seen in Body and Parentage*, London: Kegan Paul, Trench, Trubner & Co., 1886, pp. 42–7, 7.)

The skeleton gives to the human figure its height and general conformation. The external appearance of the body is determined by the skin with its varying degrees of pigment, covering hair, and underlying fat—fat being a distinctly cutaneous appendage. Which is the more attractive, a beautiful skin and complexion, or a good figure, is a question of perennial interest. The Northern King in Tennyson's 'Princess' declares that men hunt women 'for their skins:' some men prefer to hunt them for their bones. So far as general configuration is concerned, muscle or flesh plays a slighter part.

I have endeavoured to show that there are in both sexes two leading groups of tendencies in character. I venture to affirm that there are also two general tendencies in the grouping of bodily characteristics. Neither bodily nor mental characteristics are miscellaneous collections of fragments; they run together in more or less uniform clusters. With one particular kind of skeleton and skin there will be associated a particular kind of nervous organisation, and therefore one particular kind of character. In the active and less impassioned bias the skin tends to be rosy or less pigmented; the hair growth is slighter—slighter on the head and eyebrows in women; less extended or, if extended, more sparingly distributed on the face in man. Mr. Havelock Ellis, in his able work on 'Man and Woman', remarks that women, as regards hair growth and other matters also, have gone beyond men in the path of evolution; if this be granted, the less impassioned woman, especially when endowed with high capacity and refined feeling, has travelled furthest from our remote ancestors. In the active temperament the spinal curves of dorsum and neck are markedly developed, giving, with some change in the position of the ribs, a distinctly convex or round or even globular appearance to the back.

In the more impassioned and less active temperament, on the other hand, it will be found that the skin is more opaque, and rosiness, if present, will be less transparent or even, though not unpleasingly so, muddy. The hair growth of head and eyebrows, and in men, of the face, is longer and more thickly planted. The construction of the skeleton too is different: the spinal curves are less marked and therefore the head is carried more or less upright—it may be defiantly and inartistically upright; the dorsum or back has a flat or even concave appearance between the shoulders—the concavity being perceptible through closely fitting garments in both sexes. The ribs seem to throw themselves backwards, projecting posteriorly on both sides of the spinal column as if striving to embrace it; in the less impassioned figure the ribs and thorax generally tend to fall forwards away from the spine. The upper limbs, being attached to the ribs, stand, with them, either backwards or forwards.

It is curious that with the pinker skin and more curved spine there is a somewhat greater tendency to obesity. Since making this statement in the earlier editions of this book I have, as an observer, been not a little gratified to meet with an observation of Goethe's that 'brown skins rarely grow fat.' It must not be forgotten however that alcoholic drinks it may be even in small quantities tend to produce fat whatever the temperament may be.

I have so far kept marked examples only in view; but in all classifications, of either bodily or mental characteristics, sharp lines of divisions do not exist. Intermediate—often happy intermediate—gradations are constantly met with.

It is interesting to note that the stronger spinal curves of the less impassioned figure are more in favour with artists—often indeed exaggerated by them—than the more, and possibly ungracefully, erect pose of the impassioned. It has been already remarked that one authority in art states that in a well-formed woman a plumb-line dropped from the tip of the nose should fall in front of the toes. A marked cervical or neck curve, although it involves a slight stoop, gives greater fulness to the front of the neck, which artists consider to enhance a woman's beauty. Strong curvature of the neck bones (vertebræ) shortens the neck and also throws the head forwards; marked obesity gives the *appearance* of a short neck.

In women it is perhaps somewhat easier to judge of the nervous organisation and character from the nature of the hair growth, while in men the skeleton gives, it may be, the more reliable information. Baldness of both scalp and eyebrows is common and frequently early in men of both temperaments; the face growth is more persistent. In the less impassioned man the face hair is often irregular or patchy, and tends to be more abundant on the upper lip and chin and perhaps the margin of the jaw. But not very rarely the individual hairs though not thickly planted are of large diameter, and if evenly distributed may give the delusive appearance of somewhat massive growth. Nevertheless, even in these cases, the hair-area less frequently extends so far upwards along the cheek or so far downwards along the neck as in the more impassioned. Probably a baby which takes after a more impassioned parent will have, even at birth, a more marked head of hair than its brother or sister who takes after a less impassioned father or mother.

For various reasons precipitate judgment is unwise. Not only is early baldness of head-hair and of eyebrows common in men, and may, though much less frequently, occur in women, but certain states of health occasionally thin or remove the hair. Very fine hair, especially if also of light colour, in a woman's eyebrow or on a man's face may easily give the impression that the growth is more sparing than it really is. On the other hand, an erroneous judgment may easily be formed, because, when the hair-growth is not thickly planted it may nevertheless seem to be so if it is uncut and uncared for, or if the individual hairs are of large diameter and there is no tendency to baldness. It is the relative numbers, and area, and vigour of growth, not the size of individual hairs which chiefly indicate a given variety of nervous organisation. The man whose face is kept in order by shaving twice a week has distinctly less impassioned nerve than he who needs to shave twice a day if he spends his evenings in society.

In judging of the figure, or skeleton-structure, still more caution is needed. It is important to note that carrying weights habitually in early life, early exhausting habits, or labour, or ailment, or injury, and of course advancing years, tell unequivocally on the bony framework. Slight rickets in childhood increasing the spinal curves of boys and girls is not at all rare. More or less dorsal convexity and stoop is frequent in hereditary lung trouble. When marked skeleton curves are associated with abundant hair growth it will usually be found that one of these causes has been at work. It is well to note here what seems to me an important difference between the convexity left by rickets and that belonging to phthisical proclivities: in the latter there is no change in nerve action, no lessened intensity of passion; it is quite otherwise with the curves of rickets, for these are often associated with diminution of feeling. The explanation is obvious. Certain chemical elements are identical in bone and in nerve substance; if, in early life, they are deficient in one they are deficient in the other—hence arises a thwarted transmission of parental traits of character. I have observed one compensation in the slightly ricketty conformation: slow ossification leaves a large frontal skull and larger corresponding brain, and with them frequently an unusual intellectual agility.

Now and then the whole body is inclined forwards from the hip—a posture which must not be confounded with the true dorsal curve. It must not however be supposed that the characteristic dorsal convexity (vertical and transverse) is as a general rule due to mere debility. Its subjects, generation after generation, frequently possess robust health while even the most stiffly erect individuals, and their forerunners, are often ailing.

Throughout these pages it is taken for granted that bodily organisation and character are, in the main, matters of inheritence; that we are human beings because our parents were; that we are what we are mainly because they and their forerunners were what they were. Many causes however may interfere before birth with the purity of transmission; after birth, too, organisation, affecting subsequent character, is frequently modified by ailment, accident, and general surroundings.

The most important teaching, then, of these pages is, that a given cluster of characteristics run, in equal or unequal degrees, together in the passionless temperament, and that another given cluster run as uniformily in the impassioned. Next in importance is the conclusion that each temperament has its cluster of special, distinctive, bodily signs. The more marked the temperament the more marked are the signs.

Chapter VIII

Feminine Vulnerability

103. John Haslam, *Feminine Confessions*

(Excerpt from *Considerations on the Moral Management of Insane Persons*, London: R. Hunter, 1817, pp. 4–5.)

In females who become insane the disease is often connected with the peculiarities of their sex: of such circumstances those who are not of the medical profession would be unable to judge, and delicacy would prevent the relations from communicating with such persons. It ought to be fully understood that the education, character, and established habits of medical men, entitle them to the confidence of their patients: the most virtuous women unreservedly communicate to them their feelings and complaints, when they would shudder at imparting their disorders to a male of any other profession; or even to their own husbands. Medical science, associated with decorous manners, has generated this confidence, and rendered the practitioner the friend of the afflicted, and the depositary of their secrets.

104. George Man Burrows, *Menstrual Discharge*

(Excerpt from *Commentaries on Insanity*, London: Underwood, 1828, pp. 146–8.)

Various sanguiferous discharges, whether periodical, occasional, or accidental, greatly influence the functions of the mind. Some, by their suppression operating as exciting causes; others, by their influx proving critical. Among these are classed, 1, the menstrual—2, hæmorrhoidal—3, varicose—and 4, nasal and other hæmorrhages.

These are all complicated with the functions of the circulation, though the menstrual can scarcely be ranked with the others, since it is one of the most important natural functions,—while the rest are all morbid actions of the vascular system.

Every body of the least experience must be sensible of the influence of menstruation on the operations of the mind. In truth, it is the moral and physical barometer of the female constitution. Both the accession and subsequent regularity of the menses depend on the due equilibrium of the vascular and nervous systems. If the balance be disturbed, so likewise will be the uterine action and periodical discharge; though it does not follow that the mind always sympathises with its irregularities so as disturb the cerebral functions. Yet the functions of the brain are so intimately connected with the uterine system, that the interruption of any one process which the latter has to perform in the human economy may implicate the former.

Whether this evacuation be delayed beyond the period when it ought to appear, or be obstructed after being once established, or a female be arrived at the critical age when it ceases entirely; or whether the state of utero-gestation, or parturition, or lactation, be going on, they are all conditions in which the vascular system is involved.

When the menses are stopped, a sudden or gradual plethora sometimes follows in a system long accustomed to the discharge, and a consecutive local determination to some other part often ensues.

Ere the system accommodates itself to this innovation, the seeds of various disorders are sown; and especially where any predisposition obtains, the hazard of insanity is imminent.

The state of utero-gestation is a state of local determination, from which the general system seeks relief by uterine hæmorrhage. Or sometimes this local determination influences the nervous system, and superinduces those phantasies called longings, which are decided perversions or aberrations of the judgment, though perhaps the simplest modifications of intellectual derangement. These anomalous feelings have been referred to uterine irritation from mere gravitation, and so they may be; but they first induce a greater determination of blood to the uterus and its contents, and then to the brain, through the reciprocal connexion and action existing between the two organs.

Amenorrhœa or obstruction of the menstrual flux is, however, by no means so frequent a cause of insanity as is supposed. I am quite convinced that amenorrhœa is oftener a consequence of cerebral disturbance; for in numerous cases, derangement of the mind precedes the menstrual obstruction, and the discharge returns as the functions of the brain and other organs return to a healthy state. Emmenagogues, therefore, and other remedies given in insanity (vulgarly) to force the menses, may do a great deal of mischief.

Before any remedy is prescribed with this view, it behoves us to ascertain whether the amenorrhœa should be considered as a cause or an effect of the mental derangement. That it is often a cause there can be no doubt; because terror, the sudden application of cold, &c., have occasioned the instant cessation of the menses, upon which severe cerebral affections, or instant insanity, has supervened; and the senses have been restored with the discharge.

The critical period, as it is called, when menstruation ceases, is certainly a period favourable to the development of mental aberration. The whole economy of the constitution at that epoch again undergoes a revolution. The moral character, at the age when the menses naturally cease, is much changed to what it was on their first access; and every care or anxiety produces a more depressing and permanent impression on the mind. There is neither so much vital nor mental energy to resist the effects of the various adverse circumstances which it is the lot of most to meet with in the interval between puberty and the critical period.

Besides, as an author has observed, the age of pleasing in all females is then past, though in many the desire to please is not the less lively. The exterior alone loses its attractions, but vanity preserves its pretensions. It is now especially that jealousy exerts its empire, and becomes very often a cause of delirium. Many, too, at this epoch imbibe very enthusiastic religious notions; but more have recourse to the stimulus of strong cordials to allay the uneasy and nervous sensations peculiar to this time of life, and thus produce a degree of excitation equally dangerous to the equanimity of the moral feelings and mental faculties.

105. George Man Burrows, *Hysteria*

(Excerpt from *Commentaries on Insanity*, London: Underwood, 1828, pp. 191–3.)

Hysteria, which alternates with headache, vertigo, and epilepsy, sometimes degenerates into mania. Females only are generally supposed to be subjected to this affection; but males also are certainly occasionally affected by it. C. Piso, T. Willis, Sydenham, Boerhaave, Cullen, and the best authorities, attest this fact—a fact of considerable importance in the diagnosis of this disease.

Here, again, therefore, as in the acceptation and application of the word *apoplexia*, we are misled by the derivation; the radical of hysteria being ὑστερα, the uterus of vulca.

Nervous susceptible women between puberty and thirty years of age, and clearly the single more so than the married, are most frequently visited by hysteria; and such constitutions have always a greater aptitude to strong mental emotions, which, on repetition, will superinduce mental derangement, or perhaps epilepsy.

When, however, men are subject to the hysteric passion, an accession of mania is more to be apprehended than when women are so affected; because the nervous temperament is thereby characterised more strongly than is usual in the male sex, in whom, comparatively with the female sex, it is certainly a very rare disease.

In a disorder so well known, a description of the corporeal symptoms is needless; but many will be recognised as indicative of sanguineous determination to the brain and other parts. All the exciting causes of it are those which are necessary to this effect.

Salivation, which is supposed to be derived from an increased action in the capillary circulation, is a frequent symptom in hysteria. Sydenham remarks, that he has often known salivation attend for a whole week in this disease; and this is also a frequent symptom both in mania and melancholia, and also in hypochondriasis. Either an excessive flow of tears or of urine is a very common symptom and termination of this malady: this is only determination to other parts.

Every thing which diminishes the inordinate action of the heart, and relieves the over-distended vessels of the head, removes, and often instantly, the spasm ond other symptoms of the disorder.

Thus, a great flow of tears or of urine, discharge of offending ingesta from the stomach, unlacing of stays or bandages which compress too tightly the viscera, artificial or spontaneous hæmorrhages, affusion of cold water, particularly on the head, cold drink, fear, &c., by any of which actions the circulation is equalised, will terminate the affection.

Delirium is a common symptom of hysteria; and this symptom is prolonged sometimes beyond the removal of the spasm or paroxysm. The functions of the brain are probably only sympathetically affected; but as in all other sympathetic affections, if often repeated, the brain at length retains the morbid action, and insanity is developed.

Some go so far as to assert, that hysteria is of that class of maladies which, wherever it is manifested, betrays a maniacal diathesis. Occasional hysteria, however, in young and susceptible females whose nervous systems are always highly irritable, may certainly occur without any such suspicion. But habitual hysteria clearly approximates to insanity. It should, therefore, receive serious attention, and be as speedily as possible removed; more especially if it be complicated, as it often is, with hypochondriasis. And if this affection attack a male, double precaution should be taken lest it be converted into mental derangement.

106. Alfred Beaumont Maddock, *The Education of Women*

(Excerpt from *On Mental and Nervous Disorders*, London: Simpkin, Marshall & Co., 1854, pp. 16–17.)

In reading the prospectuses of the various educational establishments, from ragged schools upwards, through dame schools, day schools, seminaries, academies, colleges, and halls, which are so profusely distributed and advertised, we are struck with the immense amount of human learning which is proposed to be crammed into one small head—

> and still the wonder grew,
> That one small head should carry all he knew.

The arts, the classics, the sciences are all and each, in their several multifarious departments, to be radically taught and thoroughly conveyed to every individual. Studies, any one branch of which is the life-long object of the undivided attention of a professor, are to slide fluently from the tongue of some simpering Miss; languages, in number sufficient to convey a courier through all the countries of Europe, without a dictionary, are added to the list. The magic pencil of Turner is to be imitated in landscape drawing; the exquisite harmonies which emanate from the volant fingers of Sterndale Bennett, or Moscheles, are to find their ready parallel on the school piano. The calculating Bidder himself, is to be rivalled in his own peculiar line: and in short, from humble crochet, up to astronomy, all is to be embraced by one expansive mind, and Admirable Crichtons, are to be manufactured by the gross. More strange still it is that the victims of all this mental persecution are generally of the softer sex; thus daringly violating those natural laws of organization, which have fated the cerebral structure of woman, less qualified for these severe ordeals, than those of her brother man.

Without intending to enter into the oft-repeated argument of the relative superiority of the sexes, yet observation enables us to affirm, that in the higher powers of imagination, as well as in the severity and strictness of the reasoning faculties, the female mind must succumb to the larger scope and appliances of the male; a comparatively few instances to the contrary may be adduced, but a few exceptions do not disprove a rule. Witness the result of those powers which are more extensively cultivated by the female sex, the sister arts of music and of painting:—among the thousands of fair fingers which have sounded the strings of the harp, or have rattled over the keyboard of the pianoforte, how many have produced those glorious harmonic combinations which characterize a Handel or a Beethoven; or in painting have approached to the gorgeous splendour of a Titian or a Reubens, or to the exquisite grace and tenderness of a Raffaelle or a Correggio? Further, in throwing a rapid yet admiring glance over the poetic effusions of the softer sex, among much to praise and to delight, we seek in vain for the homely vigour of Burns, the sonorous majesty of Milton, or the exquisite universality of Shakspere.

107. Alfred Beaumont Maddock, *Insanity and Morbid Conditions of the Generative Apparatus*

(Excerpt from *On Mental and Nervous Disorders*, London: Simpkin, Marshall & Co., 1854, pp. 177–9.)

That the reproductive organs, with the urinary apparatus in close contiguity therewith, must partake of the ordinary pathological results, when unduly, unseasonably, or exorbitantly excited, seems a mere self-evident truism to affirm. Not alone are they necessarily subject to the usual advent of those physical diseases which are the inheritance of frail humanity, but also are they closely interwoven with erratic and disordered intellectual, as well as moral manifestations. In the male sex, these morbid associations arise principally, from real or fancied impotence, or from nervous exhaustion produced by too frequent, unnatural, or protracted indulgence in those sacrifices appertaining to the rites of the Paphian goddess; and in the female, in addition to the same prolific sources of derangement, from the peculiar destiny that she is intended by nature to fulfil, as the future mother of the human race. If, from each or any of the above-mentioned causes, the normal and healthy functions of this most important part of the animal economy are destroyed, or even deranged, both health and enjoyment are necessarily lost, or diminished.

In no disease whatever is a man so thoroughly conscious of his own pitiable condition; in none is he so much the victim of his own reflections as in those connected with sexual impediments. Mysterious in their nature, delicate in their manifestations, and secret in their cause they too generally escape the observation, or elude the inquiry of the practitioner; and, in truth, it may be affirmed that too little importance, and far too small an amount of investigation, have been bestowed upon these most grievous and depressing maladies. By the unaccountable neglect which this interesting branch of medical science has experienced at the hands of those, who from previous education, physiological knowledge, and social and moral opportunity, were obviously most fitted for its elucidation, it has been, as it were, forced under the protection of shameless and extortionate empirics, who, from the peculiar delicacy and secrecy under which such subjects have been shrouded, have been enabled to amass wealth, from the threefold miserable victims of debility, ignorance, and rapacity.

The astonishing effect which a morbid condition of the generative apparatus produces on every faculty of the mind, would seem almost incredible, were it not that testimony, unhappily too abundant, exists of its truth. With failure of all the muscular powers, with haggard or bloated countenance, ulceration in various parts of the body, dimness and imperfect vision, coldness of the spine, distressing faintness, and frequently with slow or hectic fever, the sufferer is dragged down miserably to an early grave. In addition to this brief enumeration of the various physical disorders to which he is subjected, the baneful ravages upon his mind are yet infinitely more deplorable. One of the earliest effects experienced in general, is failure of memory; diminution of sight, hearing, and readiness of perception, follow in due course; and impediment or loss of judgment proceeds in steady march. By gloom of the most afflicting and melancholy character he is perpetually overpowered. Society loses all its charms, and even that solitude for which he often pines, affords him no relief—there, brooding over his misfortunes, they become aggravated by the intensity of his own miserable reflections. With perpetual restlessness of body, and anguish and remorse preying on his heart, he either sinks into a condition of physical atrophy, or a state of mental idiocy more or less complete closes the horrid scene; unless goaded on by desperation and despair, he voluntarily deprives himself of his wretched and unenviable existence.

Deplorable as are the causes, conditions, and results of these unhappy maladies; truly miserable as are the too-oft self-imolating victims of voluptuous imprudence, yet some drops of honey remain at the bottom of that Circean cup, so fatally mingled with poisonous ingesta.

108. John Millar, *Amenorrhoea*

(Excerpt from *Hints on Insanity*, London: Henry Renshaw, 1861, p. 32.)

Mental derangement frequently occurs in young females from Amenorrhœa, especially in those who have any strong hereditary predisposition to insanity. The age of the patient, the absence of the accustomed uterine function, and the chlorotic look, will at once point to the cause of the mischief. Attention ought therefore to be directed to the establishment of the periodic discharge; and this we have always been able readily to effect by improving the general health, and by giving the ordinary mistura ferri three times a day, together with an aloetic pill at bed-time. The system is soon charged with blood, and an occasional warm hip-bath, or leeches to the pubis will accomplish all we desire, and be followed by complete mental recovery.

109. Henry Maudsley, *Suppression of the Menses*

(Excerpt from *Body and Mind*, London: Macmillan & Co., 1873, pp. 87–9.)

The monthly activity of the ovaries which marks the advent of puberty in women has a notable effect upon the mind and body; wherefore it may become an important cause of mental and physical derangement. Most women at that time are susceptible, irritable, and capricious, any cause of vexation affecting them more seriously than usual; and some who have the insane neurosis exhibit a disturbance of mind which amounts almost to disease. A sudden suppression of the menses has produced a direct explosion of insanity; or, occurring some time before an outbreak, it may be an important link in its causation. It is a matter also of common experience in asylums, that exacerbations of insanity often take place at the menstrual periods; but whether there is a particular variety of mental derangement connected with disordered menstruation, and, if so, what are its special features, we are not yet in a position to say positively. There is certainly a recurrent mania, which seems sometimes to have, in regard to its origin and the times of its attacks, a relation to the menstrual functions, suppression or irregularity of which often accompanies it; and it is an obvious presumption that the mania may be a sympathetic morbid effect of the ovarian and uterine excitement, and may represent an exaggeration of the mental irritability which is natural to women at that period. The patient becomes elated, hilarious, talkative, passing soon from that condition into a state of acute and noisy mania, which may last for two or three weeks or longer, and then sinking into a brief stage of more or less depression or confusion of mind, from which she awakens to calmness and clearness of mind. In vain we flatter ourselves with the hope of a complete recovery; after an interval of perfect lucidity, of varying duration in different cases, the attack recurs, goes through the same stages, and ends in the same way, only to be followed by other attacks, until at last, the mind being permanently weakened, there are no longer intervals of entire lucidity. Could we stop the attacks, the patient might still regain by degrees mental power; but we cannot. All the resources of our art fail to touch them, and I know no other form of insanity which, having so much the air of being curable, thus far defies all efforts to stay its course. We should be apt to conclude that it was connected with the menstrual function, were it not that periodicity is more or less the law of all nervous diseases, that its attacks often occur at uncertain intervals, and, more decisive still, that it is not confined to women, but occurs perhaps as often in men. Whether connected or not, however, in any way with the generative functions, it certainly presents features of relationship to epilepsy, and occurs where the insane neurosis exists; and if I were to describe it in a few words, I should designate it an epilepsy of the mind.

110. Henry Maudsley, *The Female Life Cycle*

(Excerpt from *Body and Mind*, London: Macmillan & Co., 1873, pp. 90–2.)

The natural cessation of menstruation at the change of life is accompanied by a revolution in the economy which is often trying to the mental stability of those who have a predisposition to insanity. The age of pleasing is past, but not always the desire, which, indeed, sometimes grows then more exacting; there are all sorts of anomalous sensations of bodily distress, attesting the disturbance of circulation and of nerve functions; and it is now that an insane jealousy and a propensity to stimulants are apt to appear, especially where there have been no children. When positive insanity breaks out, it usually has the form of profound melancholia, with vague delusions of an extreme character, as that the world is in flames, that it is turned upside down, that everything is changed, or that some very dreadful but undefined calamity has happened or is about to happen. The countenance has the expression of a vague terror and apprehension. In some cases short and transient paroxysms of excitement break the melancholy gloom. These usually occur at the menstrual periods, and may continue to do so for some time after the function has ceased. It is not an unfavourable form of insanity as regards probability of recovery under suitable treatment.

Continuing the consideration of the influence of the generative organs in the production of insanity, I come now to puerperal insanity. Under this name are sometimes confounded three distinct varieties of disease—that which occurs during pregnancy, that which follows parturition and is properly puerperal, and that which comes on months afterwards during lactation.* The insanity of pregnancy is, as a rule, of a marked melancholic type, with suicidal tendency; a degree of mental weakness or

* 'The Insanity of Pregnancy, Puerperal Insanity, and Insanity of Lactation.' By J. Batty Tuke, M.D.

apparent dementia being sometimes conjoined with it. Other cases, however, exhibit much moral perversion, perhaps an uncontrollable craving for stimulants, which we may regard as an exaggerated display of the fanciful cravings from which women suffer in the earlier months of pregnancy. We can hardly fail, indeed, to recognise a connection between the features of this form of insanity and the strange longings, the capriciousness, and the morbid fears of the pregnant woman. The patient may be treated successfully by removal from home; but if the disease be allowed to go on, there is no good ground to expect that parturition will have a beneficial effect upon it; on the contrary, the probability is that it will run into a severe puerperal insanity, and from that into dementia.

Puerperal insanity proper comes on within one month of parturition; and, like the insanity of pregnancy, occurs most often in primiparæ. The statistics of the Edinburgh Asylum show that in all the cases occurring before the sixteenth day after labour, as most cases do, the symptoms were those of acute mania; but in all the cases which occurred after the sixteenth day they were those of melancholia. In both forms, but especially in the latter, there is sometimes a mixture of childishness and apparent dementia. The mania is more likely than the melancholia to get well. It is of an acute and extremely incoherent character, a delirious rather than a systematized mania, marked by noisy restlessness, sleeplessness, tearing of clothes, hallucinations, and in some cases by great salacity, which is probably the direct mental effect of the irritation of the generative organs. Suicide may be attempted in an excited, purposeless way. The bodily symptoms, contradicting the violence of the mental excitement, indicate feebleness; the features are pinched; the skin is pale, cool, and clammy; and the pulse is quick, small, and irritable. We may safely say that recovery takes place in three out of four cases of puerperal mania, usually in a few weeks; the patient, after the acute symptoms have subsided, sinking into a temporary state of confusion and feebleness of mind, and then waking up as from a dream. I may add the expression of a conviction that no good, but rather harm, is done by attempting to stifle this or any other form of acute insanity by the administration or large doses of opium.

111. Henry Maudsley, *Hysteria*

(Excerpt from *Body and Mind*, London: Macmillan & Co., 1873, pp. 79–80.)

We might make of *hysterical* insanity a special variety. An attack of acute maniacal excitement, with great restlessness, rapid and disconnected but not entirely incoherent conversation, sometimes tending to the erotic or obscene, evidently without abolition of consciousness; laughing, singing, or rhyming, and perverseness of conduct, which is still more or less coherent and seemingly wilful, —may occur in connection with, or instead of, the usual hysterical convulsions. Or the ordinary hysterical symptoms may pass by degrees into chronic insanity. Loss of power of will is a characteristic symptom of hysteria in all its Protean forms, and with the perverted sensations and disordered movements there is always some degree of moral perversion. This increases until it swallows up the other symptoms: the patient loses more and more of her energy and self-control, becoming capriciously fanciful about her health, imagining or feigning strange diseases, and keeping up the delusion or the imposture with a pertinacity that might seem incredible, getting more and more impatient of the advice and interference of others, and indifferent to the interests and duties of her position. Outbursts of temper become almost outbreaks of mania, particularly at the menstrual periods. An erotic tinge may be observable in her manner of behaviour; and occasionally there are quasi-ecstatic or cataleptic states. It is an easily curable form of derangement, if the patient be removed in time from the anxious but hurtful sympathies and attentions of her family, and placed under good moral control; but if it be allowed to go on unchecked, it will end in dementia, and it is especially apt to do so when there is a marked hereditary predisposition.

112. Henry Maudsley, *Nymphomania*

(Excerpt from *Body and Mind*, London: Macmillan & Co., 1873, pp. 82–3.)

Take, for example, the irritation of ovaries or uterus, which is sometimes the direct occasion of *nymphomania*—a disease by which the most chaste and modest woman is transformed into a raging fury of lust. Some observers have, without sufficient reason I think, made of *nymphomania* a special variety, grouping under the term cases in which it was a prominent symptom. But it certainly occurs in forms of mania that are quite distinct—in puerperal mania, for example, in epileptic mania, and in the mania sometimes met with in old women; and the cases in which it does occur have not such characteristic features as warrant the formation of a definite group. We have, indeed, to note and bear in mind how often sexual ideas and feelings arise and display themselves in all sorts of insanity; how they connect themselves with ideas which in a moral mental state have no known relation to them; so that it seems as inexplicable that a virtuous person should ever have learnt, as it is distressing that she should manifest, so much obscenity of thought and feeling.

113. Andrew Wynter, *Inheritance of Insanity in the Female Line*

(Excerpt from *The Borderlands of Insanity*, London: Robert Hardwicke, 1875, pp. 52–3.)

It is agreed by all alienist physicians, that girls are far more likely to inherit insanity from their mothers than from the other parent, and that the same rule obtains as regards the sons. The tendency of the mother to transmit her mental disease is, however, in all cases stronger than the father's; some physicians have, indeed, insisted that it is twice as strong. In judging of the chances of an individual inheriting mental disease, or, indeed, of the insane temperament, it may not be unadvisable to study the general likeness and character. If the daughter of an insane mother very much resembles her in feature and in temperament, the chances are that she is more likely to inherit the disease than other daughters who are not so like. And the reason is obvious; for if the general physical aspect and the temperament are alike, it points to a similar likeness in the structure of the body and nerve. The mental likeness is, however, the most important of the two, as we often see children partaking of the father's features and of the mother's temperament. In such cases the child would possibly inherit the mother's insane temperament, transmuted into some disorder of the nervous system, such as hysteria, epilepsy, or neuralgia; for nothing is more common than to find mere nervous disorders changed, by transmission from parent to child, into mental disorders, and *vice versâ*.

114. Andrew Wynter, *The Constraints of the Female Role*

(Excerpt from *The Borderlands of Insanity*, London: Robert Hardwicke, 1875, pp. 59–63.)

We all know the ease with which hysterical depression makes but too many seek what they euphemistically term 'support' under such circumstances.

Beginning with sal-volatile, and ascending by graduated steps, such as red lavender, eau de Cologne, to sherry and spirits, it may easily be conceived that the liberal prescription of brandy by a celebrated physician, as one of the most efficacious and universal of remedies in diseases (usual amongst them) was calculated but too rapidly to be accepted and acted upon. Hence the necessity for the reasoning that 'alcohol in whatever form should be prescribed with as much care as any powerful drug; and that the sanction of its use should be so framed as not to be interpreted as a sanction for excess, or necessarily for the continuance of its use when the occasion is past.'

But let us ask, is there no other cause of this female intemperance besides the injurious misuse of the physician's prescriptions? Have the changes which have taken place in social life anything to answer for?

Within these last twenty years the railway may be said to have driven female society farther and farther into the country. The man goes forth to his labour in the morning and returns in the evening, leaving his wife, during the whole of the day, to her own devices. Whilst our residences were in town, they always had that intensely feminine refreshment, shopping, to solace their *ennui;* but shops now being out of the question, what have our wives to do, especially the childless ones, under the present miserable views as regards their education? It has been, we think, well said that the working man goes to the public house for light and cheerful society as much as for beer. After the muscular fatigues of the day, he requires some social recruitment of this kind. May we not ask if some recruitment for the woman's mind is not required after the humdrum housekeeping labours for the day are accomplished? We think this cannot be denied. As it is, she is left to her own devices, and if there is no family to be attended to, we know that these devices are not of too intellectual an order. In short, arrangements of society and the railways have banished our wives from all the amusements and excitement of town, and they are thrown upon their own resources with but very imperfectly educated minds. The result is, in many cases, where this incipient form of insanity is present, a fatal appeal to the bottle. As long as ladies are ashamed to put their hands to any useful matter, and are untrained to any intellectual work, they cannot help getting into mischief. For this reason we believe that the great cure for the evil that has begun to show itself within the sacred precincts of home, is a good intellectual training for women. If our wives knew anything of art, if they could draw, paint, model, or write, we should hear far less of the sherry-bottle. The few hours that elapsed before the husband's return from business would be bridged over by some occupation that delighted and satisfied the mind; at least the demon that, unknown to themselves, exists within themselves, may not be called into life.

It certainly is deplorable to think that the delicate sense of woman for beauty, her appreciative faculties, her delicate touch, and mental fibre should be wholly lost on the world's work. All that man wants intellectually she is fitted by nature to supply; but unfortunately Mrs. Grundy stands resolutely in the way, and it is thought beneath her position and dignity to do anything useful or ornamental in life, especially if she is paid for it. As long as we bring up young girls with these absurd and snobbish notions how can we expect that anything but evil can come of it?

115. Furneaux Jordan, *The Physical Constitution of Battered Wives*

(Excerpt from *Character as Seen in Body and Parentage*, London: Kegan Paul, Trench, Trubner & Co., 1886, pp. 1–5.)

Several years ago I noticed that a very large proportion of the women who came into hospital suffering from injuries inflicted by their husbands had, as a rule, something peculiar in their personal appearance. The peculiarity or peculiarities seemed common to all of them. They certainly had not been assaulted because they were old or plain. We are sometimes told, as a danger of unbelief, that men would put aside wives who had lost their youthful looks. Many of these women were young, some were very pretty, and their husbands were believers. In truth it is neither 'belief' nor 'unbelief,' but certain congenital impulses of character, based in great measure on organisation, but influenced in no unimportant degree by environment and training, which mainly determine the conduct of men and women. As Carlyle affirmed, both the best men and women and the worst are found in all varieties of opinion and belief.

I came slowly to see that the skin of the assaulted women was often clear, delicate, perhaps rosy. Their hair-growth was never heavy nor long, and the eyebrows were spare and refined. Their upper spinal curves were so formed as to give a somewhat convex appearance to the back and shoulders and a more or less forward pose to the head. This bodily conformation, by the way, is a favourite one with artists, one of whom states that, in a well-formed woman, a plumb-line dropped from the tip of the nose should fall in front of the toes. The friends and neighbours usually let it be known that these unfortunate women whom they brought had sharp tongues in their heads and an unfailing—unfailing by repetition—supply of irritating topics on which to exercise them.

A comparatively small number of injured and sometimes even dead women were brought in of a wholly different character and different bodily organisation. Their injuries were much more serious. They had been assaulted not by merely provoked men, but by husbands or paramours acting under the impulse of ungovernable and perhaps well-founded jealousy, and with clearly murderous intent. In nearly all cases the assailed women and the assailing men were women and men of but poor intellectual endowment. The women of the smaller class were impassioned, but usually weak pleasure-loving and self-indulgent also. The two classes of women possessed widely different organisations—different in skin and hair and skeleton, and surely different also in brain and nerve. In the smaller and more impassioned class the spine was straighter, the head and neck and shoulders were held upwards and backwards; the hair-growth was abundant and the eyebrows marked.

Mr. Ruskin, in a few paragraphs of remarkable interest, declares that bishops should watch rather than rule; that their place is at the mast-head—not at the helm. A bishop, he says, not only ought to know everybody in his diocese, he ought also to know why Bill and Nancy knock each other's teeth out. In strict truth bishops are not trained to understand Bill and Nancy, and for eighteen centuries they have done but little for them. Bill and Nancy are what they are chiefly from organisation and inheritance, and in great measure also, no doubt, from circumstance. When fully matured, however, a body-guard of bishops could not keep them straight, especially Bill, who is usually, and on physiological grounds, the greater sinner. Bill and Nancy will do better when we come to see that the improvement of educational, social, and moral methods have more to do with physiologists than with bishops.

Although there are features of character which make for riches or for poverty, and notwithstanding also that riches and poverty tell on character, yet there is no one feature which is confined to the poor or to the well-to-do. The unimpassioned tradeswomen who entreats a magistrate to protect her from a brutal husband, and the delicately born but erring (impassioned) lady who is summoned to the Divorce Court resemble in organisation and proclivity their humbler sisters who are brought into hospitals with bruised bodies or with fatal wounds.

Neither is there any feature of character which is peculiar to one sex. The fidgetty and querulous wife who involuntarily provokes a foolish husband, is often in body, mind, and character, the counterpart of her fidgetty and querulous father. The quiet easy-going man is often the repetition of his tranquil and affectionate mother. The difference of sex is small and secondary, when compared with the fundamental differences of character.

The potency of nerve organisation is not enforced here for the purpose of extenuating domestic cruelty, or excusing the domestic savage. But every truth, if it is a truth, explains other truths—for there is no truth gleanable by moral methods which ought not to be gleaned, and no sin greater (our scientific ethical teachers tell us) than the sin of forming judgments on insufficient and untested data. Look at two men of average—certainly not strong—character and organisation. They may be much alike in many ways. Both are but moderately wise and self-restrained. One marries a certain combination of skin, and hair, and bone, and nerve; he is happy and content, and thinks that everybody else, if they were only as wise and virtuous as he, would also be happy and content. The other, marrying quite another sort of anatomical combination, finds life arid and burdensome and gradually turns to violence and folly. The first often does not know why he is happy and good; the second but dimly perceives why he is unhappy and bad. Both are to a certain degree the creatures of organisation and parentage. The first has usually no charity for the second; perhaps he sits in a judicial, or editorial, or other chair of authority, and proclaims his own virtue by denouncing the shame of his neighbour. A change of place on the marriage morning would have changed their lives and views. These sentences would need but little change if they began with the words 'Look at two women,' and consider the matter from the woman's point of view. If Mary Stuart's first husband had been a Bothwell, much else in her life would have been different. The less impassioned men and women are perhaps not well fitted, however willing, to judge their impassioned brothers and sisters. The more emotional also are too insensible to the merits of the active and less emotional.

Here, then, was a clue, not to every nook and corner, but still to a wide range of character. Material for observation is everywhere around us—in domestic, in social, and in public life; in the school, in the committee-room, in parliament; in the theatre, the law court, the church; in history, biography, and fiction; in all written and spoken words, and in all writers and speakers themselves.

Chapter IX

Idiocy, Criminal Lunacy and Pauper Lunacy

116. Alexander Morison, *Degrees of Imbecility*

(Excerpt from *Outlines of Mental Diseases*, Edinburgh: MacLachlan & Stewart, 1824, pp. 102–9.)

In Congenital Idiotism, the intellectual faculties have never been developed. It commences with life, or shews itself very early; while Dementia does not take place till after puberty.

It exists in various degrees, from complete idiotism to what is termed Imbecility.

The last stage of Dementia of Fatuity has been termed *acquired* Idiotism.

Congenital Idiots rarely live to a great age; and the more complete the state of idiotism is, the shorter time do they live.

There is frequently something faulty in the formation of the head, and the position of the eyes of idiots; their mouth is gaping, and slavers; their lips are thick; their gums are unhealthy, and their teeth soon decay; some are deaf, or deaf and dumb; they are often lame; their sensibility, physical and moral, is obtuse; they are deficient in sensation, perception, and attention. Some are in constant motion; some laugh; others weep; occasionally they are prone to mischief.

Idiotism sometimes prevails in families, and is often conjoined with palsy or epilepsy.

The *Cretins* of Switzerland are the idiots met with in the narrow valleys of the mountainous districts. They are often deaf and dumb, and the other senses are imperfect; they frequently have enlargement of the thyroid gland.

Children born in perfect health, but apparently of a scrofulous constitution, have continued to improve in body and mind until some years after birth, when they have become Idiots; on the other hand, cases have occurred, where, in early youth, the mental faculties have made an unexpected development, and have emerged from threatened idiotism.

In idiotism, when congenital, the treatment is limited to the preservation of cleanliness, and the encouragement of occupation; the general health must be attended to, and every precaution ought to be taken to prevent idiots from procreating.

Mental deficiency is of two kinds:

The one, in which there is Imbecility, or a weak state of all the Faculties. The other, in which there is Imbecility of one or several of the Faculties; and there are different degrees from what has legally been termed *non compos mentis*—that degree of imbecility which renders the person incompetent to the management of himself and his affairs—to the ordinary standard of intellect.

Under the term Imbecile, then, are included those in whom all the intellectual faculties manifest themselves to a certain extent, and who are capable of partial education. They are also subject to violent emotions, as fear, anger, lust, and grief; while Idiots have neither intellect nor affections, or at least in a very obscure degree.

Sometimes a propensity to music and mimicry is shewn by the imbecile; they are likewise frequently given to steal—have occasionally committed murder—and are sometimes made the instruments of crimes by villains. Houses and stacks of corn have been burnt in this way.

The mind may be weak from birth, or it may be enfeebled by disease, at any period of life.

The causes of imbecility are—hereditary disposition—scrofula—epilepsy—convulsions—severe illness, or injury done to the head in early infancy, and hydrocephalus.

Some have attributed the production of imbecile children to hard labour, to fright, or other violent emotions, affecting the mother during pregnancy.

In cases of mental deficiency, much has been effected by a well directed education, in conducting which, the principal object must be to improve the power of attention, and encourage the particular bent of the capacity.

When *hereditary* disposition to insanity exists in a family, much discrimination is required in conducting the education of the children.

Imbecility, fickleness and indecision, violent temper, and timidity, each require a different management—to strengthen feeble faculties—to restrain violent passions—and to encourage timid dispositions.

Dotage—The mental imbecility of old age is hardly to be regarded as a disease. The different senses and faculties fail by degrees: of the latter, the memory is generally the first to fail. Senile imbecility is sometimes prematurely induced by excesses.

Is weakness of one or more of the mental faculties—of perception or apprehension—judgment—memory—volition, &c.

When the perception is feeble or dull, the term *Dullness* or *Stupidity* has been employed. This is sometimes hereditary, or it may proceed from defective education—from intemperance—and corporeal diseases.

There is a striking difference in this respect among certain nations.

Impaired Memory may be a natural defect—or it may be the consequence of various diseases—injuries of the head—habits of inattention—old age, &c.

When the judgment is remarkably deficient, there is a general and unusual degree of *Credulity*. In most cases of this description, the judgment is naturally weak; but in others, credulity is in some measure voluntary, from indolence.

Indecision or *Fickleness* is also natural or acquired. Firmness and consistency of character may be greatly promoted by judicious management in youth: hence the importance of early habits of governing the will by the reason, and of restraining the impulse of the moment. Indecision is often the first striking symptom of incipient insanity.

Disorders of Attention are conspicuous in the various genera of insanity, and of mental imbecility.

The mind, in thinking, may be in a *passive* state, when thoughts follow each other independent of volition, as in musing, dreaming, and mania, or when entirely occupied by objects of sense, or in an *active* state, when the mind exercises command or controul over its thoughts, or changes its condition.

The relative degrees of these states in different individuals powerfully influence character, command of thought being much increased by cultivation and exercise.

The term *Absence of Mind* is applied when the attention is wandering, and does not readily yield to the dictates of the will—a state nearly allied to the suspension of thought during sleep.

Absence of mind is very unfavourable to acquiring knowledge, since the other faculties are dependent on the vigour of the attention.

It is a curious fact that perception of objects may subsist in absence of mind, though for a time we may remain unconscious of their presence.

The term *Abstraction of Mind* is employed, when the attention is fixed with consent of the will on some ideas not connected with surrounding objects. This state may be occasioned by intense study, or by overwhelming passion.

That of *Studium Inane*, or *Brown Study*, has been applied to the state of mind which takes place when the attention is voluntarily relaxed, and allowed to indulge in passing ideas.

As the faculty of attention is capable of being invigorated, it is of the utmost importance to cultivate it in early life, being more readily arrested by certain objects than others; and it is important to ascertain these, to select them, in the first instance, for cultivation, and the attention may afterwards be transferred to other pursuits. In the treatment of all the varieties of partial weakness of mind, corporeal causes are, if possible, to be removed, and mental instruction suited to the case assiduously cultivated.

The improvement of the strongest faculties tends directly to invigorate the others.

117. George Man Burrows, *Idiocy*

(Excerpt from *Commentaries on Insanity*, London: Underwood, 1828, pp. 505–6.)

Idiocy is a congenital or an acquired defect of the intellectual faculties.

Pinel says, idiocy consists in an obliteration, more or less absolute, of the functions of the understanding and the affections of the heart. But to this definition I object, as to *aliénation mentale*, that it implies a previous possession of intelligence. Obliteration, therefore, can only apply to idiocy acquired subsequent to the development of an understanding.

Congenital idiocy may originate in mal-conformation of the cranium, or of the brain itself. Acquired idiocy proceeds from mechanical injury of the cranium, by which the functions of the brain are lesed or impeded, or from an injury or disease which that organ has sustained: it follows also from excess in sensual pleasures, habitual drunkenness, excessive depletions of blood, masturbation, extenuating diseases, study too intense or wrong directed, and from profound moral causes, as terror, fright, extreme joy, &c.

In the congenital state, the external senses are often wanting or defective, as well as the intellectual, and life is commonly of short duration; in the acquired, the external senses may be quite alienated, or be only partially affected, but they have been once perfect, and life may be protracted to old age.

Absolute idiocy admits of no cure. The mental faculties and external senses have been so impaired by injuries done to the head, as to give all the characters of idiocy to a person; and yet a surgical operation, or nature herself, has restored those faculties. When depraved only by the vices and moral impressions referred to, the mental faculties have been restored by the access of fever, a paroxysm of violent mania, or by such means as have directly or indirectly, imparted fresh energy to the brain. But in this latter case the event of recovery shews that the mental faculties were in a state of demency, rather than of idiocy. For idiocy signifies an irremediable condition of the mental faculties; demency, of whatever duration, except when there is organic lesion of the brain, or it be the effect of old age, implies a capability of their restoration.

Whenever the term idiocy is applied to a fatuous condition of the understanding, unfortunately it is construed into incurability. From this confounding of terms I fear that some are consigned to oblivion, who, being only in a state of acute demency, might have become useful members of society. However degraded the mind appears, the origin of that state should be carefully inquired into: if it proceeds from a defect of nature, there is nothing to be done but what compassion for a hapless fellow-being dictates; if it be from injury to the head, the skill of surgery may sometimes afford relief; if from disease, excessive depletion, extenuation, or moral cause, provided no organic change in the organ of intelligence has followed, means which invigorate the constitution and restore the suspended energies of the brain may still effect a cure.

To describe the characters which denote idiocy were quite superfluous. There are doubtless different grades of incapacity as well as of capacity; but they cannot be disguised, and need not delineation.

118. James Cowles Prichard, *The Etymology of the Word 'Idiot'*

(Excerpt from *On the Different Forms of Insanity in Relation to Jurisprudence*, London: Hippolyte Ballière, 1847, pp. 202–3.)

There are few expressions which have undergone greater changes of meaning than 'idiot,' and 'idiotism.' The original meaning of the word 'idiot' is, as every one knows, 'a private man,' or one who has not a public office; thence it came to signifying a person incapable of such an employment, and a person of mean capacity. In English law, 'idiot' originally meant, any person by unsoundness of mind of whatever description, unable to take care of himself and his property, and to fulfil the ordinary duties of his station. The word 'idiota,' is joined in the oldest writs with 'fatuus,' and the definition is given 'fatuus et idiota, ita quod regimini sui ipsius, terrarum, tenementorum et cattallorum suorum non sufficit.' The officer to whom writs of inquisition, 'de idiotâ inquirendo' were issued, was originally the escheater, or a person appointed to inquire what casual profits accrued to the king's estate, and he was directed to examine whether the person in question was 'idiota et fatuus à nativitate suâ an alio tempore.' If such person was found to have been an idiot, according to the definition, from his birth, the escheator was entitled, as it seems, to declare his lands forfeited to the king, and to take possession of them in the king's name.

119. Henry Maudsley, *The Animality of Idiots*

(Excerpt from *Body and Mind*, London: Macmillan & Co., 1873, pp. 48–52.)

In the conformation and habits of other idiots the most careless observer could not help seeing the ape. A striking instance of this kind is described by Dr. Mitchell, Deputy Commissioner in Lunacy for Scotland. 'I have never,' he says, 'seen a better illustration of the ape-faced idiot than in this case. It is not, however, the face alone that is ape-like. He grins, chatters, and screams like a monkey, never attempting a sound in any way resembling a word. He puts himself in the most ape-like attitude in his hunts after lice, and often brings his mouth to help his hands. He grasps what he brings to his mouth with an apish hold. His thumbs are but additional fingers. He has a leaping walk. He has heavy eyebrows, and short hair on his cheek or face. He is muscular, active, and not dwarfish. He sits on the floor in ape fashion, with his genitals always exposed. He has filthy habits of all kinds. He may be called an idiot of the lowest order; yet there is a mischievous brute-like intelligence in his eye. His head is not very small, its greatest circumference being twenty inches and a half, but in shape it strongly exhibits the ape-form of abnormality.'

Pinel has recorded the case of an idiot who was something like a sheep in respect of her tastes, her mode of life, and the form of her head. She had an aversion from meat, and ate fruit and vegetables greedily, and drank nothing but water. Her demonstrations of sensibility, joy, or trouble, were confined to the repetition of the ill-articulated words *bé, ma, bah.* She alternately bent and raised her head, and rubbed herself against the belly of the girl who attended her. If she wanted to resist or express her discontent, she tried to butt with the crown of her head; she was very passionate. Her back, her loins, and shoulders were covered with flexible and blackish hairs one or two inches long. She never could be made to sit on a chair or bench, even when at meals; as soon as she was placed in a sitting posture she glided on the floor. She slept on the floor in the posture of animals.

There is now under care, in the West Riding Asylum, a deformed idiot girl who, in general appearance and habits, has, according to Dr. Browne, striking features of resemblance to a goose; so much so, that the nurses who received her described her as just like 'a plucked goose.' Her father died in the asylum, and her mother's sister was also a patient in it at one time. She is 4 ft. 2 in. in height, has a small head, and thin and scanty hair, so that the crown of the head is partially bald. The eyes are large, round, prominent, and restless, and are frequently covered by the eyelids, as if by a slow forcible effort at winking. The lower jaw is large, projecting more than one inch beyond the contracted upper jaw, and possesses an extraordinary range of antero-posterior, as well as lateral, movement; the whole configuration of the lower part of the face having a somewhat bill-like appearance. The neck is unusually long and flexible, and is capable of being bent backwards so as actually to touch the back between the scapulæ. The cutis anserina is general over the body, but is most marked on the back and dorsal aspects of the limbs, where it looks exactly as if it had been just deprived of feathers. The inferior angles of the scapulæ stand prominently out, and moving freely with the movements of the arms have precisely the appearance of rudimentary wings. The girl utters no articulate sounds, but expresses pleasure by cackling like a goose, and displeasure by hissing or screeching like a goose, or perhaps like a macaw. When angry, she flaps her arms against her sides, and beats her feet upon the floor. She knows her own name and understands one or two short sentences, such as 'Come here' and 'Put out your hand.' She recognizes the persons who attend upon her and feed her, and is much agitated if touched by a stranger. She cannot feed herself, but swallows voraciously all that is put into her mouth, showing no preference for one article of diet over another. She is dirty in her habits, and no amount of attention has improved her in this respect. She is very fond of her bath, cackling when she is put into it, and screeching when she is taken out of it.

It is a natural question, Whence come these animal traits and instincts in man? Whence was derived the instinct which taught the idiot woman to gnaw through the umbilical cord? Was it really the reappearance of a primitive instinct of animal nature—a faint echo from a far distant past, testifying to a kinship which man has almost outgrown, or has grown too proud to acknowledge? No doubt such animal traits are marks of extreme human degeneracy, but it is no explanation to call them so; degenerations come by law, and are as natural as natural law can make them. Instead of passing them by as abnormal, or, worse still, stigmatizing them as unnatural, it behoves us to seek for the scientific interpretation which they must certainly have. When we reflect that every human brain does, in the course of its development, pass through the same stages as the brains of other vertebrate animals, and that its transitional states resemble the permanent forms of their brains; and when we reflect further, that the stages of its development in the womb may be considered the abstract and brief chronicle of a series of developments that have gone on through countless ages in nature, it does not seem so wonderful as at the first blush it might do, that it should, when in a condition of arrested development, sometimes display animal instincts. Summing up, as it were, in itself the leading forms of the vertebrate type, there is truly a brute brain within the man's; and when the latter stops short of its characteristic development as *human*—when it remains arrested at or below the level of an orang's brain, it may be presumed that it will manifest its most primitive functions, and no higher functions.

120. Henry Maudsley, *The Criminal Psychosis*

(Excerpt from *Body and Mind*, London: Macmillan & Co., 1873, pp. 128–31.)

Now, if there be a class of persons who are without the moral sense, who are true moral imbeciles, it is the class of habitual criminals. All observers who have made them their study agree that they constitute a morbid or degenerate variety of mankind, marked by peculiar low physical and mental characteristics. They are scrofulous, often deformed, with badly formed angular heads, are stupid, sluggish, deficient in vital energy, and sometimes afflicted with epilepsy. They are of weak and defective intellect, though excessively cunning; and not a few of them are weak-minded and imbecile. The women are ugly in features, and without grace of expression or movement. The children, who become juvenile criminals, do not evince the educational aptitude of the higher industrial classes; they are deficient in the power of attention and application, have bad memories, and make slow progress in learning; many of them are weak in mind and body, and some of them actually imbecile. At the end of the best part of a life spent among prisoners, a prison surgeon declares himself to be mainly impressed with their extreme deficiency or perversion of moral feeling, the strength of the evil propensities of their nature, and their utter impracticability; neither kindness nor severity availing to prevent them from devising and doing wrong day by day, although their conduct brought on them further privations. Their evil propensities are veritable instincts of their defective nature, acting, like instincts, in spite of reason, and producing, when not gratified, a restlessness which becomes at times uncontrollable. Hence occur the so-called 'breakings-out' of prisoners, when, without apparent cause, they fall into paroxysms of excitement, tear their clothing and bedding, assault the officers, and altogether behave for a time like furious madmen.

We may take it, then, on the authority of those who have had the best opportunities of observation, that there is a class of criminals formed of beings of defective physical and mental organization; one result of the defect, which really determines their destiny in life, being an extreme deficiency or complete absence of moral sense: that an absence of moral sense may be a congenital vice or fault of organization. The experience of medical practice certainly confirms this view. From time to time we are consulted about perplexing cases of what might be called moral insanity, or, more properly, moral imbecility, in children of the better classes. Though born in good circumstances of life, and having every advantage of education, they cannot by any care or training be made to learn and behave like other children; they display no affection whatever for parents, brothers, or sisters, and no real appreciation of the difference between right and wrong—no love for the one, no remorse for the other; they are inherently vicious, and steal and lie with a skill that it is hard to believe could ever have been acquired—are, in fact, instinctive thieves and liars; everything that their vicious nature prompts them to desire is for them right, and they exhibit a remarkable cunning in gratifying their evil propensities; they are the hopeless pupils of any master who has anything to do with them, and are sure to be expelled from any school to which they may be sent. In the end, all those who have to do with them are constrained to ascribe to defect what at first seemed simple badness. Now what we commonly find in these cases, when we are able to push satisfactory inquiry into their hereditary antecedents, is that they come of families in which insanity or some allied neurosis prevails. This is the interesting fact to which I wish to draw attention.

In addition to the entire absence of perversion of moral sense, without feeling of remorse, which experience of habitual criminals brings prominently out, other important facts which we learn from an investigation of their family histories are, that a considerable proportion of them are weak-minded or epileptic, or become insane, or that they spring from families in which insanity, epilepsy, or some other neurosis exists, and that the diseases from which they suffer, and of which they die, are chiefly tubercular diseases and disease of the nervous system. Crime is not, then, always a simple affair of yielding to an evil impulse or a vicious passion, which might be checked were ordinary control exercised; it is clearly sometimes the result of an actual neurosis which has close relations of nature and descent to other neurosis, especially the epileptic and the insane neuroses; and this neurosis is the physical result of physiological laws of production and evolution. No wonder that the criminal *psychosis*, which is the mental side of *neurosis*, is for the most part an intractable malady, punishment being of no avail to produce a permanent reformation. A true reformation would be a *re*-forming of the individual nature; and how can that which has been forming through generations be *re*-formed within the term of a single life? Can the Ethiopian change his skin, or the leopard his spots?

121. Henry Maudsley, *The Criminal Class*

(Excerpt from *Body and Mind*, London: Macmillan & Co., 1873, pp. 66–7.)

The observations of intelligent prison surgeons are tending more and more to prove that a considerable proportion of criminals are weak-minded or epileptic, or come of families in which insanity, epilepsy, or some other neurosis exists. Mr. Thompson, surgeon to the General Prison of Scotland, has gone so far recently as to express his conviction that the principal business of prison surgeons must always be with mental defects or disease; that the diseases and causes of death among prisoners are chiefly of the nervous system; and, in fine, that the treatment of crime is a branch of psychology. He holds that there is among criminals a distinct and incurable *criminal class*, marked by peculiar low physical and mental characteristics; that crime is hereditary in the families of criminals belonging to this class; and that this hereditary crime is a disorder of mind, having close relations of nature and descent to epilepsy, dipsomania, insanity, and other forms of degeneracy. Such criminals are really *morbid varieties*, and often exhibit marks of physical degeneration—spinal deformities, stammering, imperfect organs of speech, club-foot, cleft palate, harelip, deafness, paralysis, epilepsy, and scrofula. Moreau relates a striking case, which is of interest as indicating the alliance between morbid or degenerate varieties, and which I may quote here.

The moral element is an essential part of a complete and sound character; he who is destitute of it, being unquestionably to that extent a defective being, is therefore on the road to, or marks, race degeneracy; and it is not a matter of much wonder that his children should, when better influences do not intervene to check the morbid tendency, exhibit a further degree of degeneracy, and be actual morbid varieties. I think that no one who has studied closely the causation of insanity will question this mode of production.

122. Henry Maudsley, *Native Peculiarities*

(Excerpt from *Body and Mind*, London: Macmillan & Co., 1873, pp. 42–5.)

How comes idiocy, or insanity? What is the scientific meaning of them? We may take it to be beyond question that they are not accidents; that they come to pass, as every other event in nature does, by natural law. They are mysterious visitations only because we understand not the laws of their production, appear casualties only because we are ignorant of their causality. When a blow on the head or an inflammation of the membranes of the brain has produced derangement of mind, we need not look farther for a cause: the actual harm done to structure is sufficient to account for disorder of function in the best-constituted and best-developed brain. But it is only in a small proportion of cases of insanity that we can discover such a direct physical occasion of disease. In a great many cases—in more than half certainly, and perhaps in five out of six—there is something in the nervous organization of the person, some native peculiarity, which, however we name it, predisposes him to an outbreak of insanity. When two persons undergo a similar moral shock, or a similar prolonged anxiety, and one of them goes mad in consequence, while the other goes to sleep and goes to work and recovers his equanimity, it is plain that all the co-operating conditions have not been the same; that the shock has not been the entire cause of the outbreak of madness. What, then, has been the difference? In the former case there has been present a most important element, which was happily wanting in the latter—there has been a certain hereditary neurosis, an unknown and variable quantity in the equation.

Perhaps of all the erroneous notions concerning mind which metaphysics has engendered or abetted, there is none more false than that which tacitly assumes or explicitly declares that men are born with equal original mental capacity, opportunities and education determining the differences of subsequent development. The opinion is as cruel as it is false. What man can by taking thought add one cubit either to his mental or to his bodily stature? Multitudes of human beings come into the world weighted with a destiny against which they have neither the will nor the power to contend; they are the step-children of nature, and groan under the worst of all tyrannies—the tyranny of a bad organization. Men differ, indeed, in the fundamental characters of their minds, as they do in the features of their countenances, or in the habits of their bodies; and between those who are born with the potentiality of a full and complete mental development under favourable circumstances, and those who are born with an innate incapacity of mental development under any circumstances, there exists every gradation. What teaching could ever raise the congenital idiot to the common level of human intelligence? What teaching could ever keep the inspired mind of the man of genius at that level?

The congenital idiot is deprived of his human birthright; for he is born with such a defect of brain that he cannot display any, or can only display very feeble and imperfect mental functions. From no fault of his own is he thus afflicted, seeing that he must be held innocent of all offence but the offence of his share of original sin; but it is nowise so clear that it is not from some fault of his parents. It is all too true, in many cases, there has observedly been a neglect or disregard of the laws which govern the progress of human development through the ages. Idiocy is, indeed, a manufactured article; and although we are not always able to tell how it is manufactured, still its important causes are known and are within control. Many cases are distinctly traceable to parental intemperance and excess. Out of 300 idiots in Massachusetts, Dr. Howe found as many as 145 to be the offspring of intemperate parents; and there are numerous scattered observations which prove that chronic alcoholism in the parent may directly occasion idiocy in the child. I think, too, that there is no reasonable question of the ill effects of marriages of consanguinity: that their tendency is to produce degeneracy of the race, and idiocy as the extremist form of such degeneracy. I do not say that *all* the children of such marriages may not sometimes be healthy, and *some* of them quite healthy at other times; but the general and ultimate result of breeding in and in is to produce barrenness and sterility, children of a low degree of viability and of imperfect mental and physical development, deaf-mutism, and actual imbecility or idiocy. Again, insanity in the parent may issue in idiocy in the offspring, which is, so to speak, the natural term of mental degeneracy when it goes on unchecked through generations. It may be affirmed with no little confidence, that if the experiment of inter-marrying insane persons for two or three generations were tried, the result would be sterile idiocy and extinction of the family. Certain unfavourable conditions of life tend unquestionably to produce degeneracy of the individual; the morbid predisposition so generated is then transmitted to the next generation, and if the unfavourable conditions continue, is aggravated in it; and thus is formed a morbid variety of the human kind, which is incapable of being a link in the line of progress of humanity. Nature puts it under the ban of sterility, and thus prevents the permanent degradation of the race.

123. Henry Maudsley, *The Production of Criminals*

(Excerpt from *Responsibility in Mental Disease*, London: Henry S. King & Co., 1874, pp. 29–30.)

One fact which is brought strongly out by these inquiries is that crime is often hereditary; that just as a man may inherit the stamp of the bodily features and characters of his parents, so he may also inherit the impress of their evil passions and propensities: of the true thief as of the true poet it may be indeed said that he is born, not made. This is what observation of the phenomena of hereditary action would lead us to expect; and although certain theologians, who are prone to square the order of nature to their notions of what it should be, may repel such a doctrine as the heritage of an *immoral* in place of a *moral* sense, they will in the end find it impossible in this matter, as they have done in other matters, to contend against facts. To add to their misfortunes, many criminals are not only begotten, and conceived, and bred in crime, but they are instructed in it from their youth upwards, so that their original criminal instincts acquire a power which no subsequent efforts to produce reformation will ever counteract.

All persons who have made criminals their study, recognize a distinct criminal class of beings, who herd together in our large cities in a thieves' quarter, giving themselves up to intemperance, rioting in debauchery, without regard to marriage ties or the bars of consanguinity, and propagating a criminal population of degenerate beings. For it is furthermore a matter of observation that this criminal class constitutes a degenerate or morbid variety of mankind, marked by peculiar low physical and mental characteristics. They are, it has been said, as distinctly marked off from the honest and well-bred operatives as 'black-faced sheep are from other breeds,' so that an experienced detective officer or prison official could pick them out from any promiscuous assembly at church or market. Their family likeness betrays them as fellows 'by the hand of nature marked, quoted and signed to do a deed of shame.' They are scrofulous, not seldom deformed, with badly-formed angular heads; are stupid, sullen, sluggish, deficient in vital energy, and sometimes afflicted with epilepsy. As a class, they are of mean and defective intellect, though excessively cunning, and not a few of them are weak-minded and imbecile.* The women are ugly in features, and without grace of expression or movement. The children, who become juvenile criminals, do not evince the educational aptitude of the higher industrial classes: they are deficient in the power of attention and application, have bad memories, and make slow progress in learning; many of them are weak in mind and body, and some of them actually imbecile.

* The mendicant thiefs are well known to prison officials as a class of persons of weak intellect, who tramp through the country, prowling about the different houses, and begging or stealing as the opportunity offers; and it is by them that arson, rape, and other crimes are often perpetrated. In the county of Cumberland, a few years ago, the practice of committing them to prison as soon as they crossed the border was enforced. The direct result was a considerable increase in the number of admissions into the county asylum, to which they were transferred from gaol as being persons of imbecile or unsound mind.

124. Furneaux Jordan, *The Dominancy of Organization*

(Excerpt from *Character as Seen in Body and Parentage*, London: Kegan Paul, Trench, Trubner & Co., 1886, pp. 112–13.)

Few persons now deny that to organisation, in other words to inheritance, is mainly due the existence of criminals, paupers, drunkards, lunatics, and suicides. Here again, as everywhere, the occurrence of the continuity meets us, seeing that a number of individuals are constantly hovering over the lines which divide these unfortunate individuals from each other and from the more fortunate classes. On the 'hovering,' uncertain, and weakly organised individuals circumstance undoubtedly exercises considerable influence: it cannot make them strong or self-sufficing; nevertheless to these, especially in their childhood, the promoters of practical education, morals, economics, and health cannot be too zealous in their attention. The more clearly such promoters recognise the operation of physiological hereditary law the more effective their zeal will be. In spite of all or any change of circumstance the vast majority of our population are average individuals because their parents were average individuals; their children also will certainly be average individuals. The vast majority of each generation of human beings, no matter how extreme the changes, or diverse the varieties, of encompassing circumstance, are more or less uniformly honest, kindly, and industrious because the preceding generations were fairly honest, kindly, and industrious. On these terms the very existence of society is based—based on the dominacy of organisation over the possibilities of circumstance. Even 'hoverers' over dividing lines follow 'hovering' parents and beget 'hovering' children.

125. General William Booth, *The Cab Horse Ideal of Existence*

(Excerpt from *In Darkest England and the Way Out*, London: The Salvation Army, 1890, pp. 18–19.)

What, then, is Darkest England? For whom do we claim that 'urgency' which gives their case priority over that of all other sections of their countrymen and countrywomen?

I claim it for the Lost, for the Outcast, for the Disinherited of the World.

These, it may be said, are but phrases. Who are the Lost? I reply, not in a religious, but in a social sense, the lost are those who have gone under, who have lost their foothold in Society, those to whom the prayer to our Heavenly Father, 'Give us day by day our daily bread,' is either unfulfilled, or only fulfilled by the Devil's agency: by the earnings of vice, the proceeds of crime, or the contribution enforced by the threat of the law.

But I will be more precise. The denizens in Darkest England, for whom I appeal, are (1) those who, having no capital or income of their own, would in a month be dead from sheer starvation were they exclusively dependent upon the money earned by their own work; and (2) those who by their utmost exertions are unable to attain the regulation allowance of food which the law prescribes as indispensable even for the worst criminals in our gaols.

I sorrowfully admit that it would be Utopian in our present social arrangements to dream of attaining for every honest Englishman a gaol standard of all the necessities of life. Some time, perhaps, we may venture to hope that every honest worker on English soil will always be as warmly clad, as healthily housed, and as regularly fed as our criminal convicts—but that is not yet.

Neither it is possible to hope for many years to come that human beings generally will be as well cared for as horses. Mr. Carlyle long ago remarked that the four-footed worker has already got all that this two-handed one is clamouring for: 'There are not many horses in England, able and willing to work, which have not due food and lodging and go about sleek coated, satisfied in heart.' You say it is impossible; but, said Carlyle, 'The human brain, looking at these sleek English horses, refuses to believe in such impossibility for English men.' Nevertheless, forty years have passed since Carlyle said that, and we seem to be no nearer the attainment of the four-footed standard for the two-handed worker. 'Perhaps it might be nearer realisation,' growls the cynic, 'if we could only produce men according to demand, as we do horses, and promptly send them to the slaughter-house when past their prime'—which, of course, is not to be thought of.

What, then, is the standard towards which we may venture to aim with some prospect of realisation in our time? It is a very humble one, but if realised it would solve the worst problems of modern Society.

It is the standard of the London Cab Horse.

When in the streets of London a Cab Horse, weary or careless or stupid, trips and falls and lies stretched out in the midst of the traffic, there is no question of debating how he came to stumble before we try to get him on his legs again.

Index